IMAGES
of America

VERNON AND HISTORIC ROCKVILLE

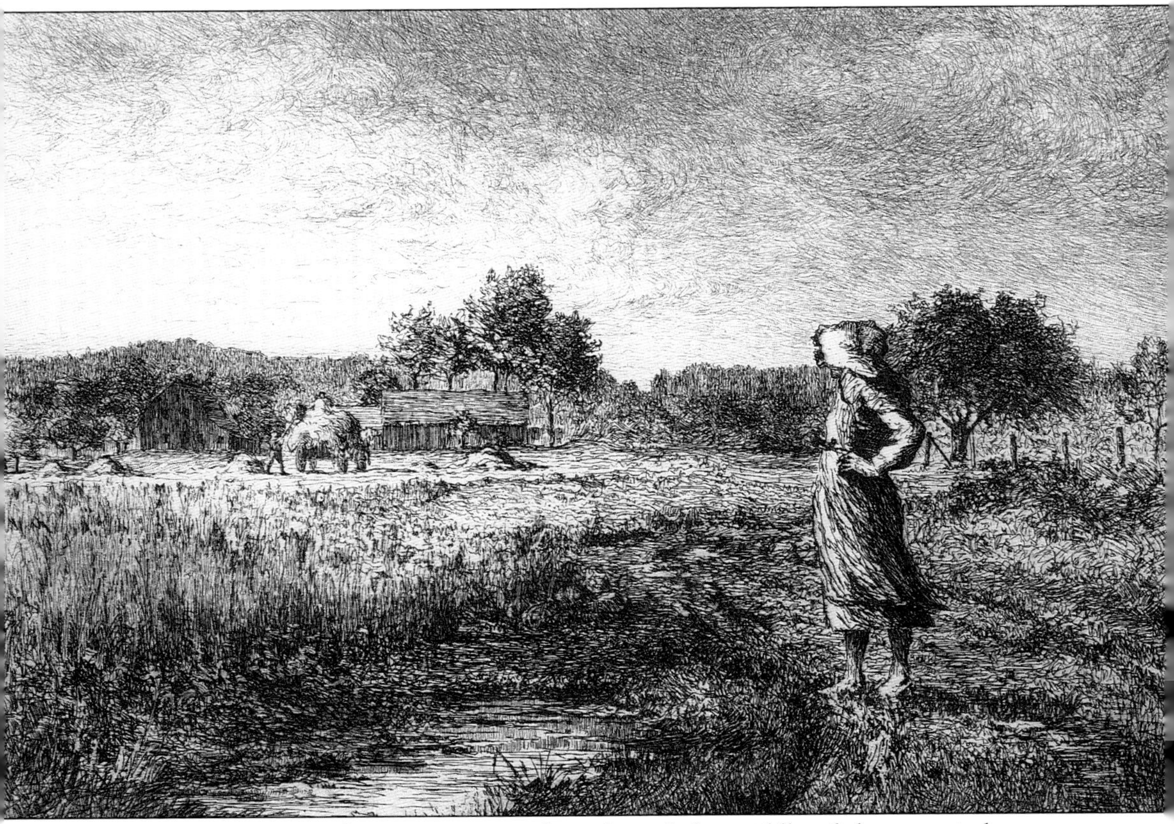

Much of the town of Vernon remained rural until the middle of the twentieth century, as shown in this etching by local artist Gustave A. Hoffman. The gambrel-roof farmhouse in the background is probably the one still standing at 100 South Street. It was owned in the mid-nineteenth century by Anson Rogers.

IMAGES
of America

VERNON AND HISTORIC ROCKVILLE

Ardis Abbott and Jean A. Luddy

ARCADIA
PUBLISHING

ISBN 978-0-7385-6479-1

Published by Arcadia Publishing
Charleston, South Carolina

Printed in the United States of America

Library of Congress Catalog Card Number: 2009921944

For all general information contact Arcadia Publishing at:
Telephone 843-853-2070
Fax 843-853-0044
E-mail sales@arcadiapublishing.com
For customer service and orders:
Toll-Free 1-888-313-2665

Visit us on the Internet at www.arcadiapublishing.com

Contents

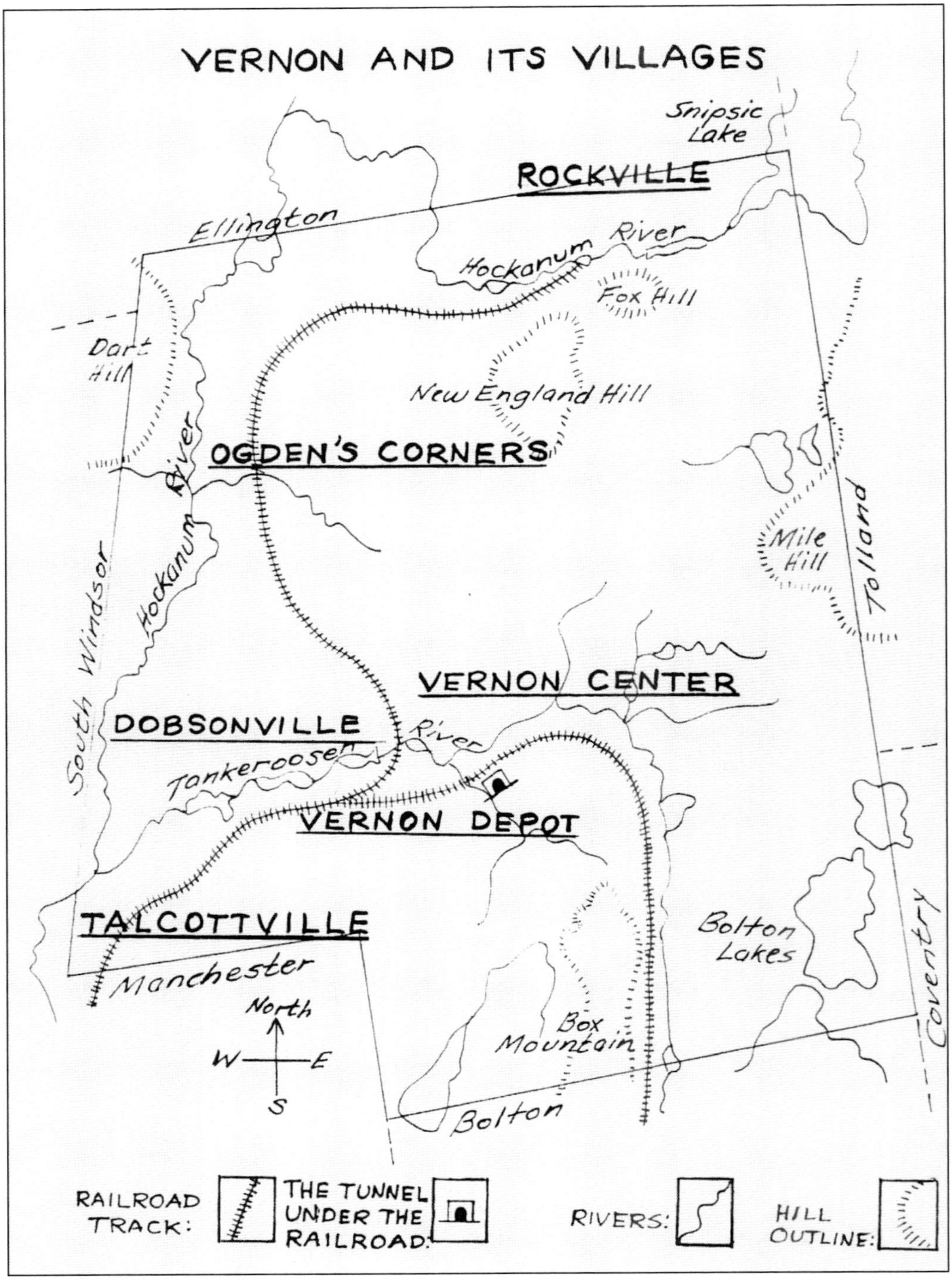

By 1870, Vernon's villages and hamlets were bound together by the Hartford, Providence and Fishkill Railroad with a spur track, the Rockville Branch Railroad, connecting Vernon Depot with Rockville. The main village centers at this time were Vernon Center, Talcottville, and Rockville.

Introduction

The town of Vernon was incorporated in 1808 by the division of the town of Bolton. Settled in 1716, the area was first known as North Bolton. Isolated by a ridge of hills from the church in Bolton, North Bolton parishioners received permission in 1762 to form an Ecclesiastical Society. With a separate religious society established, it was only a matter of time before the farmers of North Bolton successfully petitioned the General Assembly for incorporation as a town, and in 1808 the parish of North Bolton became the town of Vernon. The coming of the Hartford Turnpike in the first decade of the nineteenth century was undoubtedly a contributing factor in the establishment of the new town. The turnpike ran through Vernon and where it intersected with the major town roads, a small village, subsequently known as Vernon Center, became the bustling center of the new town.

Incorporated on the eve of the Industrial Revolution, Vernon felt the first stirrings of change when John Warburton, an English immigrant, arrived in 1796 and built a mill on the Tankeroosen River. Here he began to card wool and spin cotton yarn by machine. Warburton's manufacturing enterprise, the first cotton-spinning mill in Connecticut to become permanently established, later became the factory village of Talcottville. Warburton's success soon sparked an interest in textile manufacturing among Vernon's farmers. Several other mills were put in operation, but the small, meandering Tankeroosen River, the scene of these early experiments in mechanized textile manufacturing, provided only a limited source of water power. Several local farmers, Vernon's first manufacturing entrepreneurs, next considered the potential of the Hockanum River, located in the unsettled northeastern section of the town. From the outlet at Snipsic Lake, the Hockanum River drops in a series of cascades 254 feet over a 1.5-mile course. Each cascade soon became a potential mill site.

Francis McLean, a Vernon farmer and entrepreneur, is credited with building the first woolen factory on the Hockanum River in which all of the processes of manufacturing, from raw material to finished product, were mechanized. In 1821 McLean bought a large tract of land in what is now the center of Rockville and built a dam and water-powered factory building. In partnership with George and Allyn Kellogg and Ralph Talcott, and with an investment of $16,000, McLean had his mill in full operation by 1823. Once initiated, industrialization on the Hockanum River proceeded rapidly and by the 1880s 13 factories were in operation. The village that emerged around this industrial complex became known as Rockville, taking its name from its first manufacturing enterprise, the Rock Manufacturing Company.

Wool cloth was the main product of Rockville's factories, but silk and cotton thread, various cotton goods, and envelopes were also manufactured. Over the century, the production of fine woolens and worsteds insured the steady growth of the manufacturing village.

Expanding industry brought English, Irish, and German immigrants to Rockville. Foremost among them was George Sykes, a son and grandson of British woolen workers. In 1866, at the age of 26, Sykes came to Rockville to assume the management of the Hockanum Company mill.

In association with mill owner George Maxwell, he set the path that would lead to national recognition. At the World's Colombian Exposition in Chicago in 1893, the products of the Hockanum mills were pronounced "equal in every respect to the best made in Europe." In the 1900 Paris exposition, three Rockville mills, managed by Maxwell and Sykes, won a gold medal. The cloth for the inaugural suits of Presidents William McKinley in 1897 and Theodore Roosevelt in 1905 were made in the Rockville mills.

By 1880 Rockville was beginning to suffer growing pains as the burgeoning population encountered problems which the rural town government was unable to resolve. Rural Vernon did not feel obliged to pay for such village necessities as adequate fire protection—the mills were a constant source of danger in this respect—a police force, street lights, sewers, and sidewalks. After a decade of agitation, the city of Rockville was incorporated March 28, 1889, as a chartered city within the town of Vernon with the authority to lay a tax to pay for the needed urban amenities.

The next two decades saw great changes in the center of Rockville as the new city sought to live up to its aspirations to be "among the leading cities of the state." Following a disastrous fire in 1888, much of the old village center was rebuilt. In the adjacent residential neighborhood surrounding a small city park, a newly self-conscious middle class remodeled, removed, and rebuilt, transforming the area in high Victorian style.

In the summer of 1908, as Vernon celebrated its 100th anniversary, its citizens looked back with pride on a century of solid achievement. In the first century of its history, a wilderness had been turned into a prosperous city of nearly 8,000 people, and everyone anticipated that the Rockville textile mills would continue to assure Vernon's prosperity. In fact this was not to be the case. Vernon had reached a plateau in its development that would last until World War II. A long twilight settled over the woolen industry; the mills continued to operate but under changed conditions. In 1934 the families who had run the woolen mills for several generations sold out to M.T. Stevens & Company, the woolen division of J.P. Stevens & Company. In 1952 J.P. Stevens & Company closed the Hockanum mills. Consolidation of the town and city governments took place in 1964, and Rockville became just a "section" of the town of Vernon. Today the city of Rockville and the factory village of Talcottville are listed as historic districts on the National Register of Historic Places as well-preserved examples of nineteenth-century textile manufacturing communities, representative of the role paid by textiles in the transformation of Connecticut into a manufacturing state.

One

The Village of Vernon Center

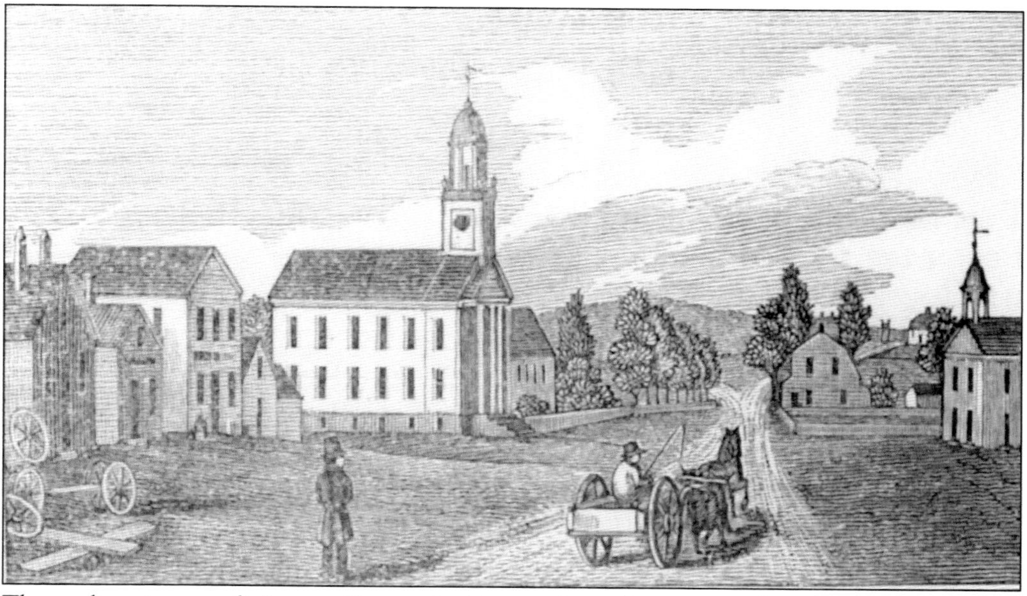

The earliest image of Vernon Center is this woodcut illustration taken from John Barber's *Connecticut Historical Collections*, published in 1836. The First Congregational Church of Vernon is in the left center, and the steepled building on the right was the school. A turnpike, opened in 1801 to connect the Hartford State House with the Tolland County Courthouse, passed through the center of the village.

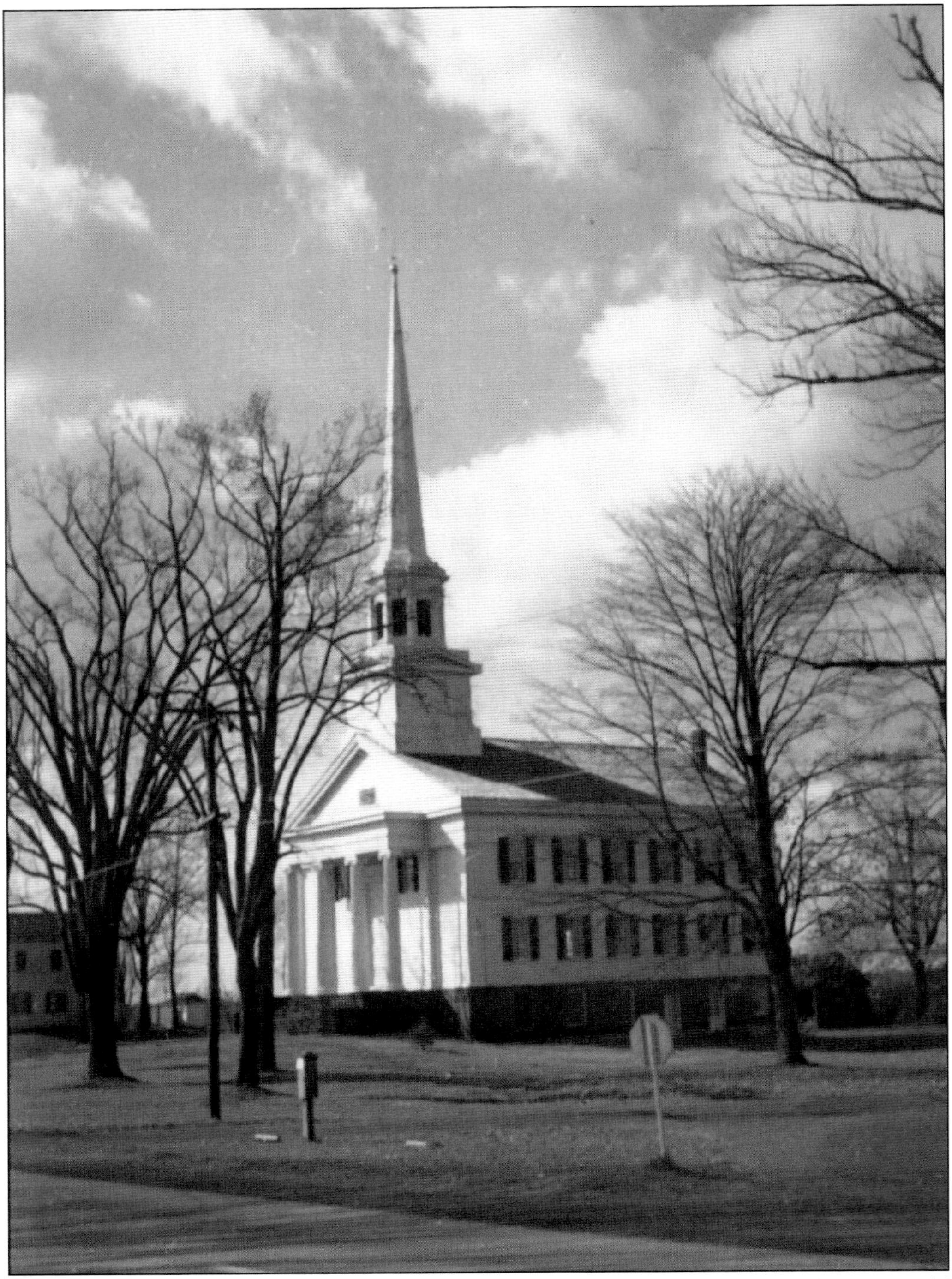

The church was the center of community life in rural New England. Each Sunday farmers would travel from their homesteads to the meetinghouse to worship and to meet their neighbors and "tell the news." The site of the first meetinghouse in Vernon, built in 1763 on Sunnyview Drive, is marked with a plaque. By the early 1820s the old meetinghouse was no longer adequate for the growing town, and in 1826 a new church was built on the corner of Hartford Turnpike and Center Road. It is shown here as it appeared about 1940.

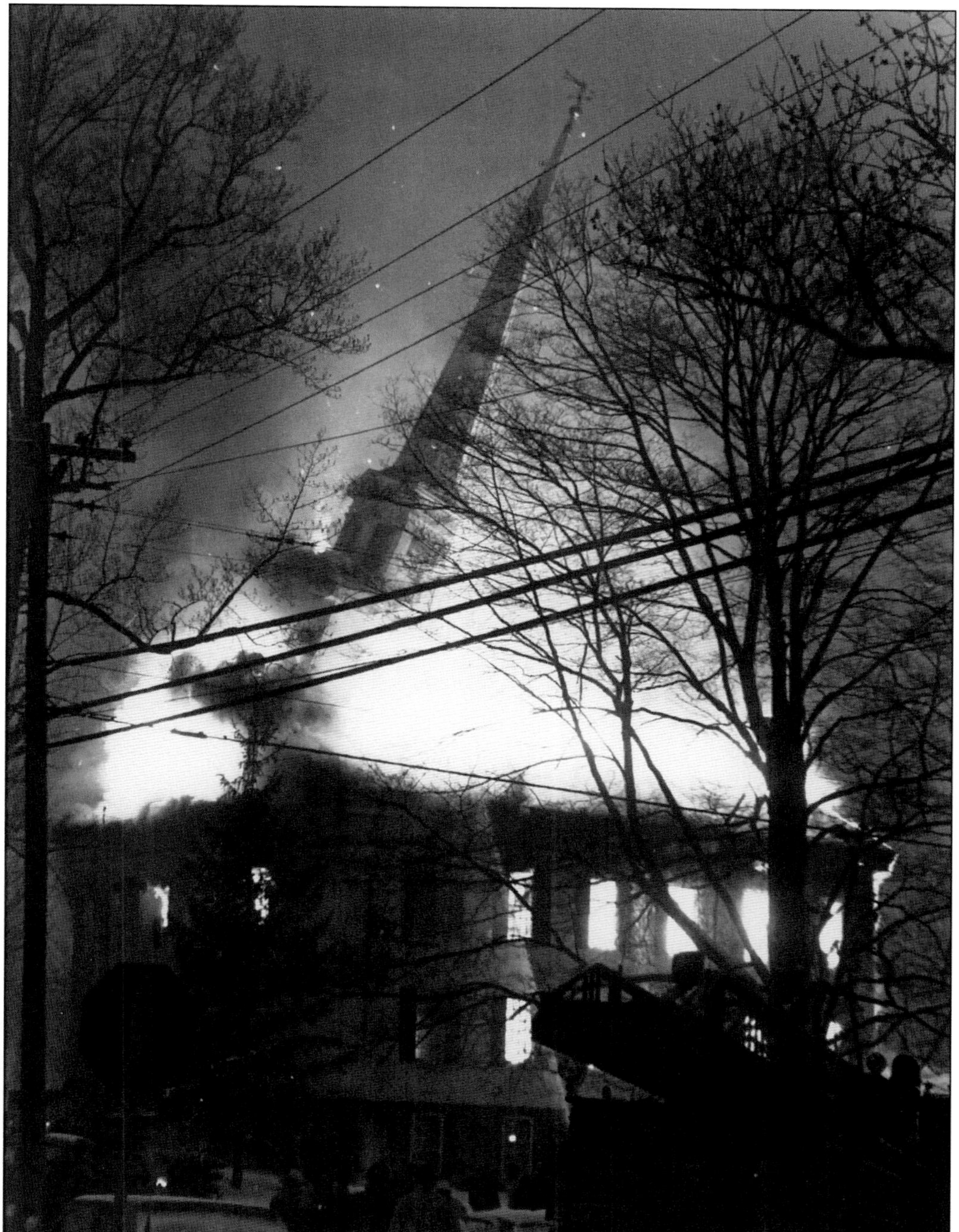

In the winter of 1965 the First Congregational Church was destroyed by fire. In this dramatic picture, photographer Joseph Saternis captures the exact moment the steeple of the venerable church collapsed. Through the efforts of the congregation, the church was rebuilt almost exactly like the earlier structure.

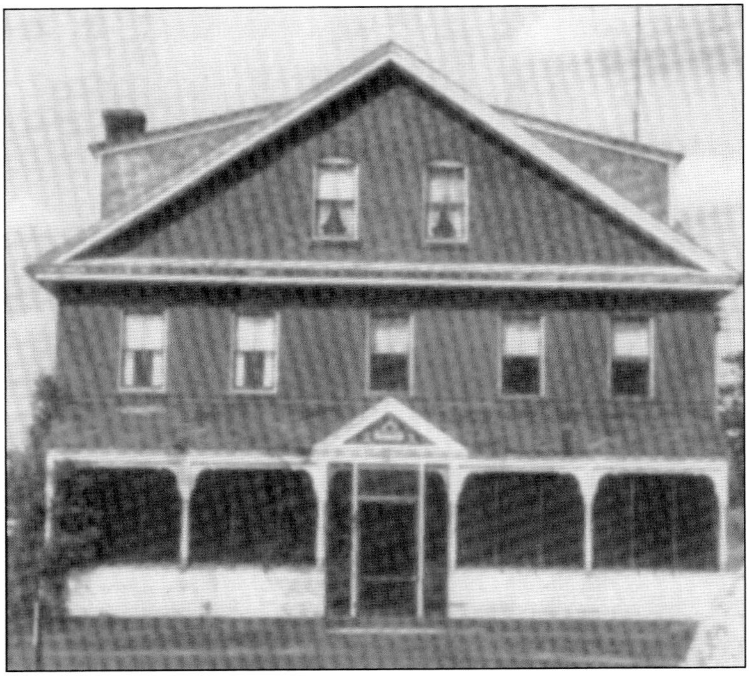

Located near the Tolland line on the Hartford Turnpike, King's Tavern was a popular stop for stagecoaches. The Marquis de Lafayette, the French aristocrat and hero of the American Revolution, stopped briefly at King's Tavern when he revisited America in 1824. After 1868 the tavern was converted to a home for local indigents. It was demolished after World War II to make way for the Lafayette shopping plaza.

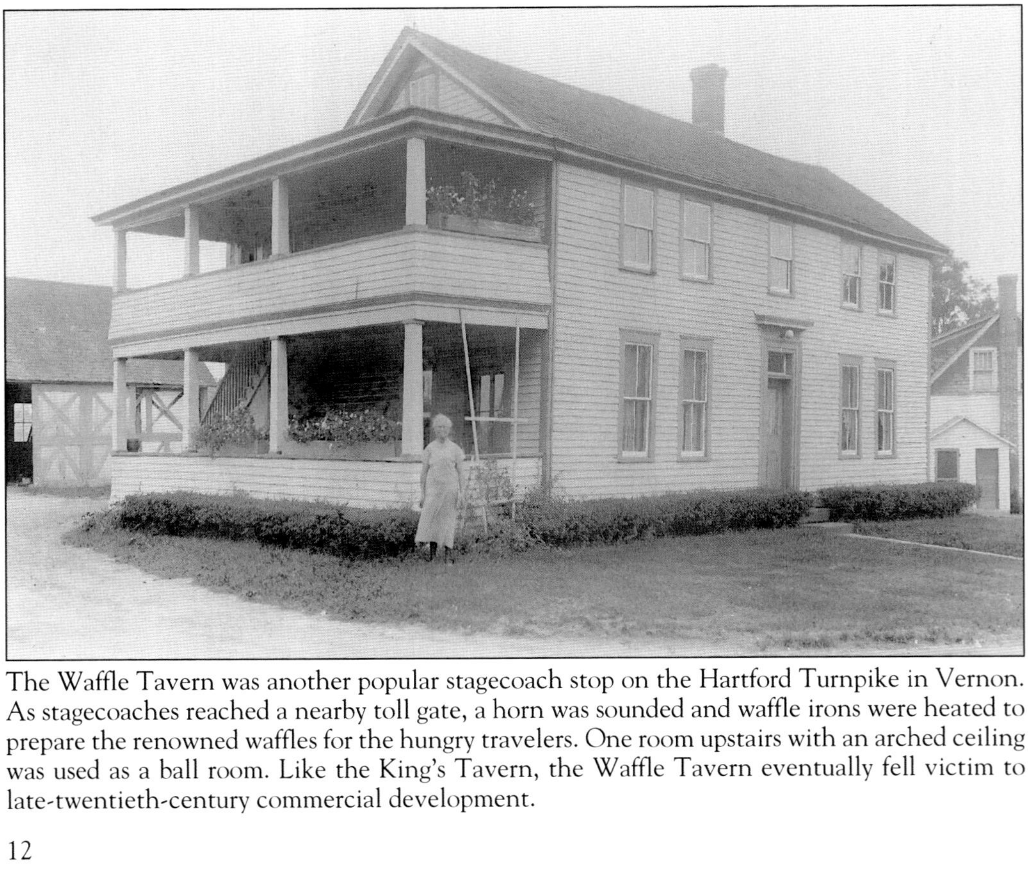

The Waffle Tavern was another popular stagecoach stop on the Hartford Turnpike in Vernon. As stagecoaches reached a nearby toll gate, a horn was sounded and waffle irons were heated to prepare the renowned waffles for the hungry travelers. One room upstairs with an arched ceiling was used as a ball room. Like the King's Tavern, the Waffle Tavern eventually fell victim to late-twentieth-century commercial development.

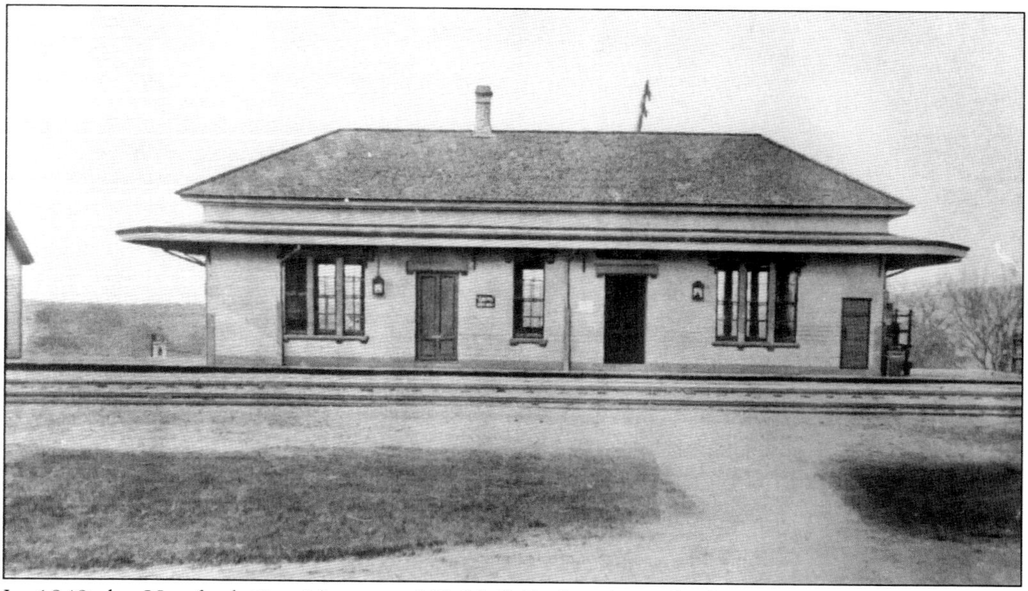

In 1849 the Hartford, Providence and Fishkill Railroad was built through Vernon. The fare to Hartford was 75¢. In 1903 the line was sold to the New York, New Haven, and Hartford Railroad Company. By 1929 passenger service on the line had decreased considerably and the company closed the depot as a cost-cutting measure.

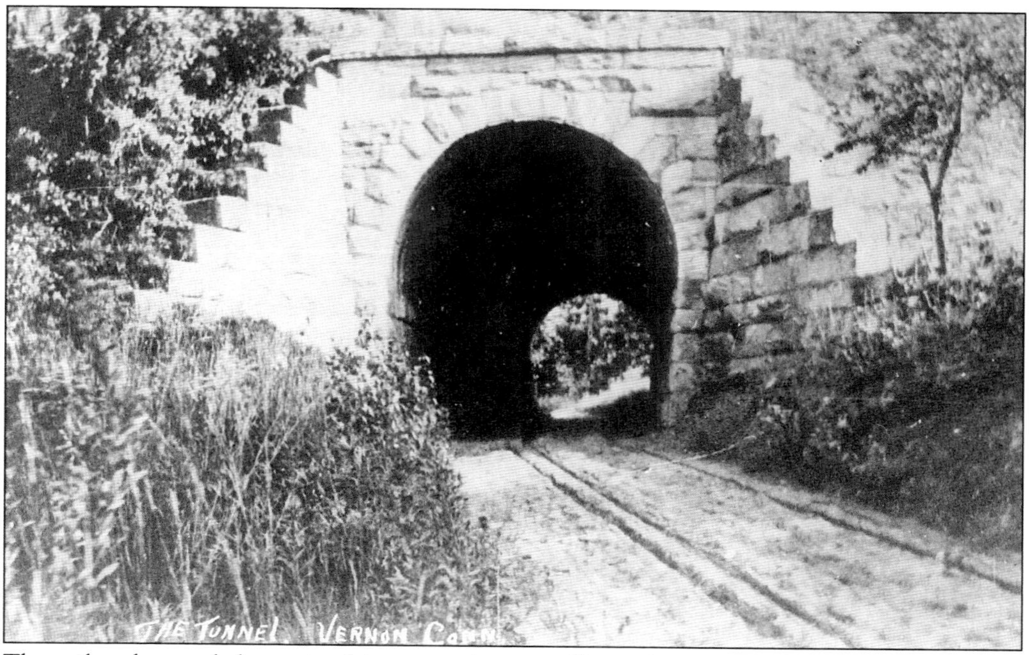

The railroad tunnel shown in this postcard view still stands on Tunnel Road. Built between 1846 and 1849 when the Hartford, Providence and Fishkill Railroad was constructed through Vernon, the tunnel—with its distinctive keystone arch—is a tribute to the engineering skill of its builders. The 108-foot tunnel consists of 30 keystone arches and was constructed with native sandstone quarried in Vernon.

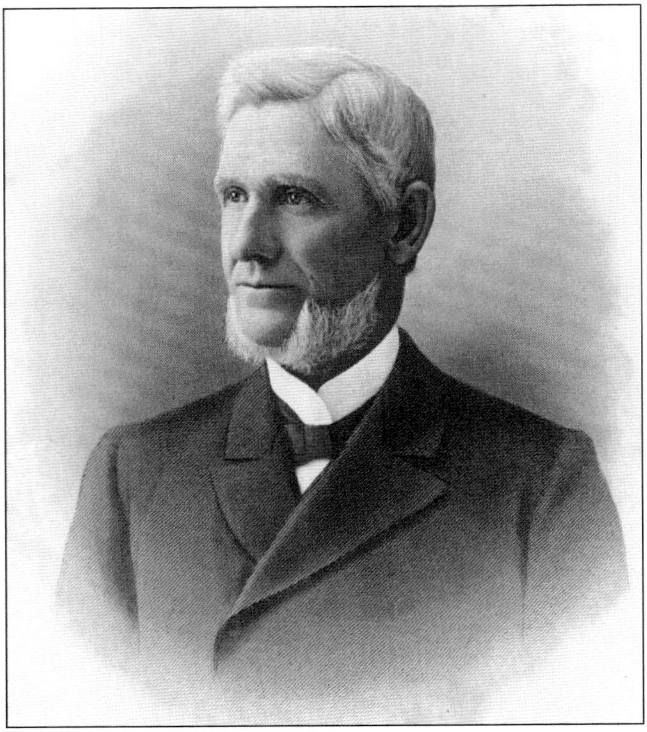

Nathan Morgan Strong was born in Vernon in 1889. In time he took over the farm first owned by his grandfather, Nathan Morgan Strong. The farm is now operated by Norman R. Strong and his son, Morgan G. Strong, making five generations of the family to operate Strong Farm.

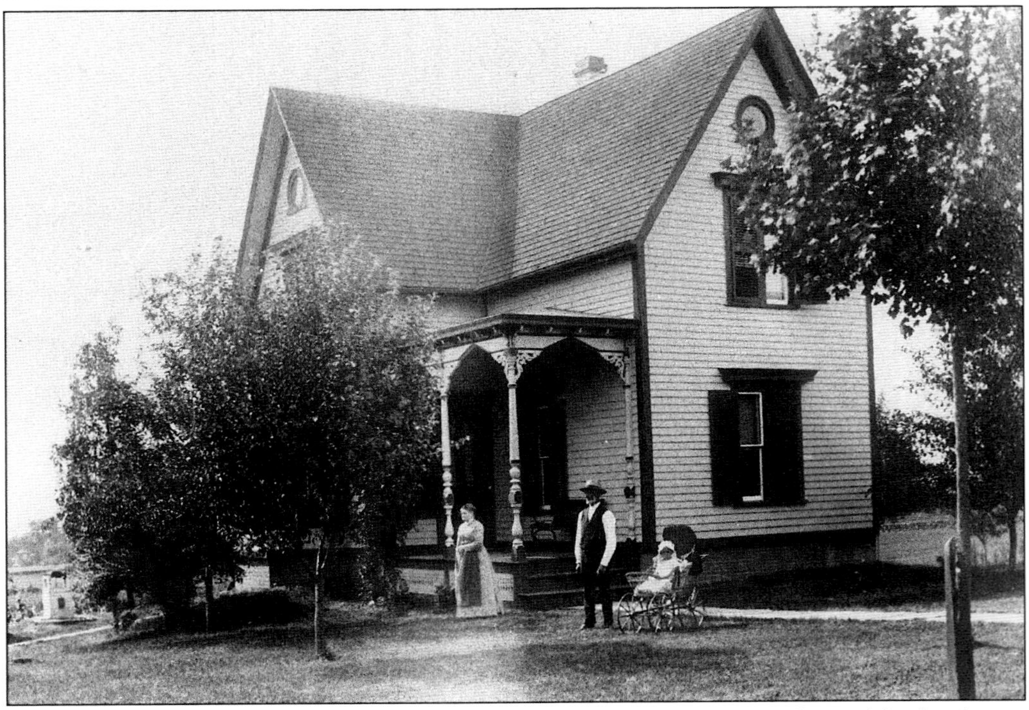

Nathan Morgan Strong and his daughter-in-law, Ella Dart Strong, pose in from of the farmhouse which he built in 1878. His namesake, N. Morgan Strong, is in the carriage. The Strongs are the last of Vernon's farm families to operate a farm in Vernon, which has become an almost fully developed suburban town.

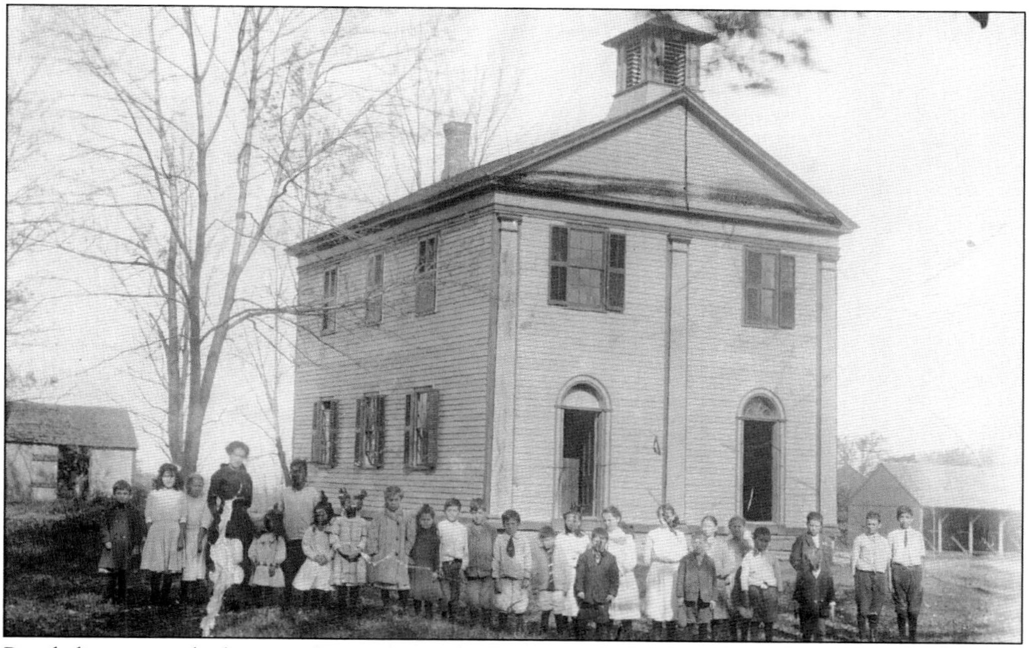

Pupils line up with their teacher to have their picture taken in front of Vernon Center School about 1910. Several schoolhouses like this existed in rural Vernon in the nineteenth century. Typically, the buildings had two doors—one for boys, the other for girls. These rural schools continued in use until more modern schools were built in the 1950s.

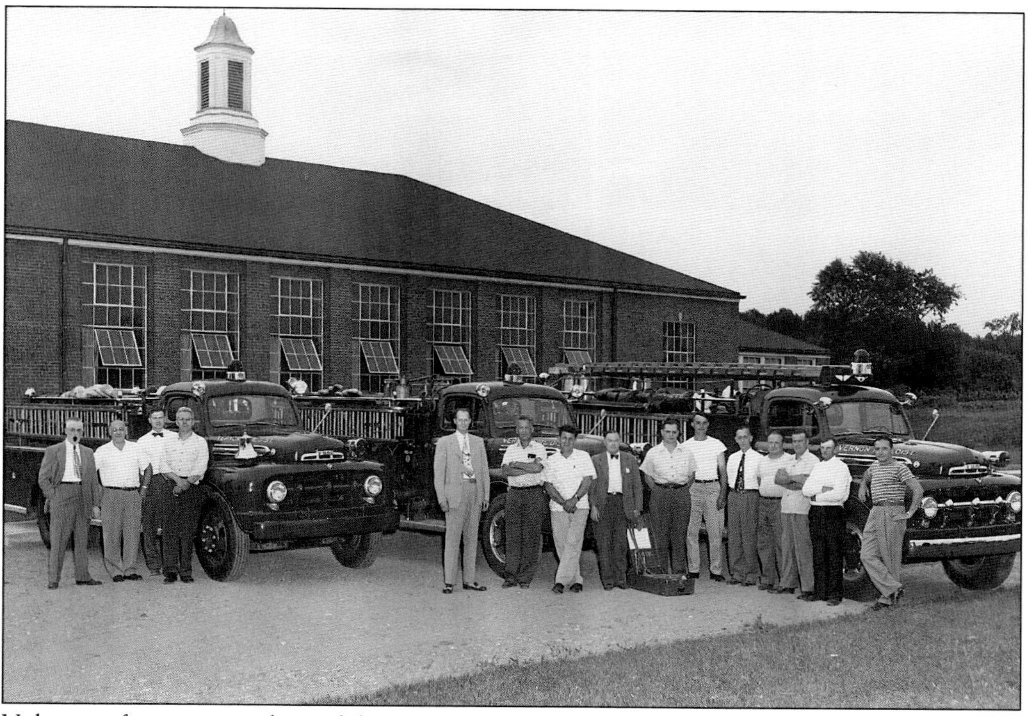

Volunteer firemen, members of the Vernon Fire District, pose with their apparatus in front of rural Vernon's first graded elementary school. Vernon Elementary School opened in 1952, and the old one-room schoolhouses soon passed into history.

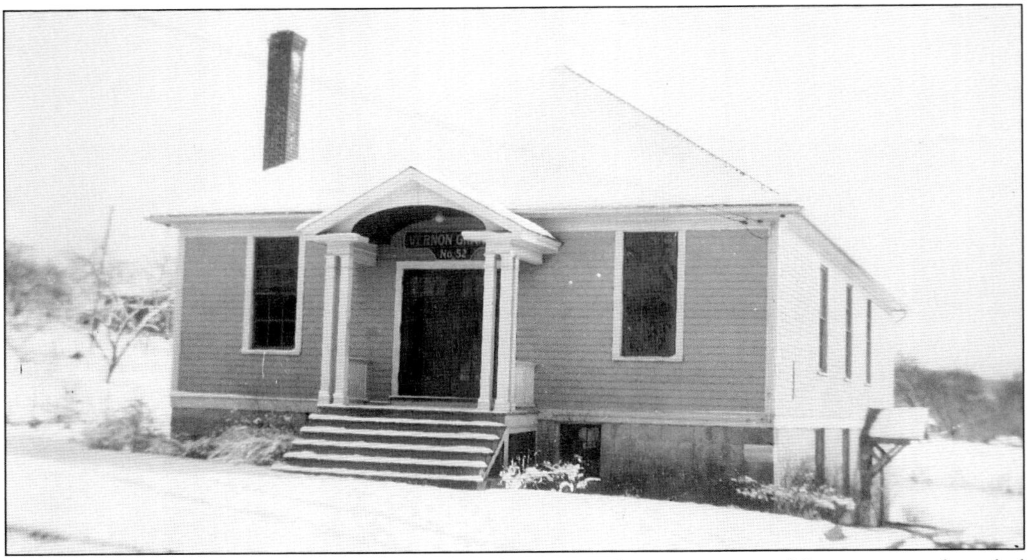

The Vernon Grange Number 52, a chapter of a national organization of farmers, was founded in 1889. Members first met in the Vernon Congregational Church, but when they wished to include dancing in their activities, church members objected. The Grangers then raised funds and built the Grange Hall in 1929. The site of many delicious suppers and lively square dances, the building now houses the Vernon Historical Society.

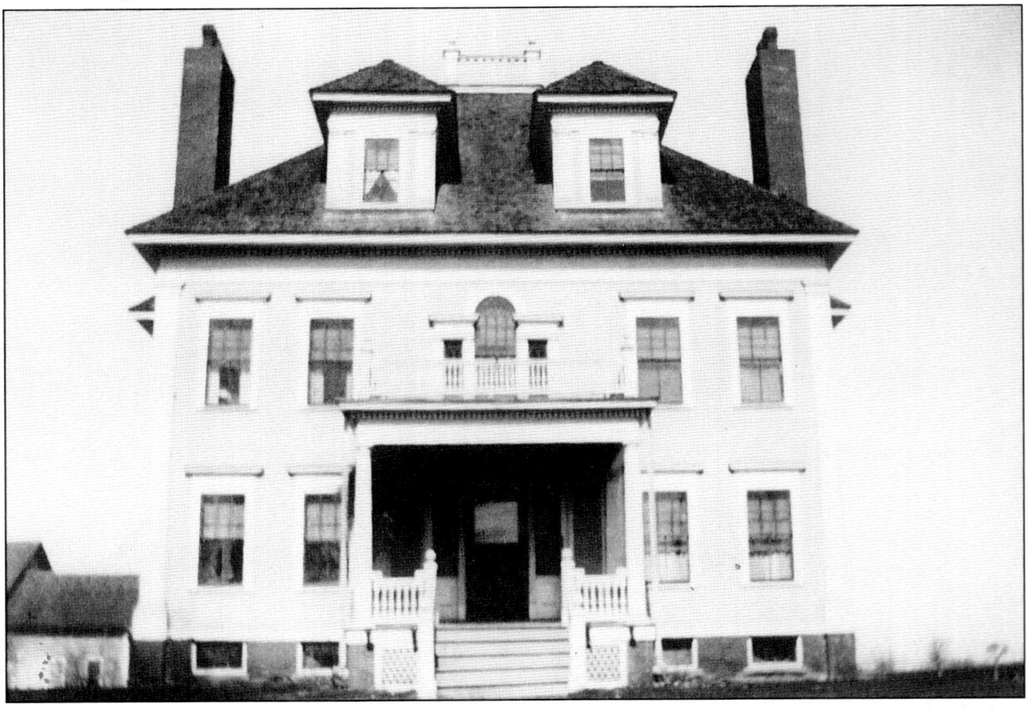

The Tolland County Temporary Home for Children was founded in 1883 to provide shelter for children without parents or from troubled families. First located in Andover and then Rockville, it was moved to this building in Vernon Center in 1900. As Social Security benefits for dependent children gradually replaced orphanages, the home was closed. The vacant building was destroyed by fire in the 1970s.

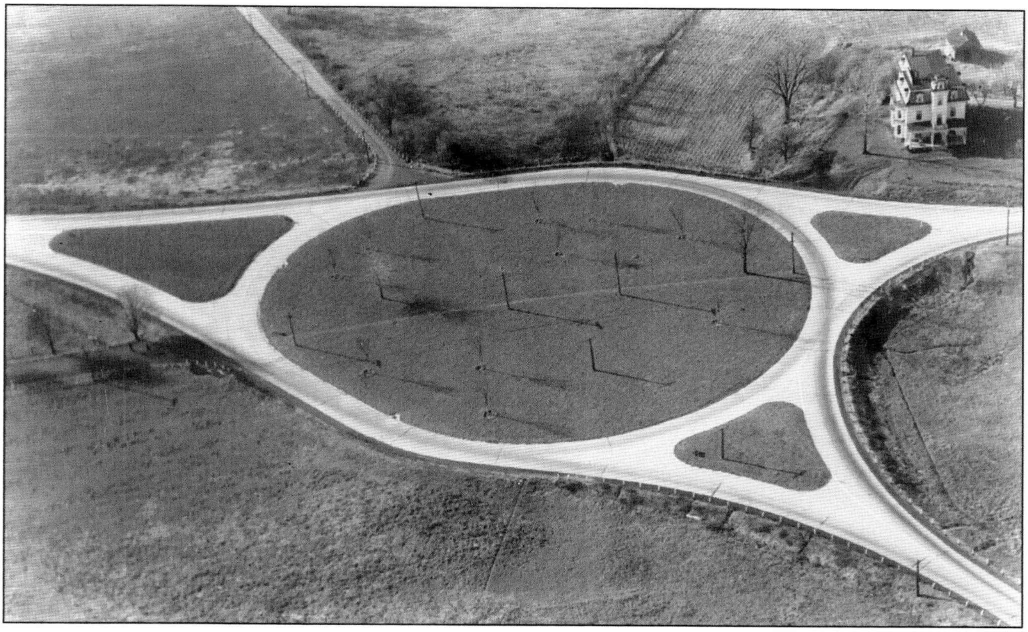

Increased use of the automobile in the 1930s led to road improvements in rural areas. This aerial view shows Vernon Circle shortly after its completion in the early 1930s. The farm in the background was known as the "goat farm" because the elderly couple who lived there kept goats.

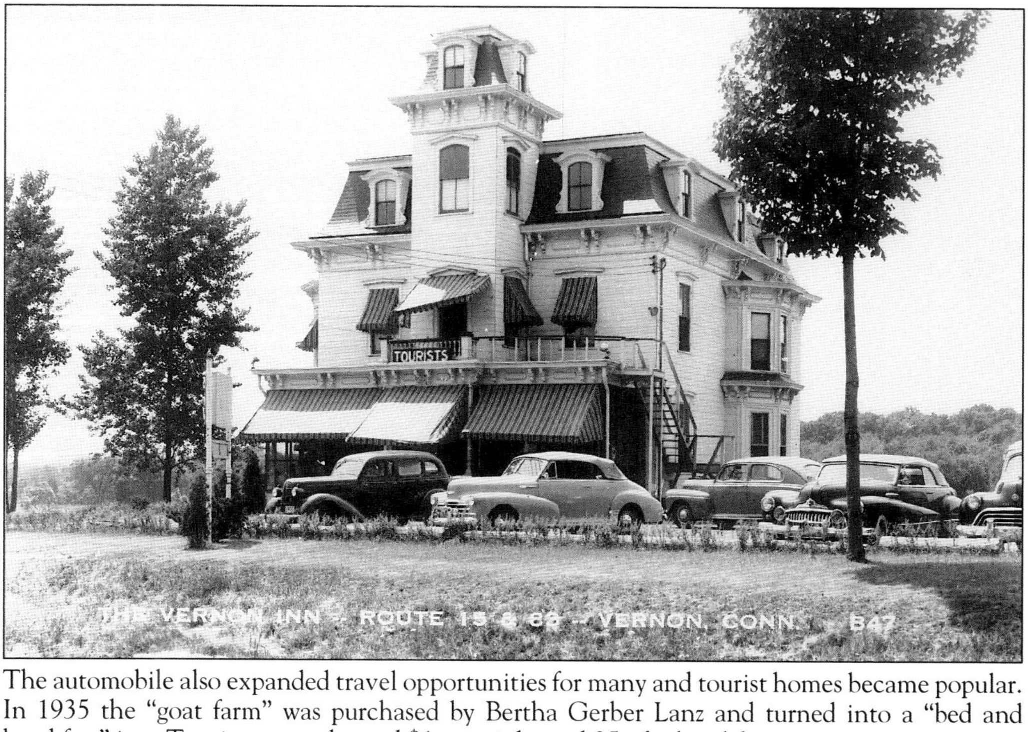

The automobile also expanded travel opportunities for many and tourist homes became popular. In 1935 the "goat farm" was purchased by Bertha Gerber Lanz and turned into a "bed and breakfast" inn. Tourists were charged $1 per night and 35¢ for breakfast.

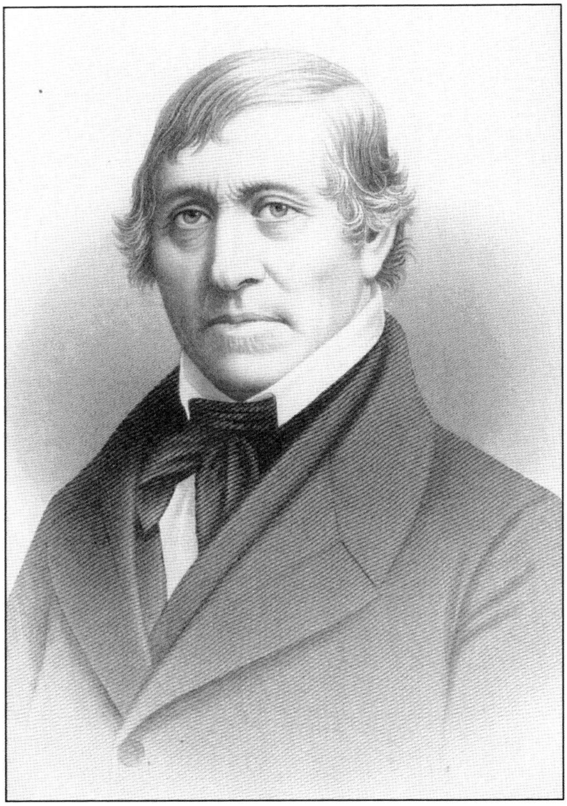

Peter Dobson was an English cotton manufacturer who emigrated to America in 1809. In 1811 he built a cotton spinning mill on the Tankeroosen and was instrumental in introducing a new fabric called satinet, a mixed cotton and wool cloth, to Connecticut. His mill was located next to the present Dobson Road bridge. The area was first called Centreville, but it was later renamed Dobsonville.

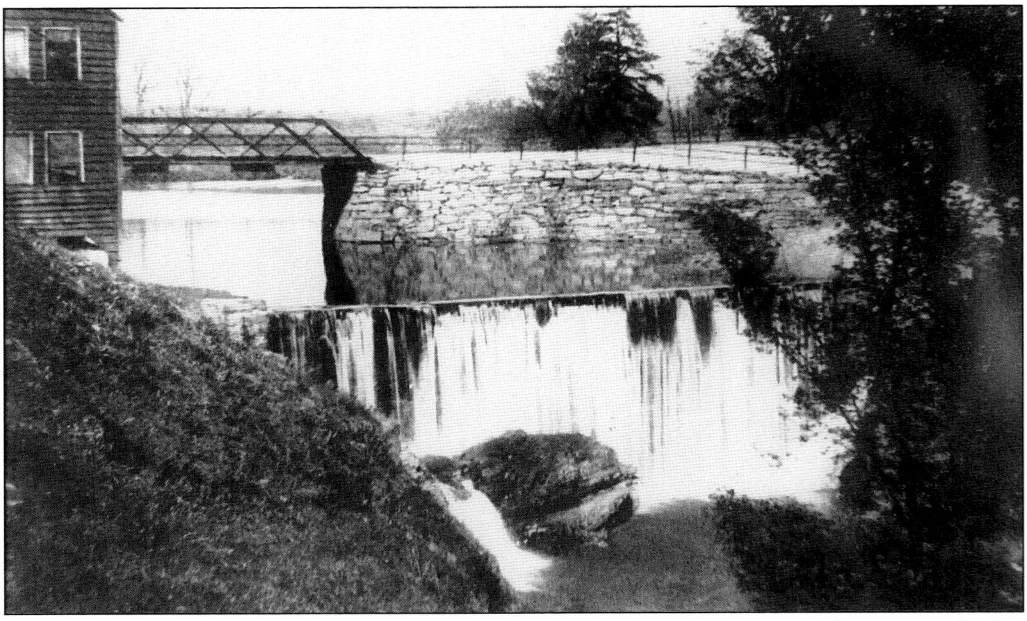

This postcard view shows the falls at the Dobson mill site. The mill later became Ackerly's Mill and produced tobacco cloth used in Connecticut's shade-grown tobacco industry. The foundations of the mill may still be seen by the Dobson Road bridge.

Two

The Village of Talcottville

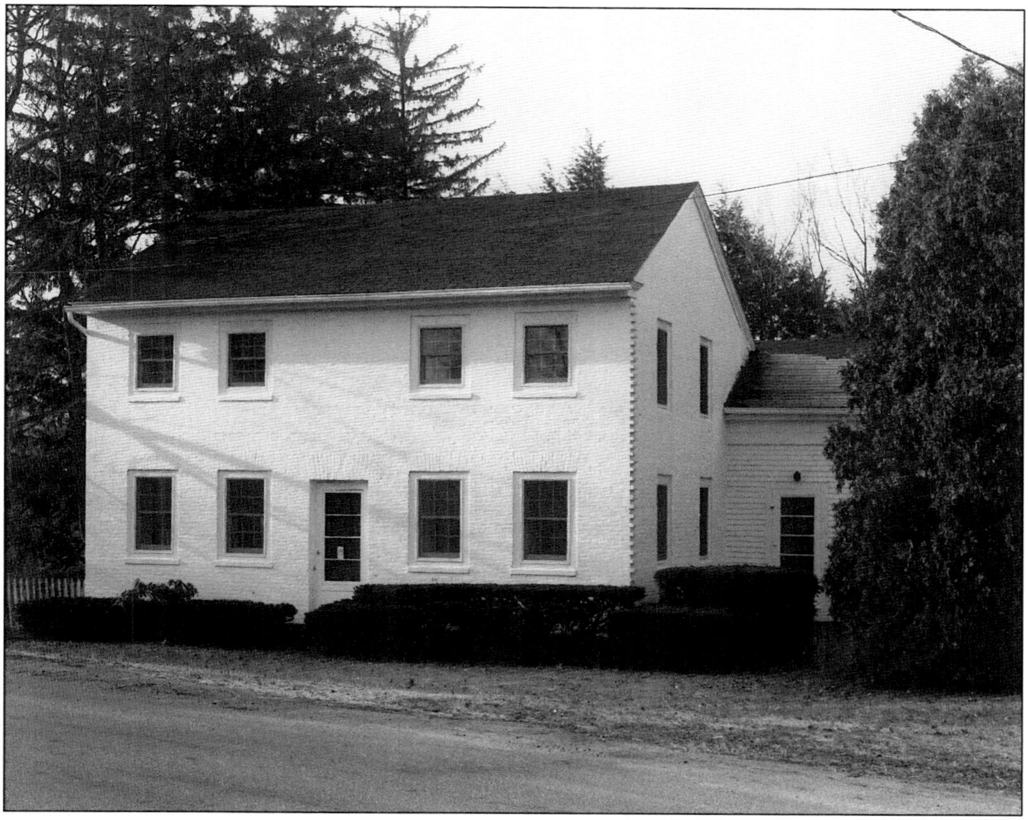

The first cotton spinning mill was built in Vernon about 1796 by an English immigrant, John Warburton. The Warburton House still stands next to the dam and mill pond in Talcottville. John Warburton's mill was purchased and expanded by a series of owners. In 1856 it was purchased by the Talcott brothers and the village surrounding it became known as Talcottville.

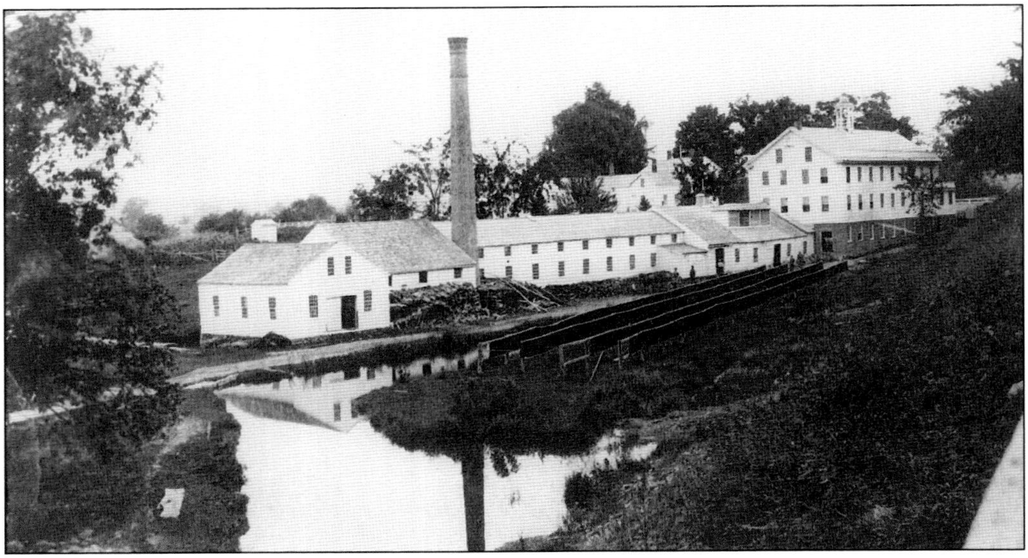

The earliest photographs of the Talcott Brothers mill were taken by Hartford photographer Richard S. Delamater in the summer of 1869. A flood in October of 1869 washed away all but the main building with its distinctive bell tower, which still remains as part of the present factory building in Talcottville.

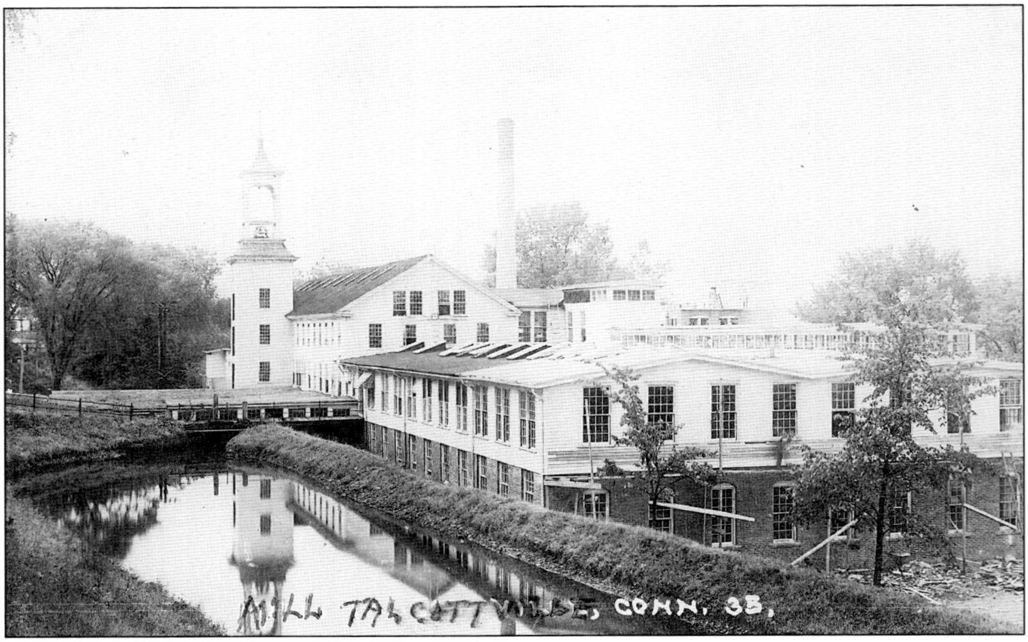

Another view of the Talcott Brothers mill showing the rebuilt factory and the mill race. The Talcott Brothers Company was organized in 1856 and continued in operation until 1950. The mill complex is no longer used for textile manufacturing.

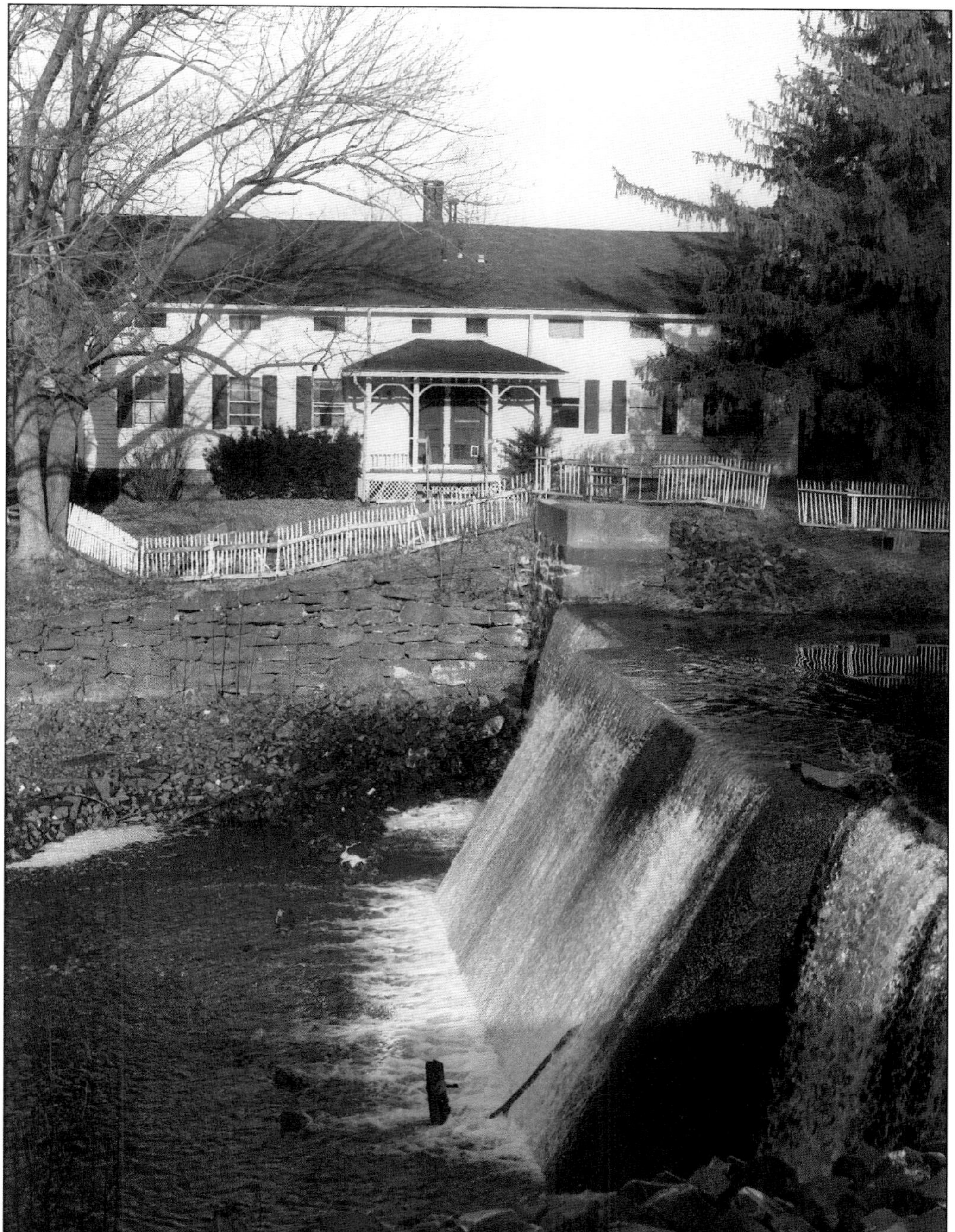

In addition to factory buildings, the first manufacturers built housing for their employees. This view shows worker's housing with the dam that provided water power for the mill in the foreground.

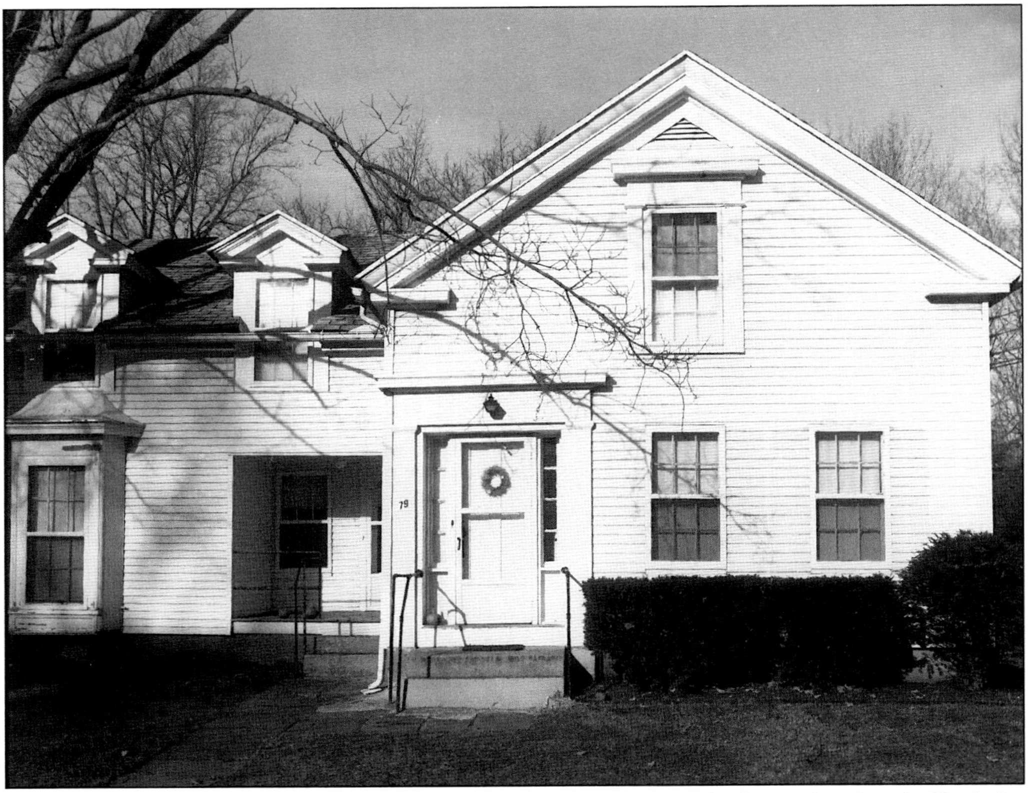

Most of the houses in the Talcottville Historic District were built in the first half of the nineteenth century by the Talcotts or previous mill owners and rented to workers. This Greek Revival-style house is a typical example.

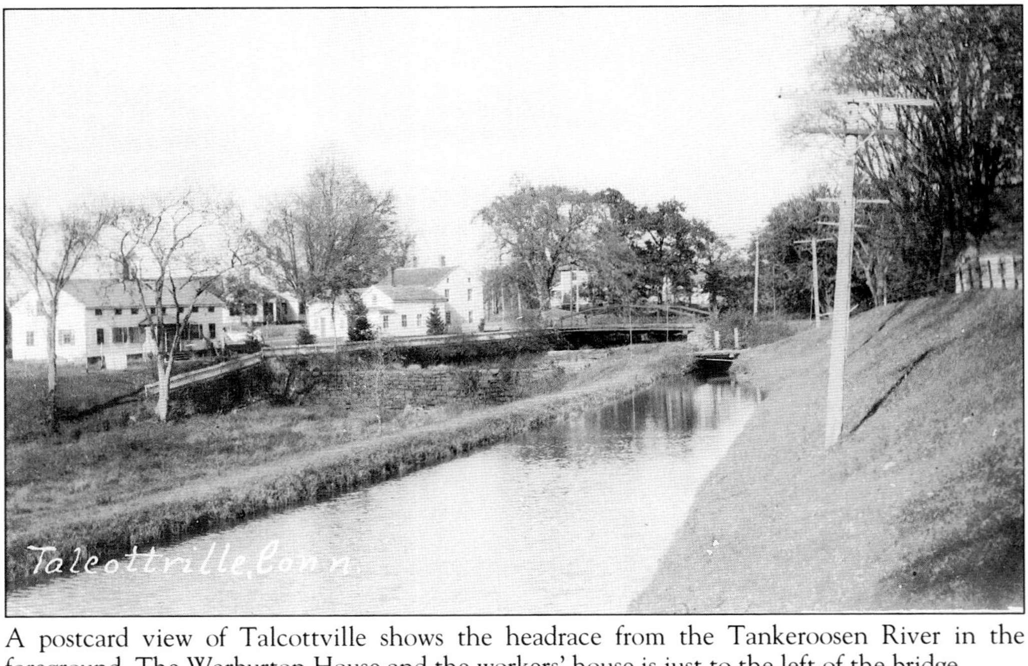

A postcard view of Talcottville shows the headrace from the Tankeroosen River in the foreground. The Warburton House and the workers' house is just to the left of the bridge.

Horace W. Talcott first went to work in the mill in 1854. At that time it was owned by Nathaniel Kellogg and the factory village was called Kelloggville. Following Kellogg's death in 1856, Talcott and his brother purchased the mill and changed the name to Talcottville.

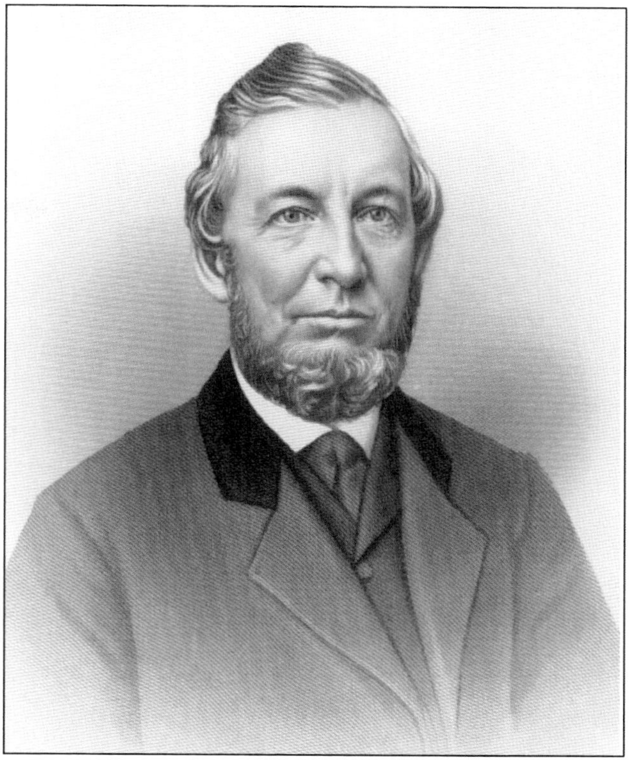

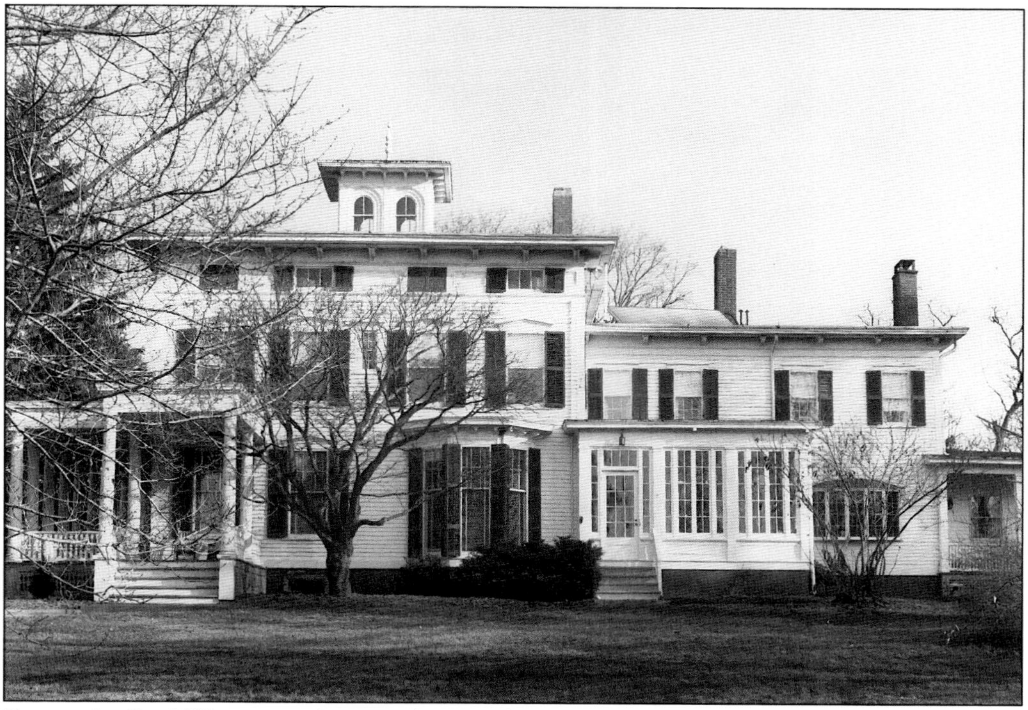

During the Civil War years, when textile manufacturing was very profitable, the Talcott brothers built identical houses on a hill overlooking their factory village. Both houses are extant, but only the H.W. Talcott House remains in its original condition.

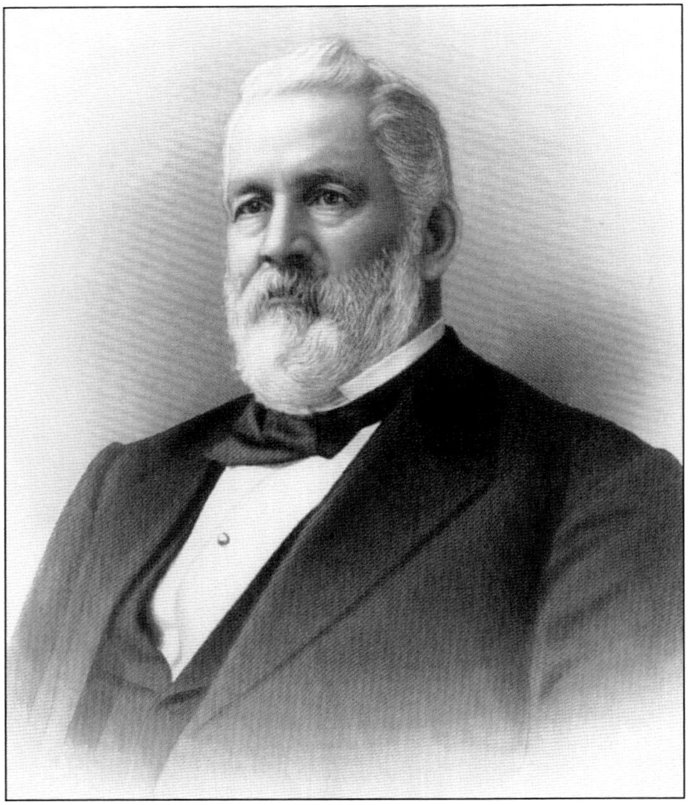

Charles D. Talcott began his career as a schoolteacher but gave that up to join his brother in the operation of Talcott Brothers Company.

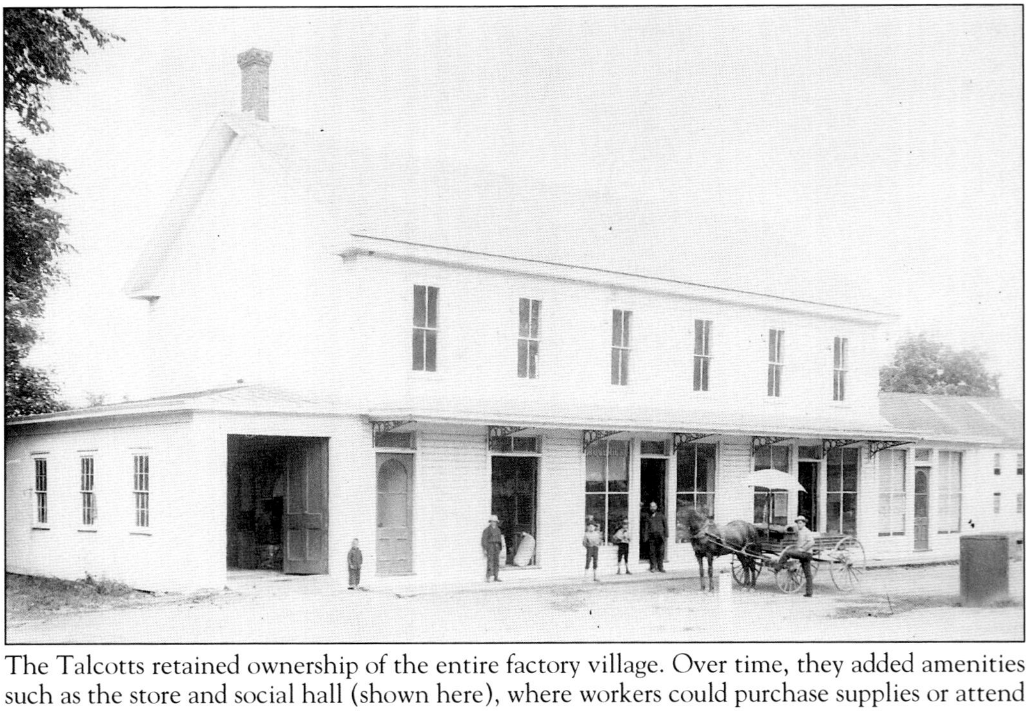

The Talcotts retained ownership of the entire factory village. Over time, they added amenities such as the store and social hall (shown here), where workers could purchase supplies or attend social events in the upstairs assembly hall.

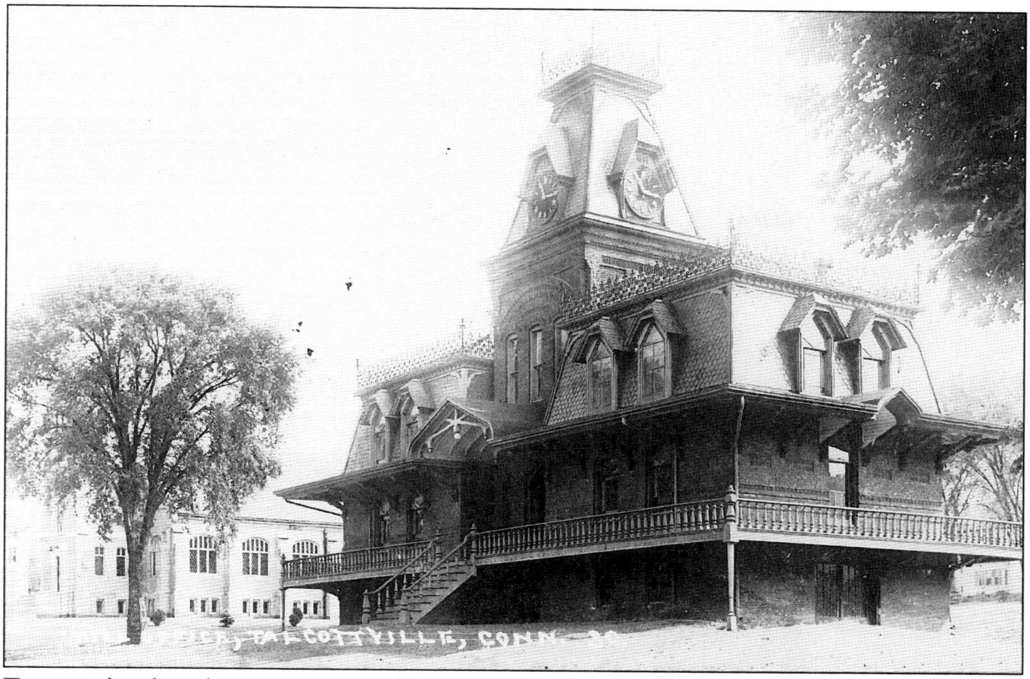

To provide what they considered wholesome entertainment for their employees, the Talcott brothers also built this imposing library with its four-sided clock tower.

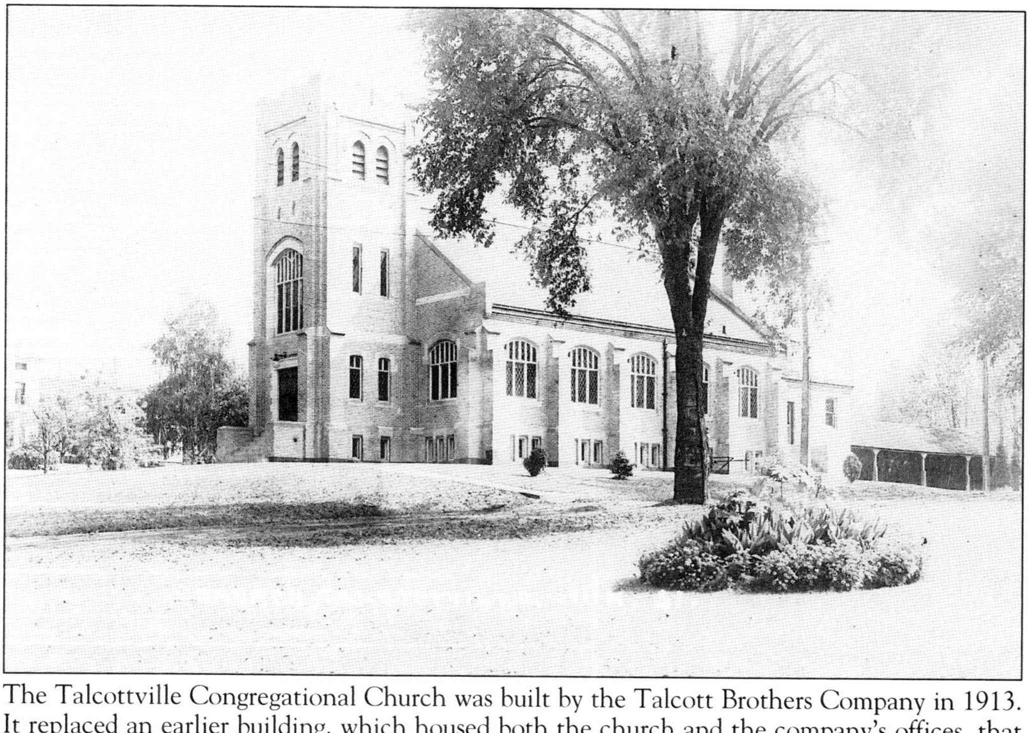

The Talcottville Congregational Church was built by the Talcott Brothers Company in 1913. It replaced an earlier building, which housed both the church and the company's offices, that had been destroyed by fire.

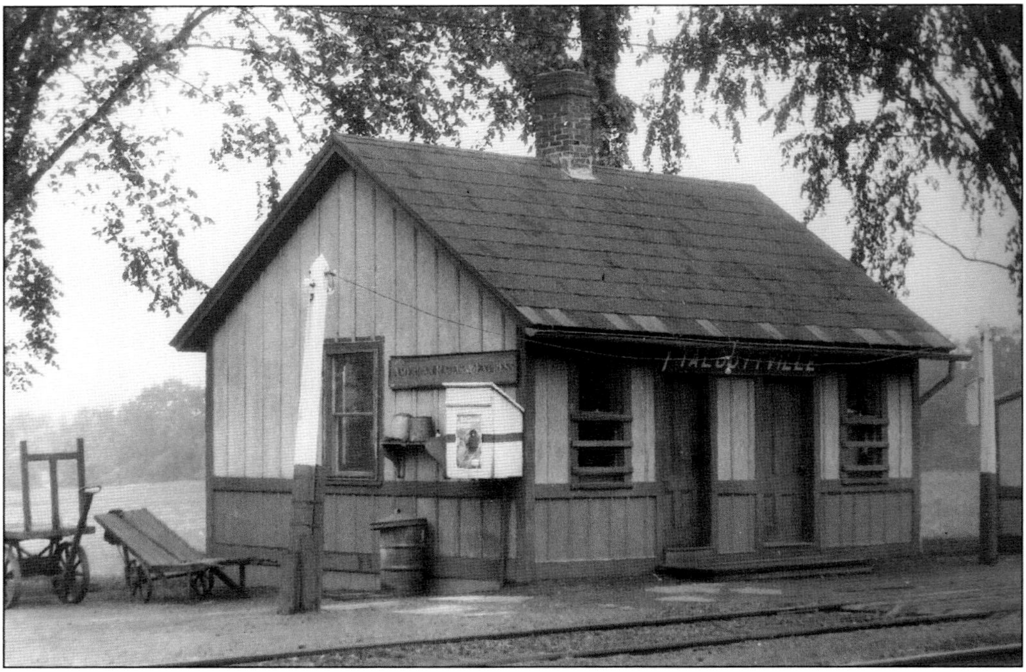

This small railroad station on the Hartford, Providence and Fishkill Railroad served the village of Talcottville.

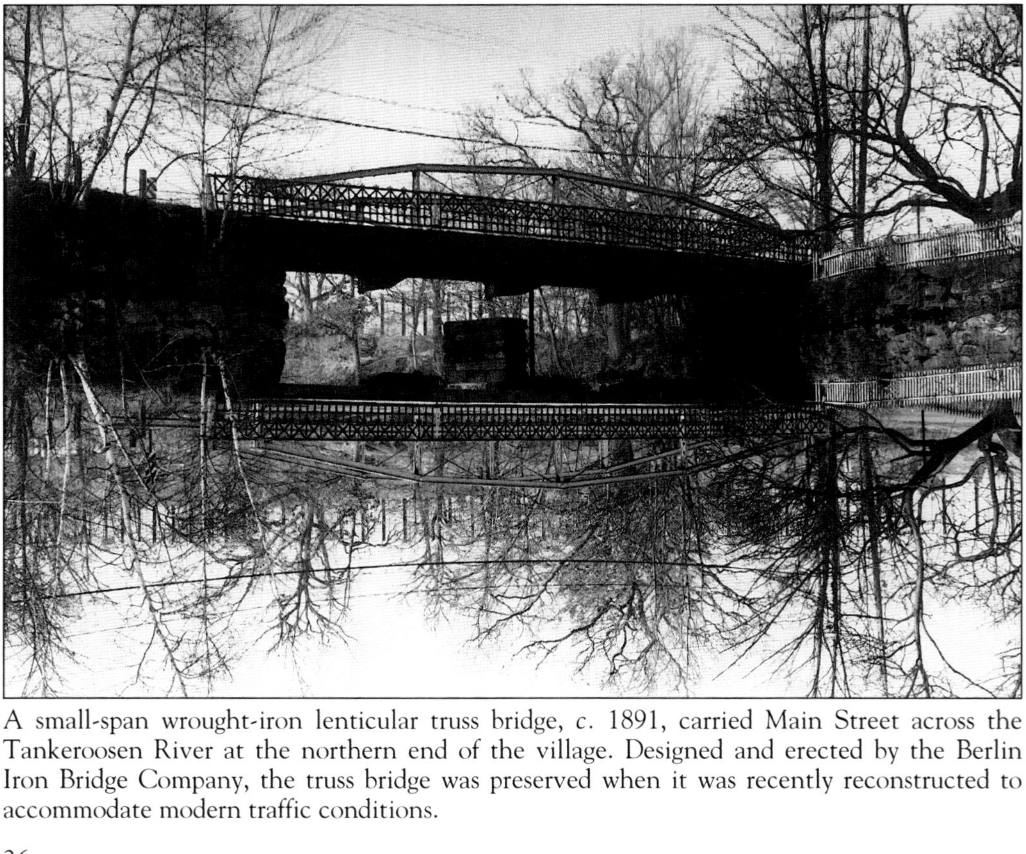

A small-span wrought-iron lenticular truss bridge, *c.* 1891, carried Main Street across the Tankeroosen River at the northern end of the village. Designed and erected by the Berlin Iron Bridge Company, the truss bridge was preserved when it was recently reconstructed to accommodate modern traffic conditions.

Three

Industry on the Hockanum River

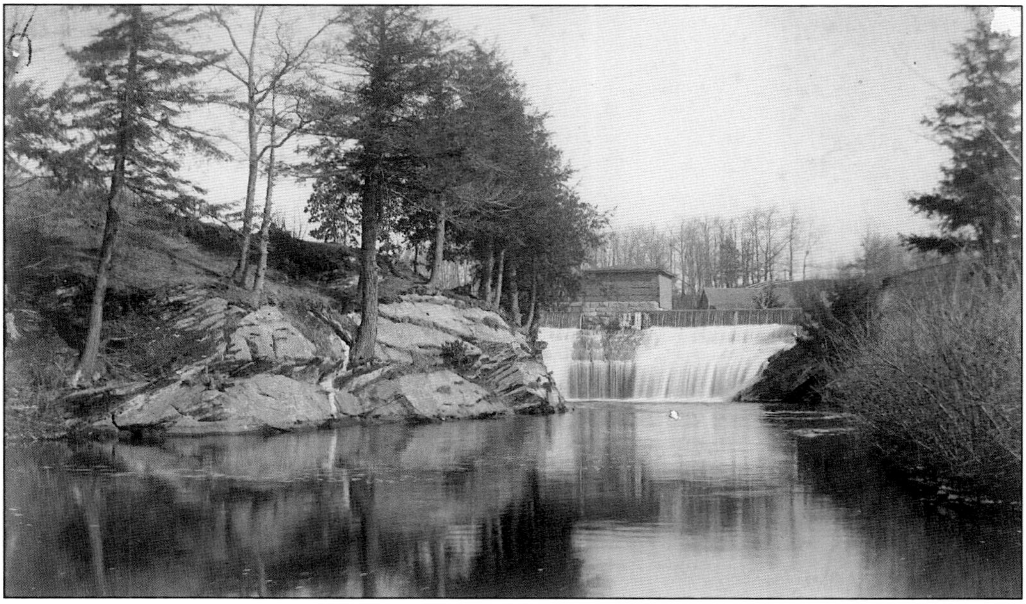

Snipsic Lake Dam was the initial source of water power for Rockville's factories. From this point, the Hockanum River falls 254 feet over a 1.5-mile course. During the nineteenth century, the dam was raised to increase the water available for power, drinking, and recreation. Industrialization in this area created the village of Rockville, which became a chartered city within the town of Vernon in 1889.

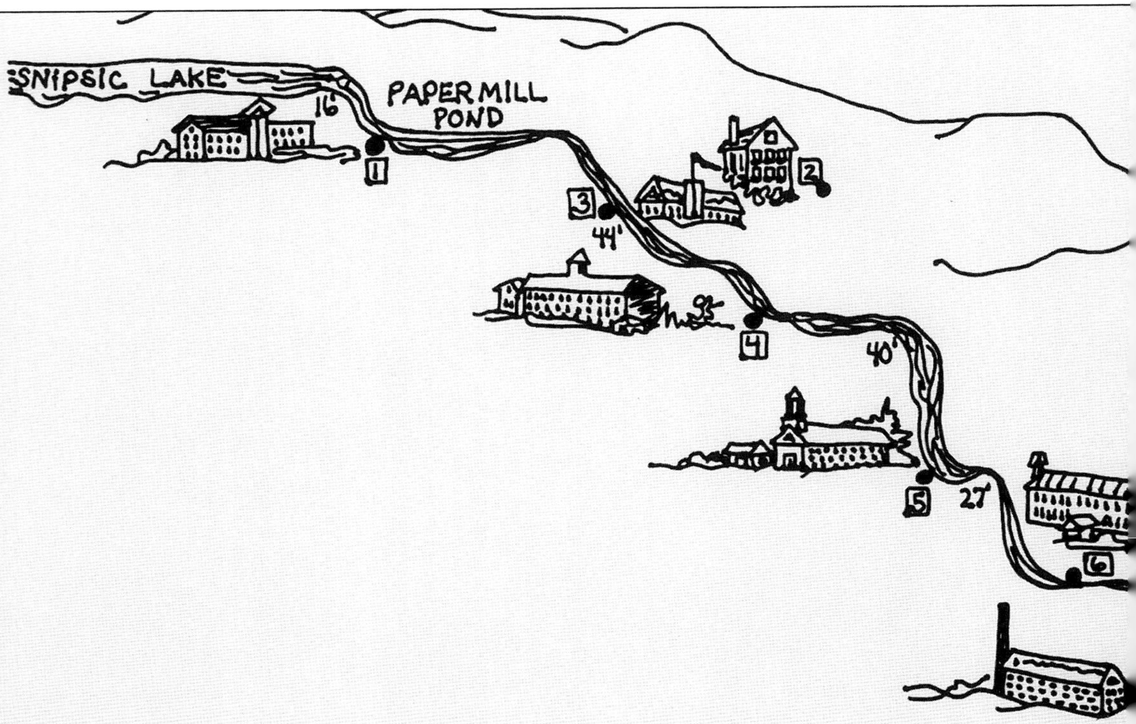

	Company	Product*
1.	Adams Manufacturing Company	Cotton Warp
2.	Cyrus White	Cotton
3.	Belding Brothers	Sewing silk
4.	Samuel Fitch and Sons	Stockinet
5.	American Mills	Cassimeres
6.	Rock Manufacturing Company	Cassimeres
7.	Leeds Company	Cassimeres
8.	White Manufacturing Company	Ginghams
9.	New England Company	Cassimeres
10.	White, Corbin & Company	Envelopes
11.	Springville Company	Satinets
12.	Hockanum Company	Cassimere
13.	Saxony Company	Cassimere

Between 1821 and 1870, 13 factories were built along the Hockanum River in Rockville. The manufacture of fine woolens became the dominant industry. The silk and cotton-thread mills

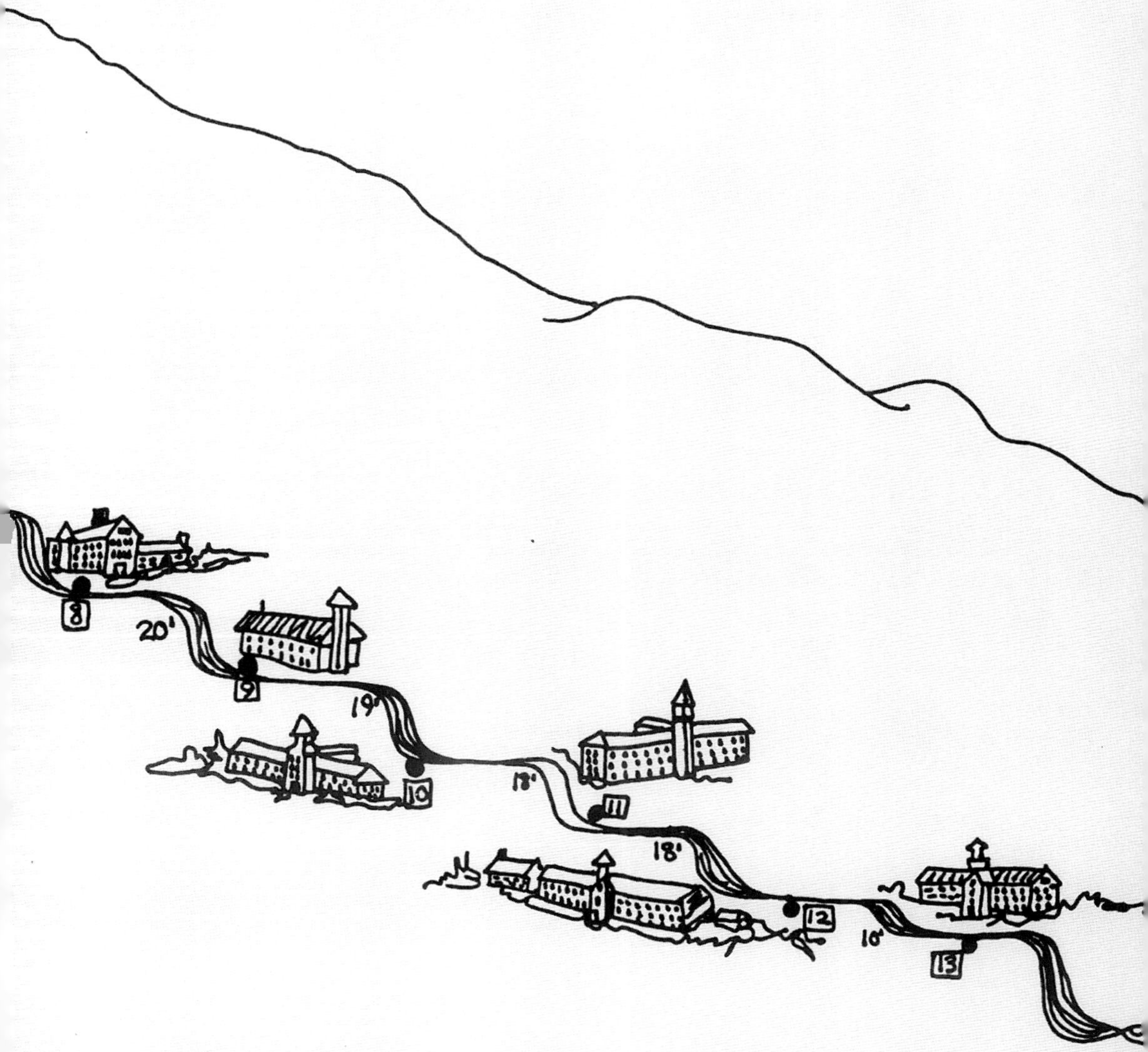

*Cassimere, a fine, tightly-woven all wool fabric.
Satinet, sturdy fabric having a cotton warp and a woolen weft.

did not survive the Great Depression, but the wool mills struggled on until 1951, when they were closed permanently.

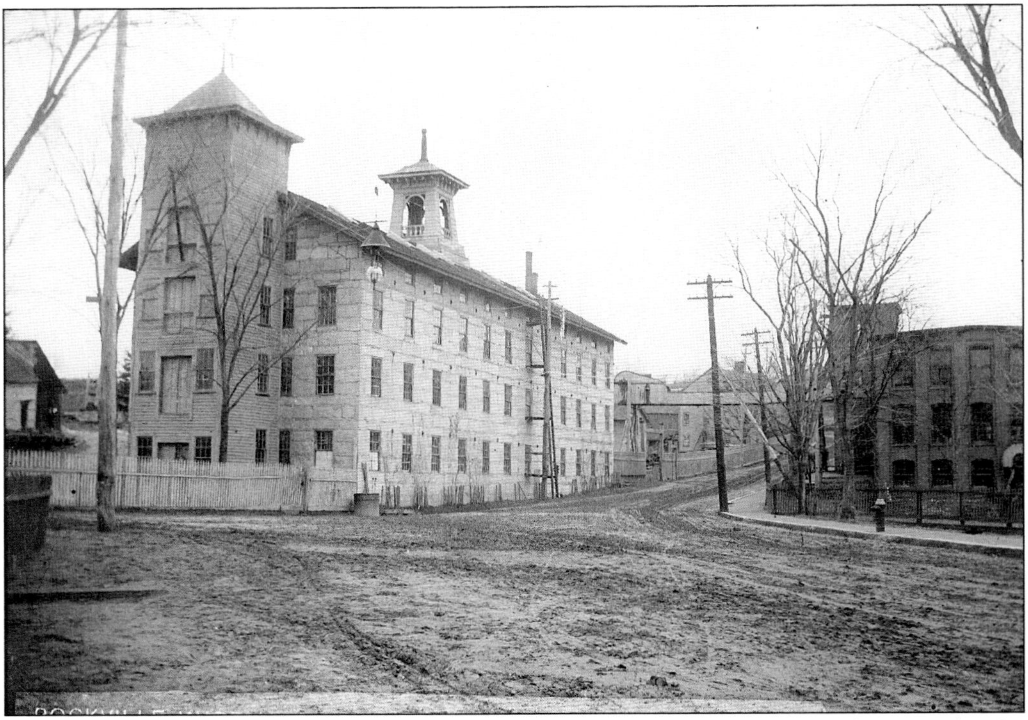

This stone mill, the oldest existing mill building in Rockville, was constructed in 1834 by the Rock Manufacturing Company. It became the Adams Manufacturing Company in 1871. Since this mill was the closest to Snipsic Dam, the owner, Henry Adams would supervise the opening of the gates every morning to send the water on its way to power all of the factories below.

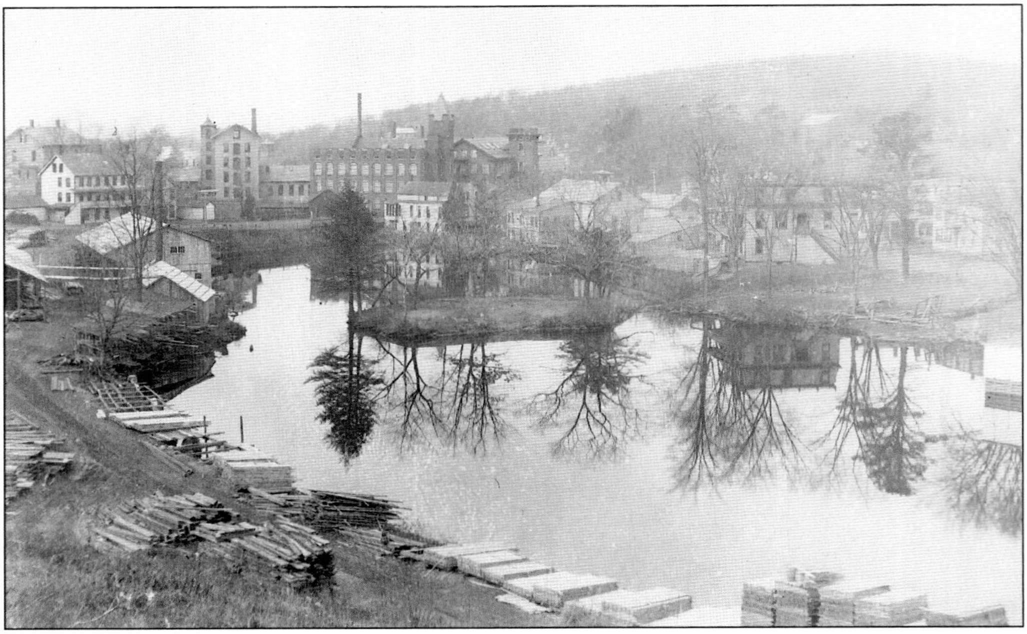

Just before beginning its descent into Rockville, the river enters Paper Mill Pond, named after Francis McLean's short-lived paper mill built in 1833 and demolished by fire in the 1860s. In its place, Albert Dart, the village blacksmith, built the three mills seen in the background.

Dart's Stone mill, certainly the most picturesque of Rockville's mills, was built by Albert Dart in 1868. Leased for several manufacturing ventures, it eventually became the property of the White Manufacturing Company, which produced gingham cloth.

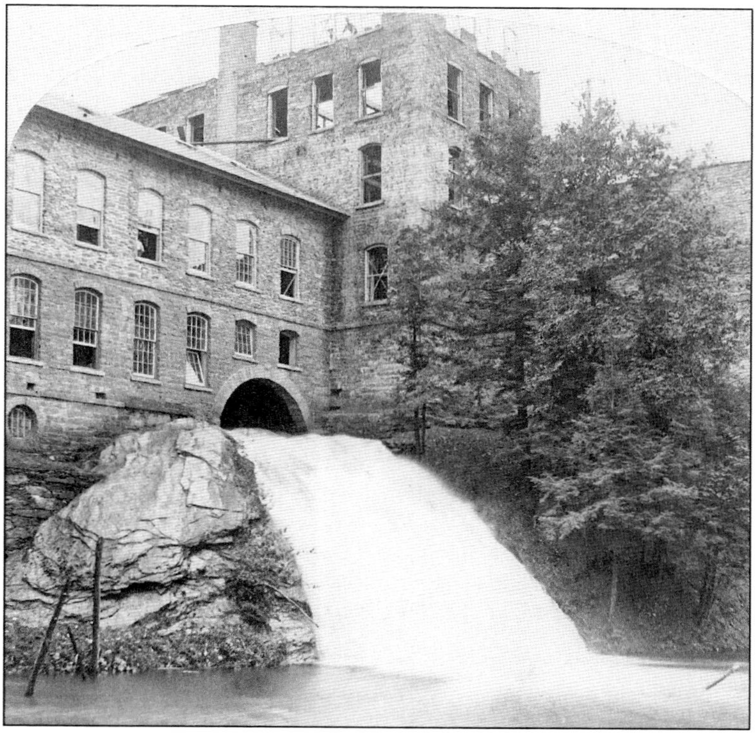

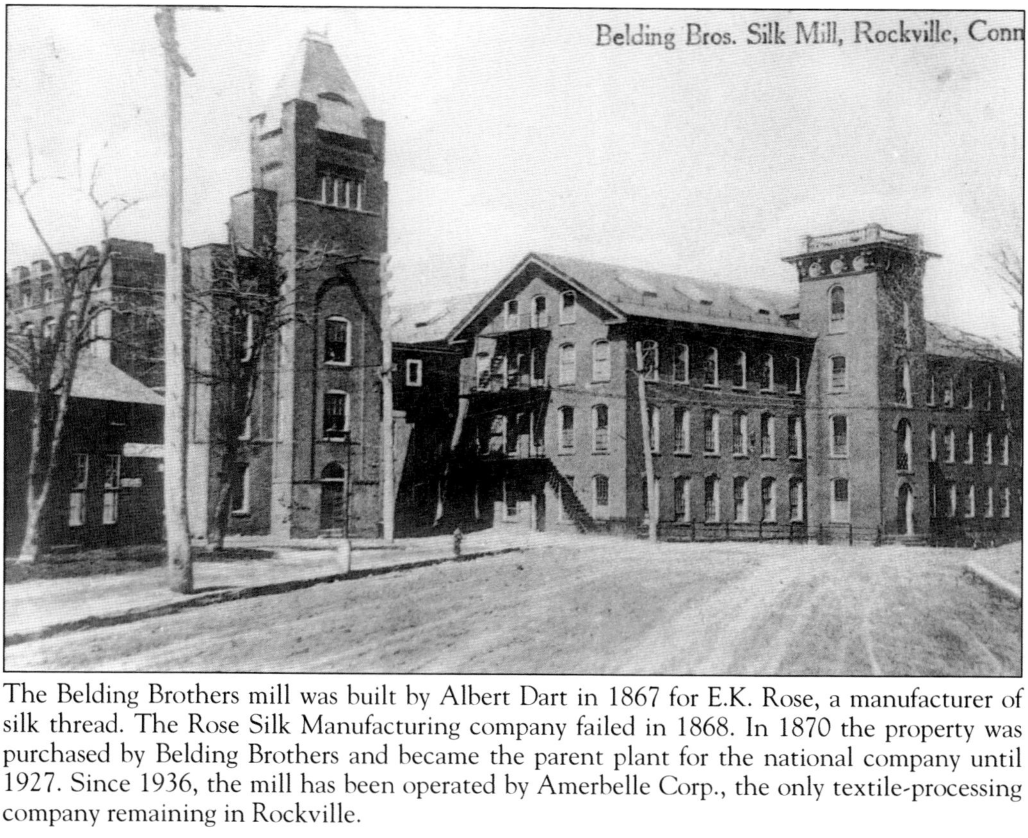

The Belding Brothers mill was built by Albert Dart in 1867 for E.K. Rose, a manufacturer of silk thread. The Rose Silk Manufacturing company failed in 1868. In 1870 the property was purchased by Belding Brothers and became the parent plant for the national company until 1927. Since 1936, the mill has been operated by Amerbelle Corp., the only textile-processing company remaining in Rockville.

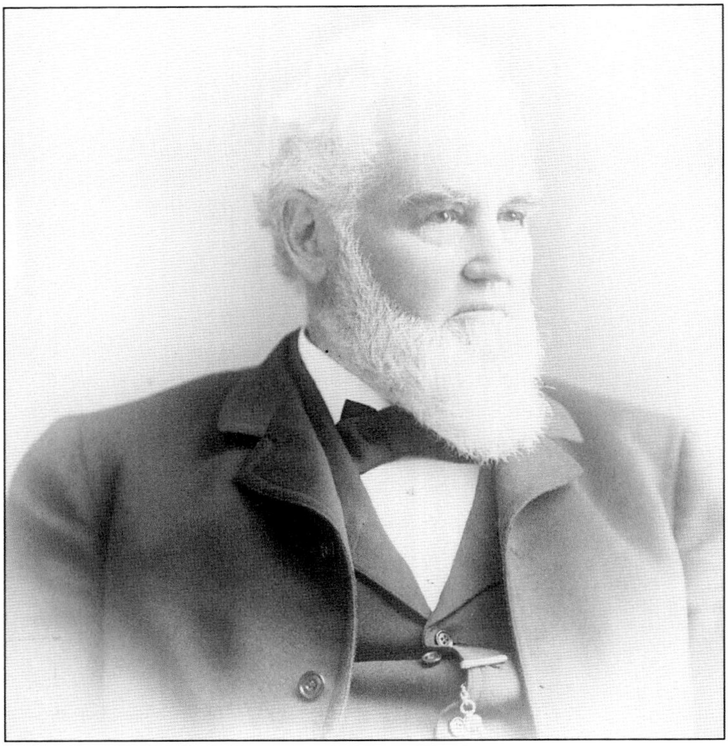

Samuel Fitch was a successful manufacturer and owner of stores and apartments in Rockville, as well as the Fitch Stockinet mill. He was elected mayor when Rockville received a city charter in 1889.

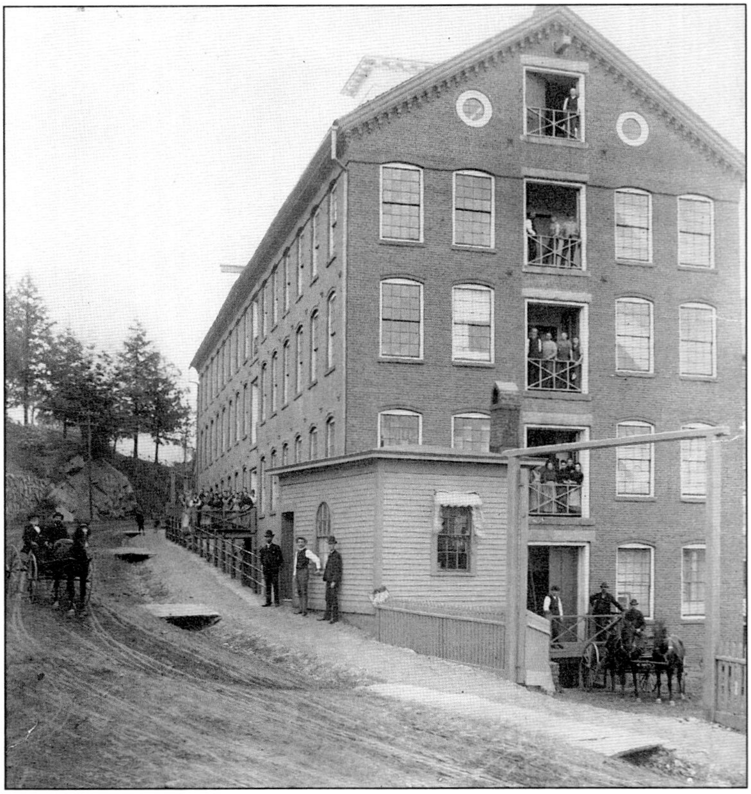

The first of Dart's mills, the Carlisle thread mill, was built in 1865. In 1874 it was purchased by Samuel Fitch and converted to the manufacture of stockinet, a cotton fabric used to line rubber boots. Pictured on the left side of the photograph are Fitch and his son Spencer in the carriage while workers pose in the doorways and windows.

Phineas Talcott, a member of one of Vernon's founding families, came to Rockville in 1847 to serve as agent of the Rock Manufacturing Company. In 1847, he became president of the American Mills Company, the joint-stock company which built the American mill.

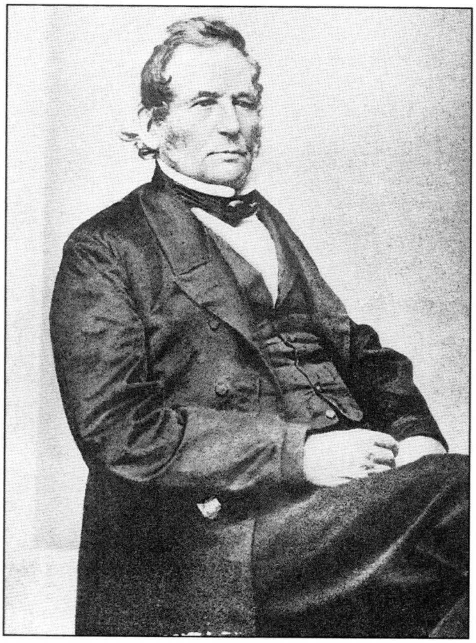

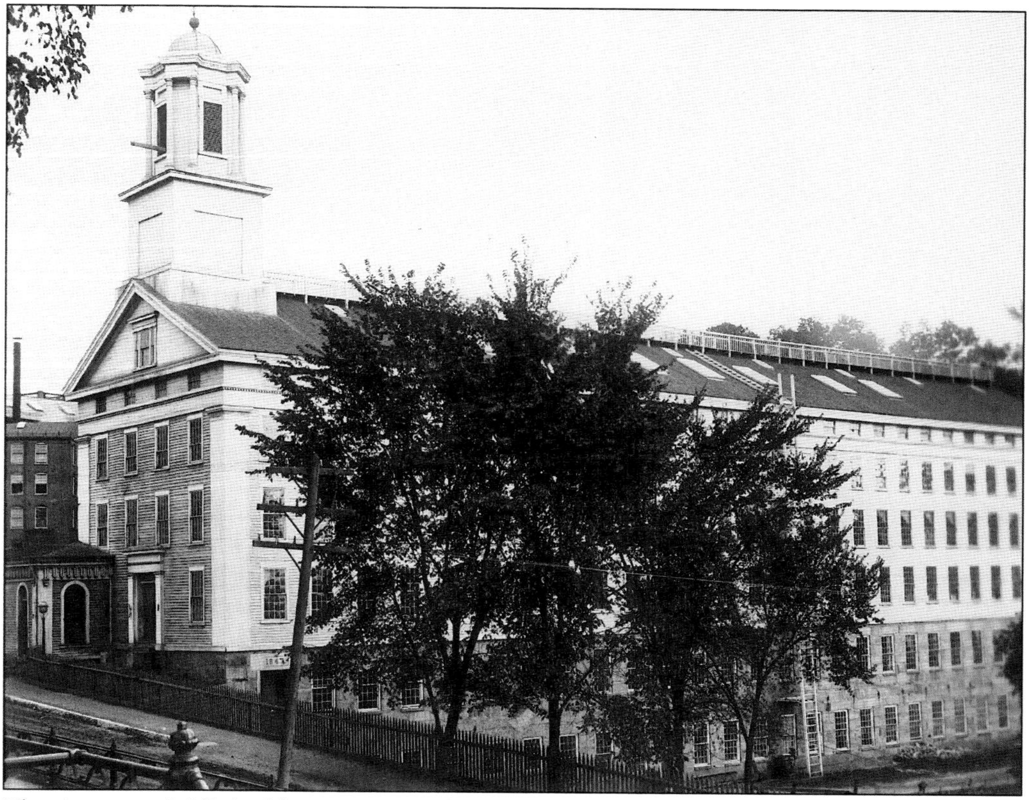

The American Mills building was erected in 1847. The company produced fancy cassimere for men's clothing. The 200-by-45-foot building rose six stories high and was embellished with Greek Revival details and a handsome bell tower. It was the largest of the early wood-framed mill buildings to be constructed in Rockville.

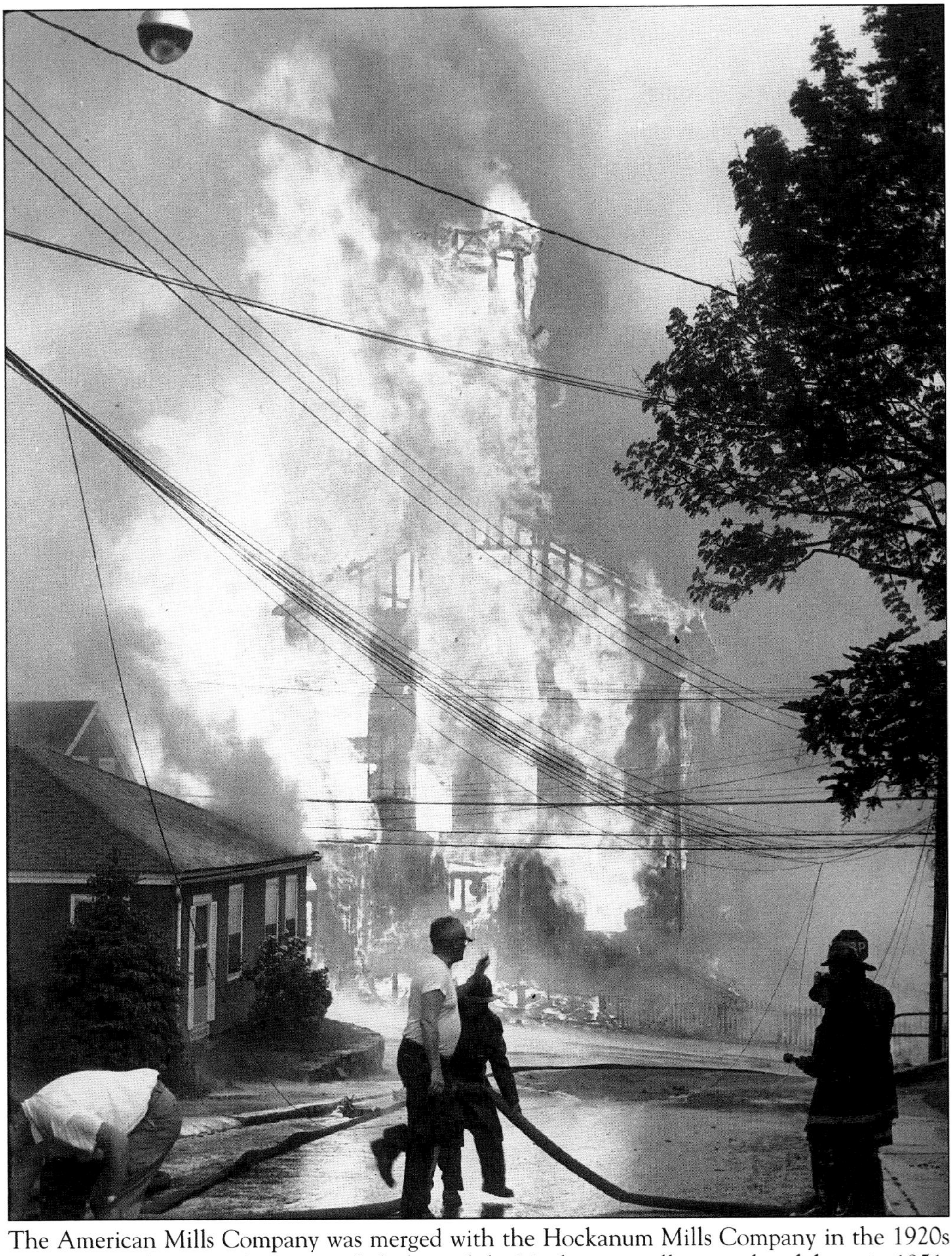

The American Mills Company was merged with the Hockanum Mills Company in the 1920s and continued to manufacture wool cloth until the Hockanum mills were closed down in 1951. In 1960 a dramatic fire consumed the American mill. Fortunately the fire was contained, but onlookers recalled that the intense heat blistered the paint on surrounding buildings.

In 1821 George Kellogg, in association with Francis McLean and Ralph Talcott, founded the Rock Manufacturing Company. Kellogg remained the leading wool manufacturer in Rockville throughout his life and was acclaimed by the American wool industry as one of its most distinguished pioneer manufacturers.

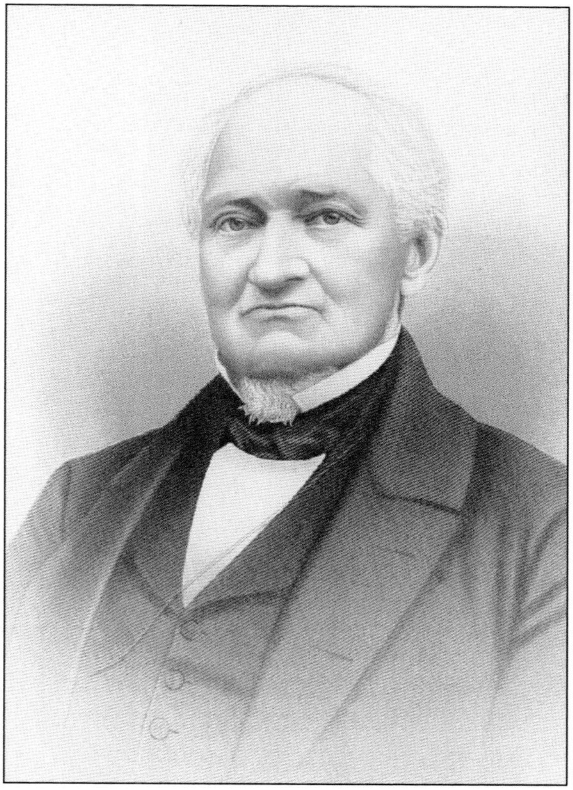

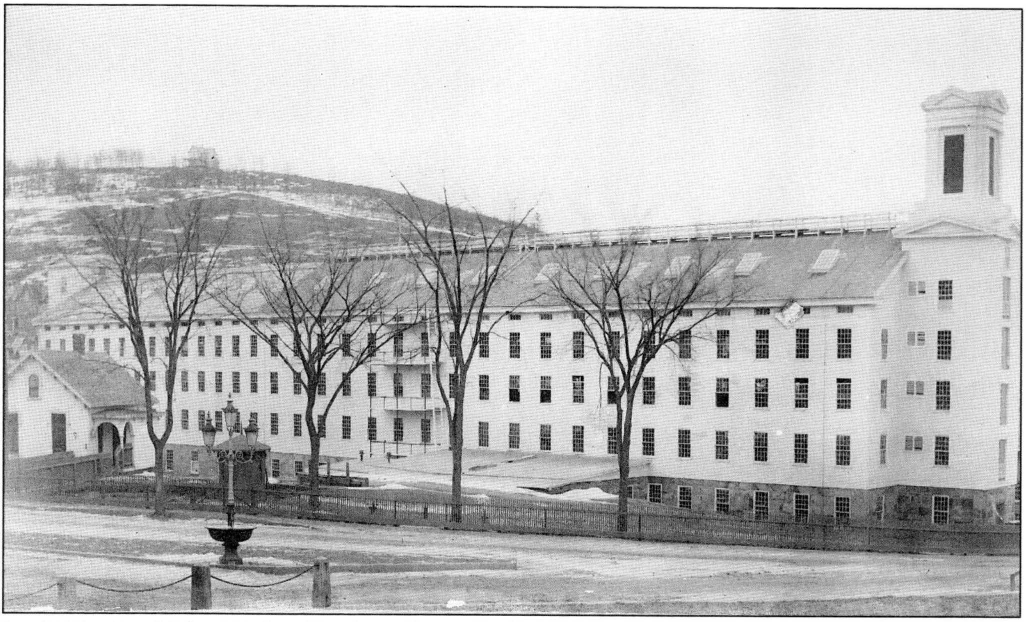

In 1821, the 80-by-30-foot Rock mill was built on the cascades of the Hockanum River in what later became Rockville. It was Vernon's first true factory in which all the processes of manufacture from raw material to finished product were combined in one place. Expanded in 1847, the building continued in use until the 1920s, when the Rock Company dissolved and the century-old building was torn down.

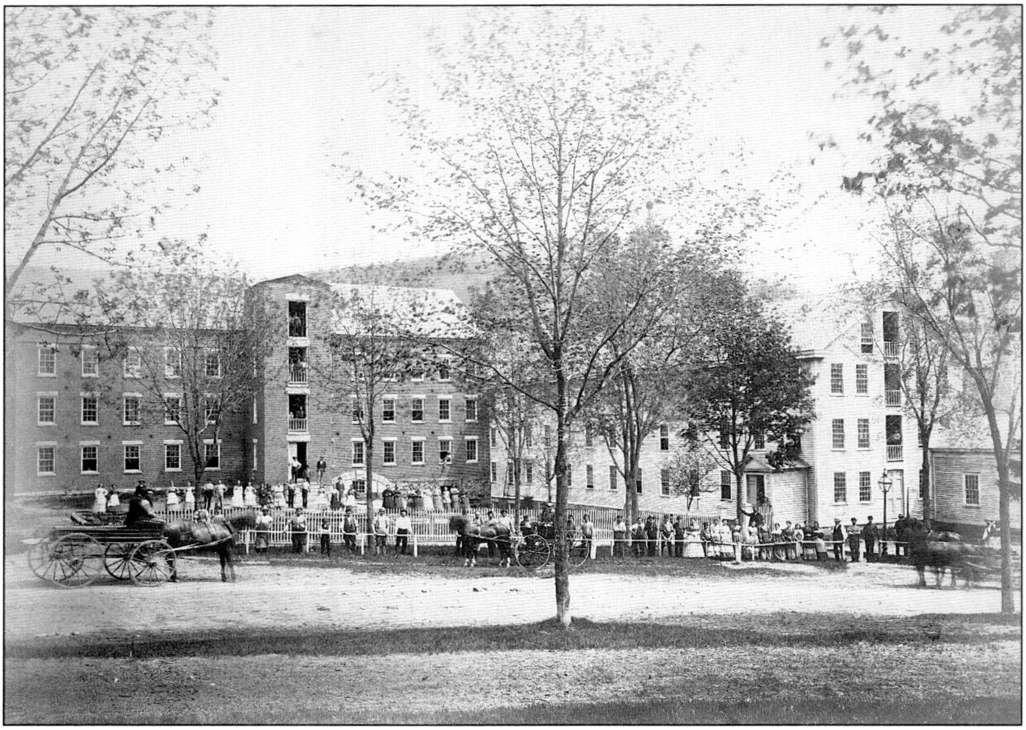

Leeds mill, an expansion of the Rock Company, was built in 1832. In 1843, it became a separate organization, the Leeds Company, but was re-incorporated into the Rock Manufacturing Company in 1873. It was located on West Main Street just opposite the Rockville General Hospital parking lot.

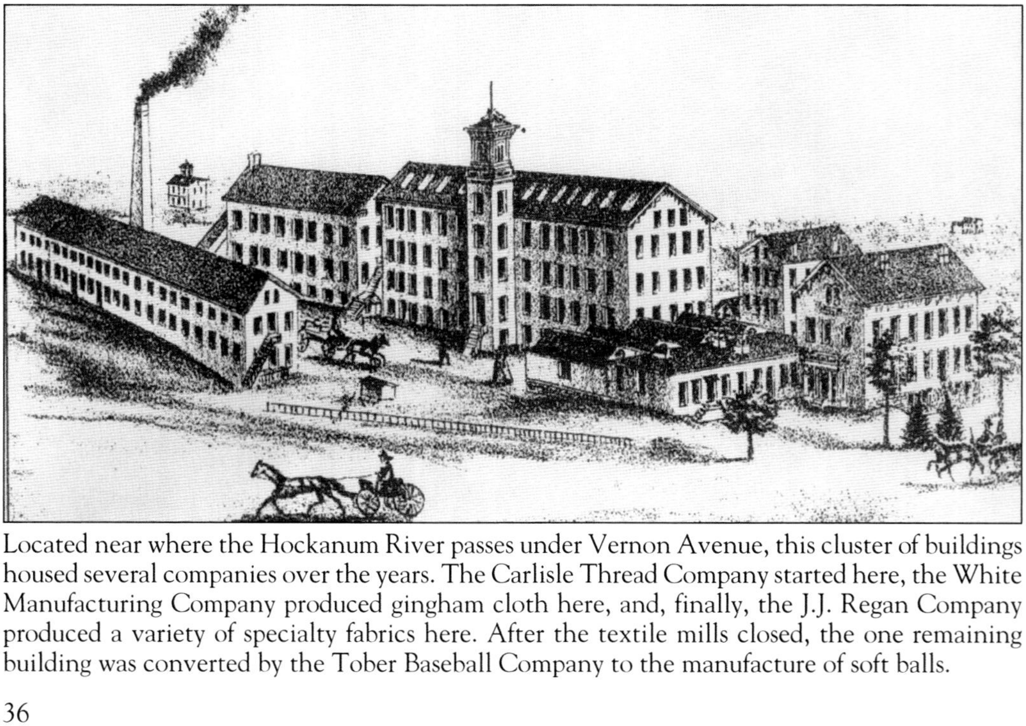

Located near where the Hockanum River passes under Vernon Avenue, this cluster of buildings housed several companies over the years. The Carlisle Thread Company started here, the White Manufacturing Company produced gingham cloth here, and, finally, the J.J. Regan Company produced a variety of specialty fabrics here. After the textile mills closed, the one remaining building was converted by the Tober Baseball Company to the manufacture of soft balls.

Allen Hammond, scion of another Vernon family and a former schoolteacher, joined George Kellogg in organizing the New England Company in 1837. He was the first of Rockville's wool manufacturers to begin using Crompton looms, which he installed in the New England mill in 1842, to manufacture all-wool cassimere.

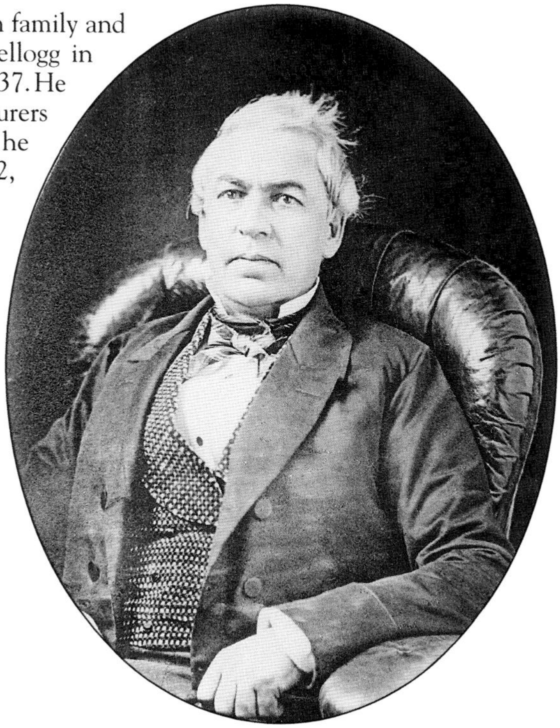

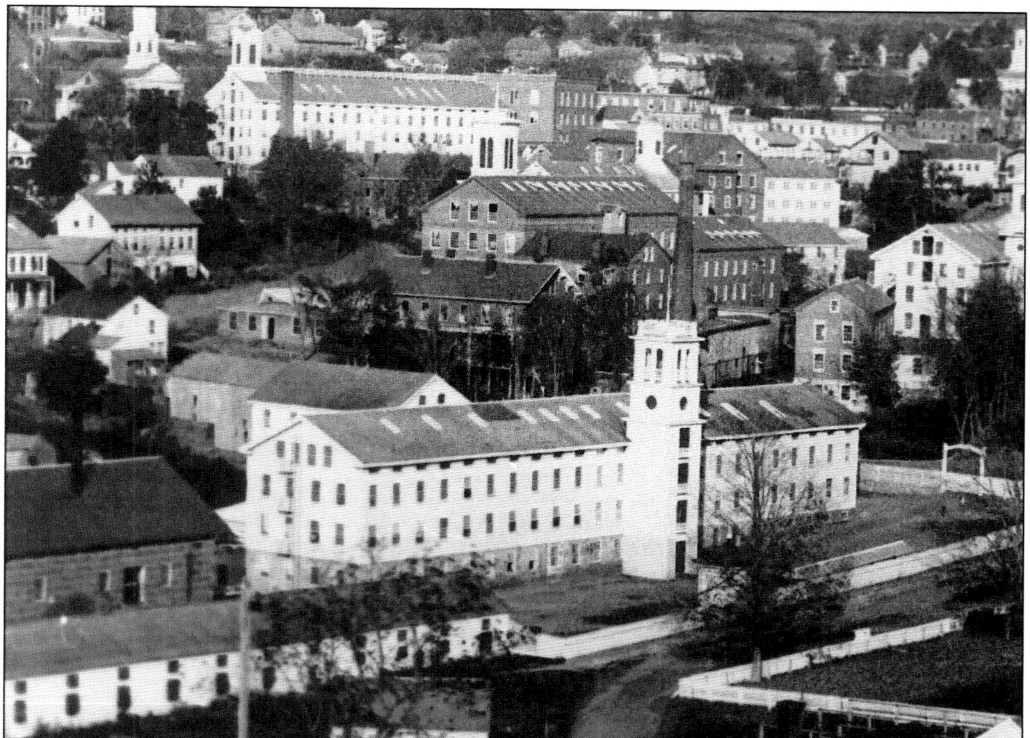

The New England mill was built in 1837, burned to the ground shortly after, and was immediately rebuilt. This view shows the mill as it appeared in the late nineteenth century.

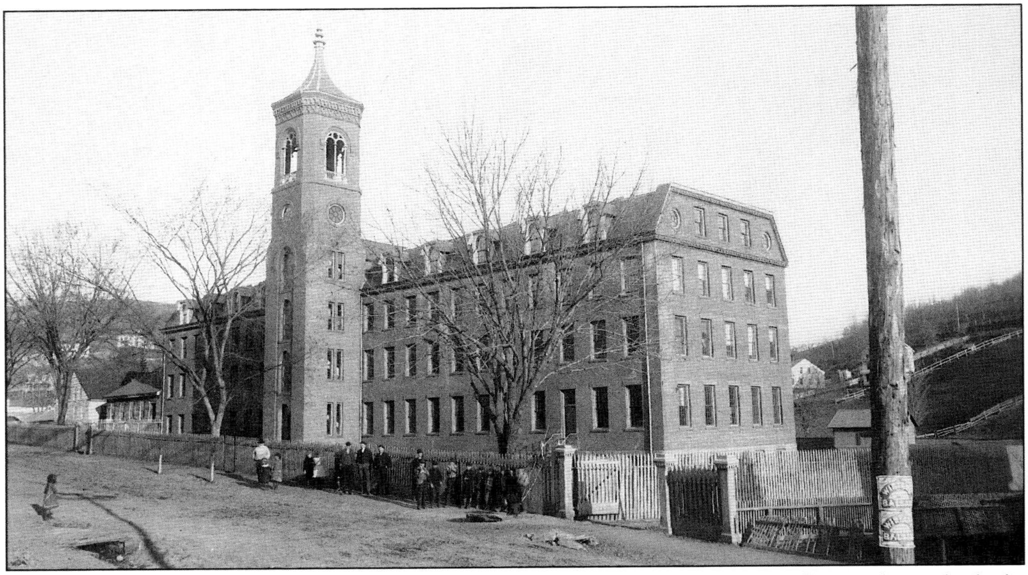

The Florence mill, built in 1864 to replace an earlier building, manufactured wool cloth. Overextended as a result of the prosperous Civil War years, the company failed in 1869, and the building subsequently became property of White, Corbin and Company, later the U.S. Envelope Company. When it was closed down in the 1970s, the building was converted to apartments for the elderly, but its original architecture has been preserved.

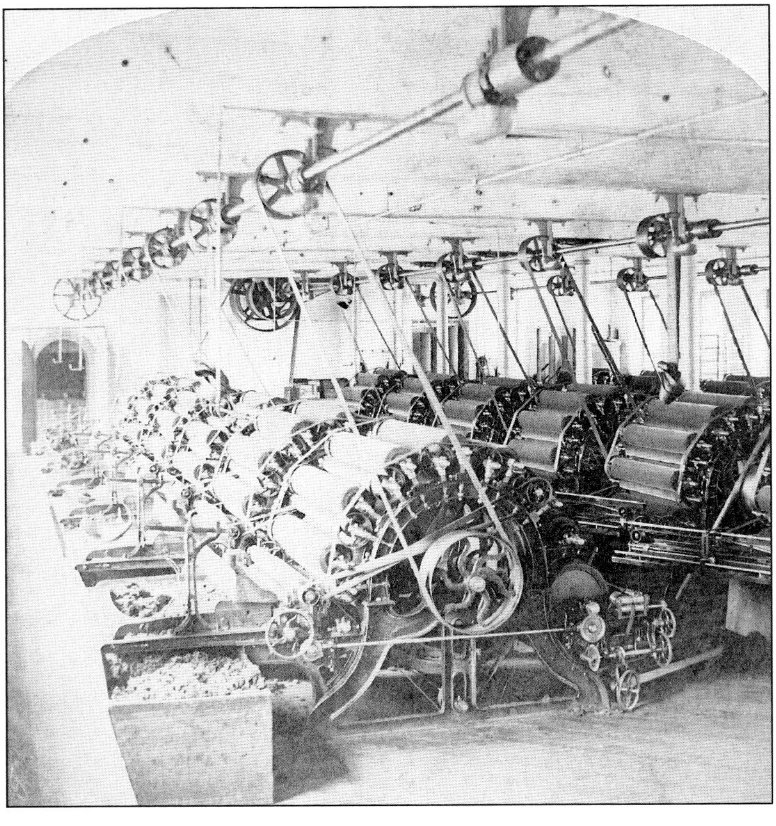

A rare 1868 stereograph provides a view of the Florence mill carding room in the period just prior to the failure of the company. At its peak, it was one of Rockville's most modern woolen mills.

Millwright Chauncey Winchell, in association with others, organized the Springville Manufacturing Company in 1833. He served as president of this small but highly profitable company for 52 years.

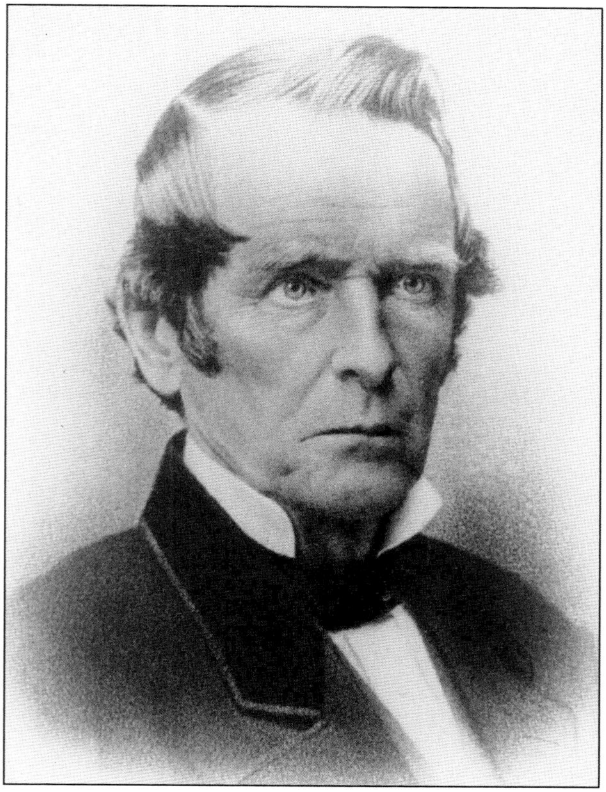

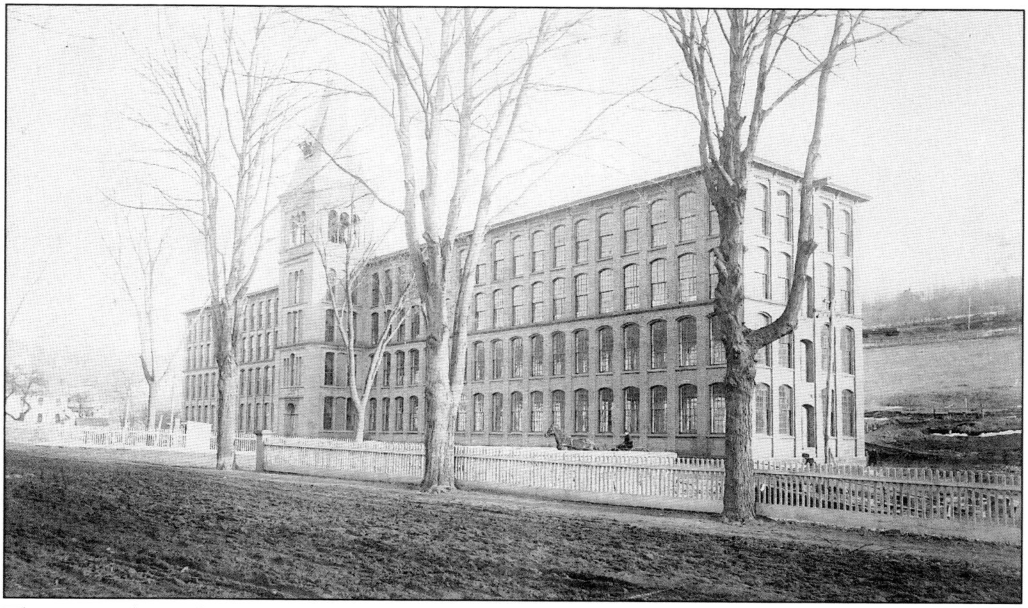

The original wood-framed Springville mill was replaced in 1886 by the brick mill shown here. Equipped with exceptionally large windows, an elevator, gas and electric lighting, and automatic sprinklers, it was considered a model manufacturing building for its time. Although recently converted to apartments, the building's historic architecture has been preserved.

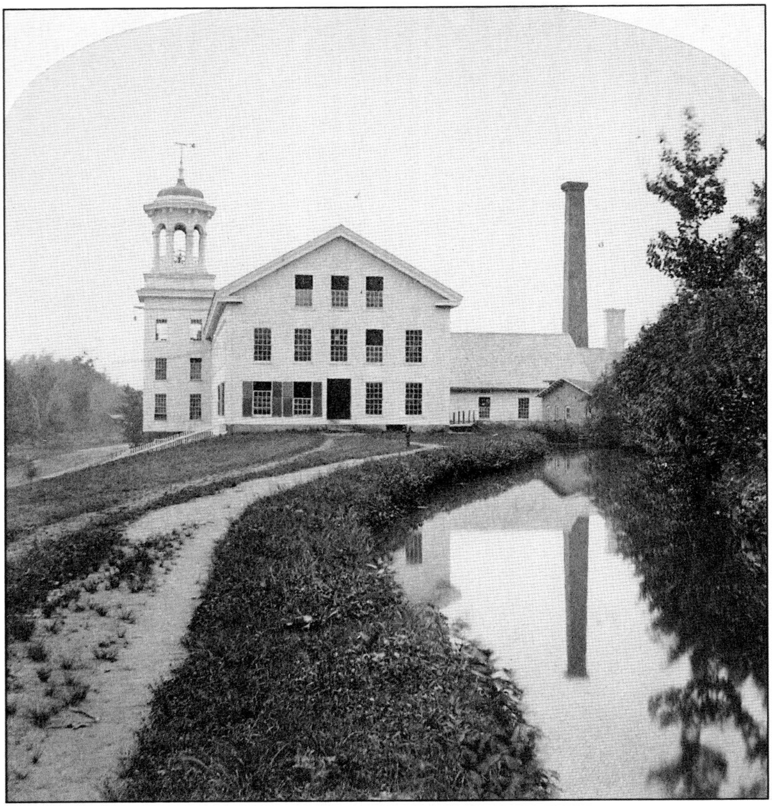

The Hockanum mill was constructed in 1855, a replica of an 1849 building destroyed by fire. The Hockanum Company, organized in 1836, merged with the other Rockville woolen mills in 1906 to form the Hockanum Mills Company, which won national and international renown for the quality of its worsted men's wear. In 1934 the company was purchased by J.P. Stevens Company, who finally closed down the mills in 1951.

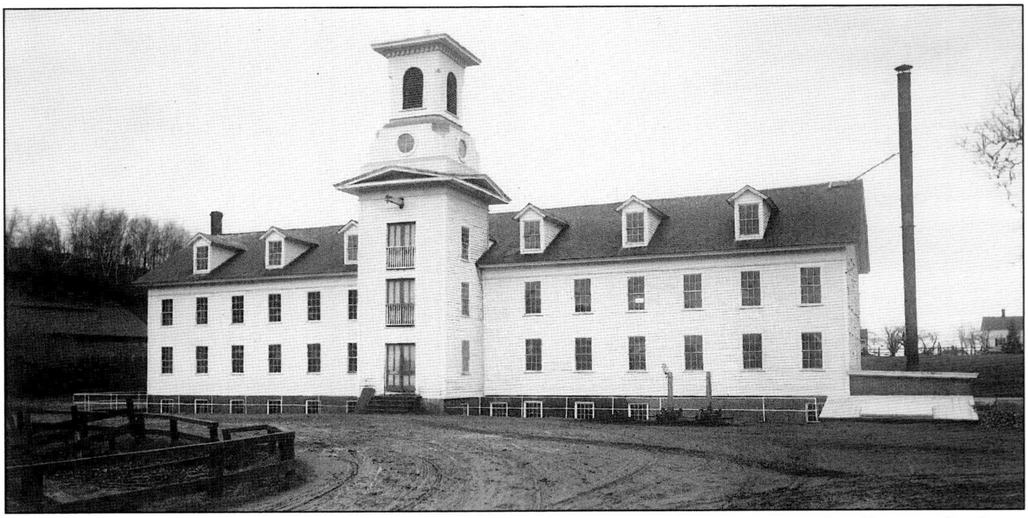

The Saxony mill, located at the lowest level of the Hockanum River in Rockville, was built in 1836. It was doubled in size and the stair and bell tower added in 1870. Following the failure of the company in 1873, the mill was purchased by the Hockanum Company. It remained in use for manufacturing purposes until recently. Sadly, it was destroyed by fire in 1994.

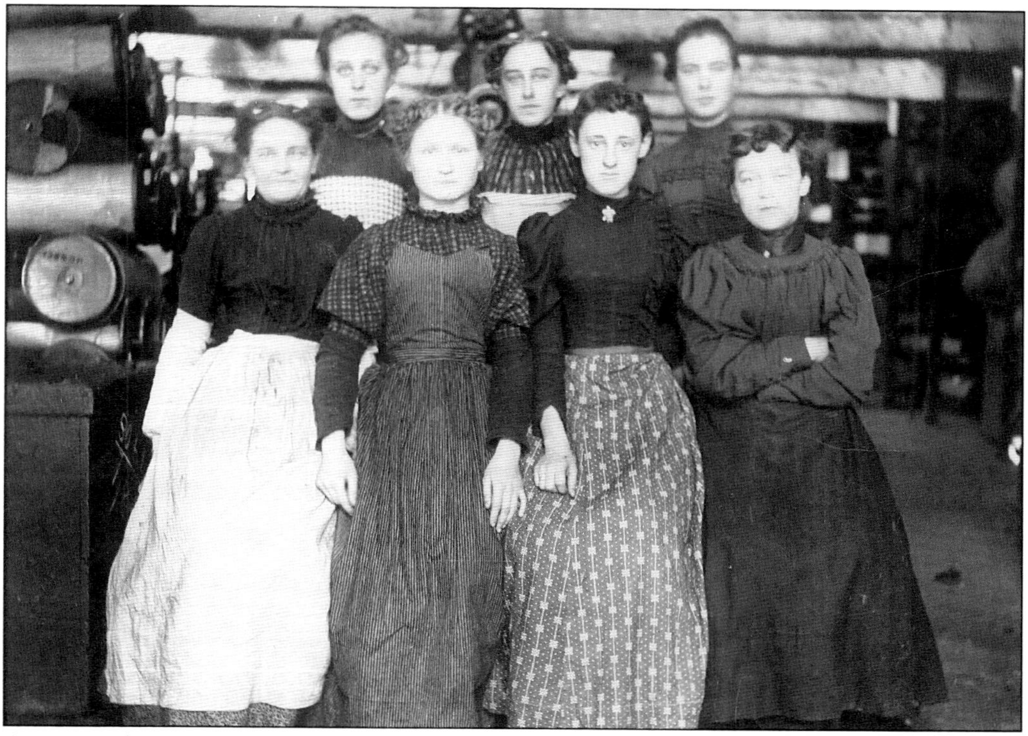

A group of young mill workers pose in front of their looms. The undated photograph was probably taken about 1900. Typically, the women wore aprons to protect their clothing from the oil used in woolen cloth production.

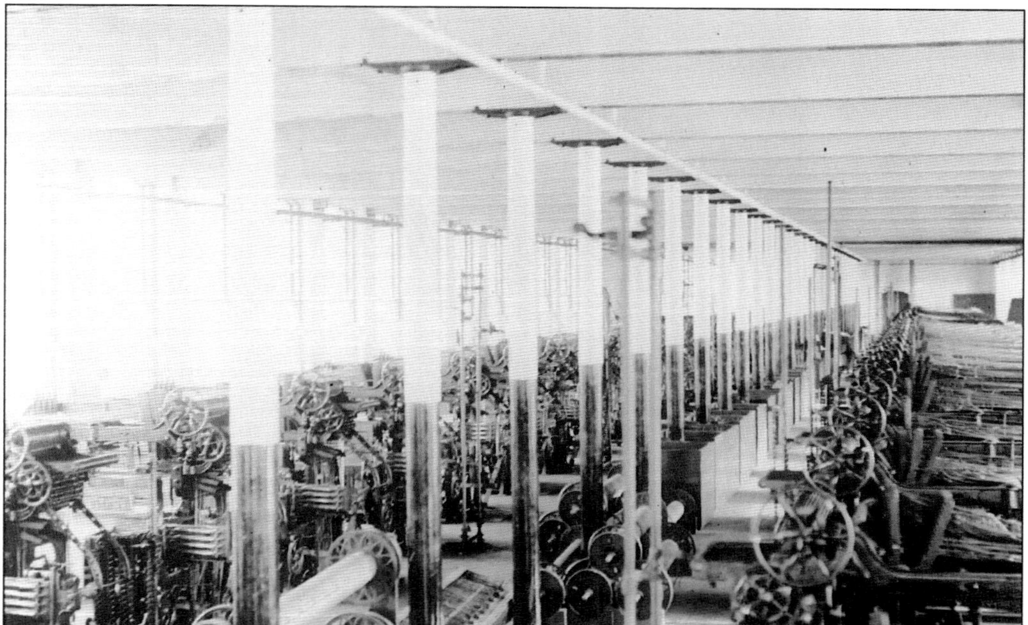

This photograph of the huge weave room in the Springville mill was taken in 1926. The deafening sound when all the looms were in operation often left long-time weavers with impaired hearing.

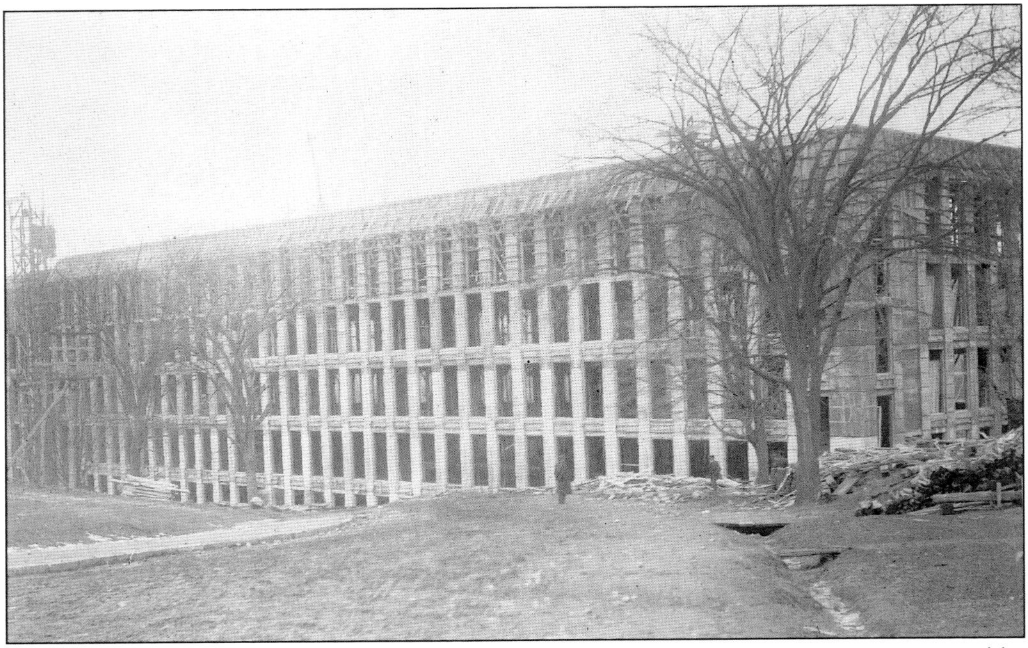

The Minterburn mill, the last of the textile mills to be built in Rockville, was constructed by the Hockanum Mills Company following the merger of 1906. Older buildings were demolished, and a modern concrete structure, 300-by-56 feet, was added to the 1834 stone mill previously owned by the Rockville Warp Mills Company. Following the closing of the woolen mills, the building became the home of Roosevelt Mills, which manufactured sweaters.

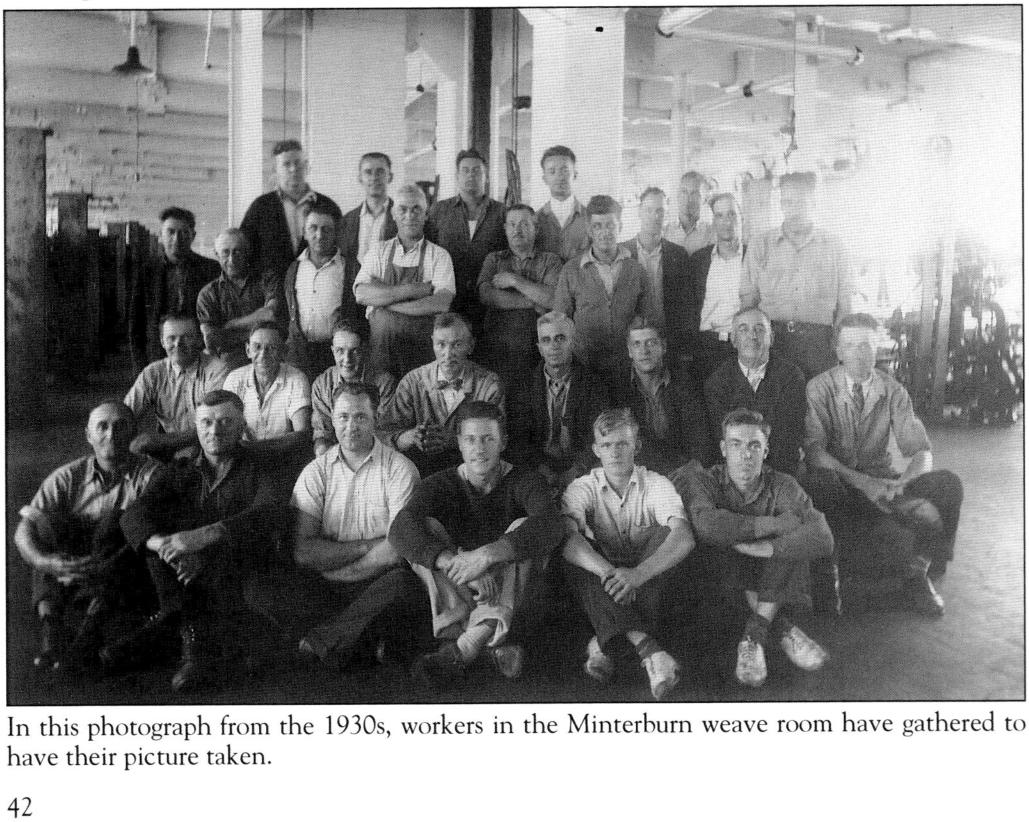

In this photograph from the 1930s, workers in the Minterburn weave room have gathered to have their picture taken.

Four

The Industrial Village of Rockville

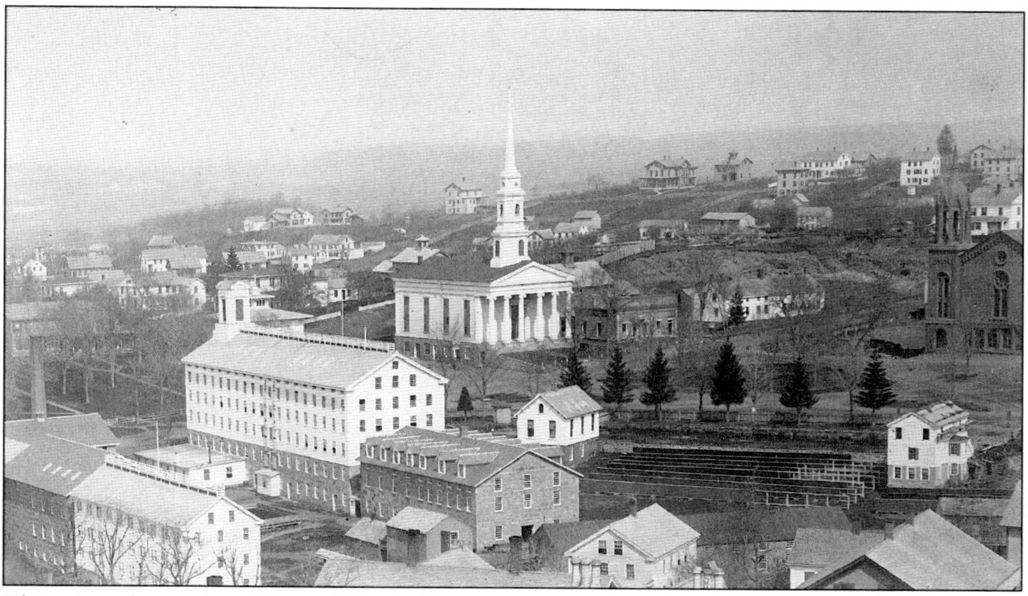

This view shows the village of Rockville as it appeared in the 1870s. Dominating the scene is the Second Congregational Church, built in 1848. To the left are the Rock Manufacturing Company buildings. In the right foreground are the tenter racks on which the fulled wool cloth was stretched to dry. On the extreme right is the Rockville Methodist Episcopal Church, built in 1867, now serving as Vernon's senior center.

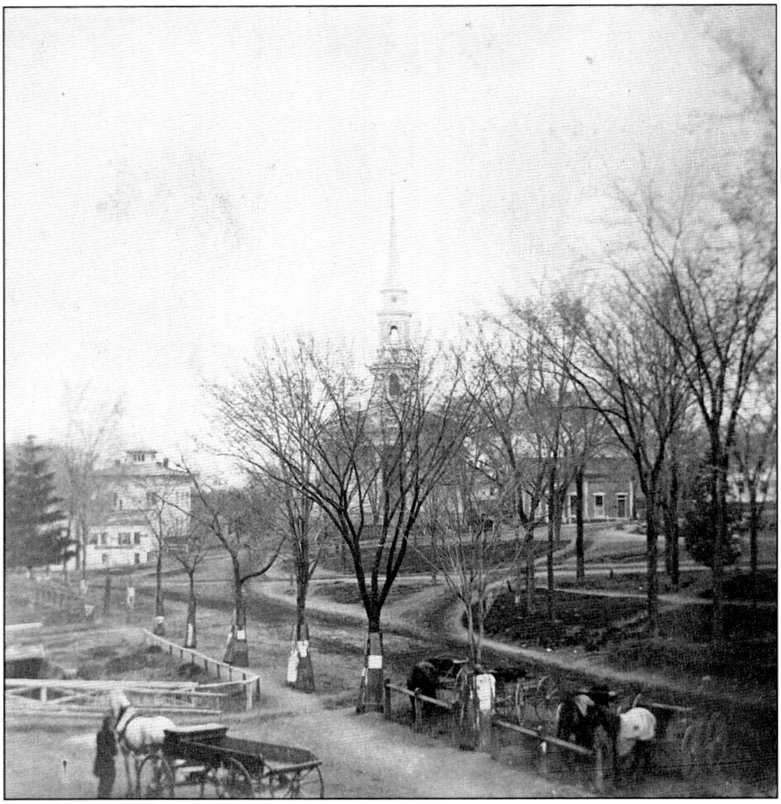

An early stereograph shows Central Park in the late 1860s planted with graceful elm trees. Walks and curbing were added later. On the left, small wooden bridges cross the canal that supplied water power for the Rock mill.

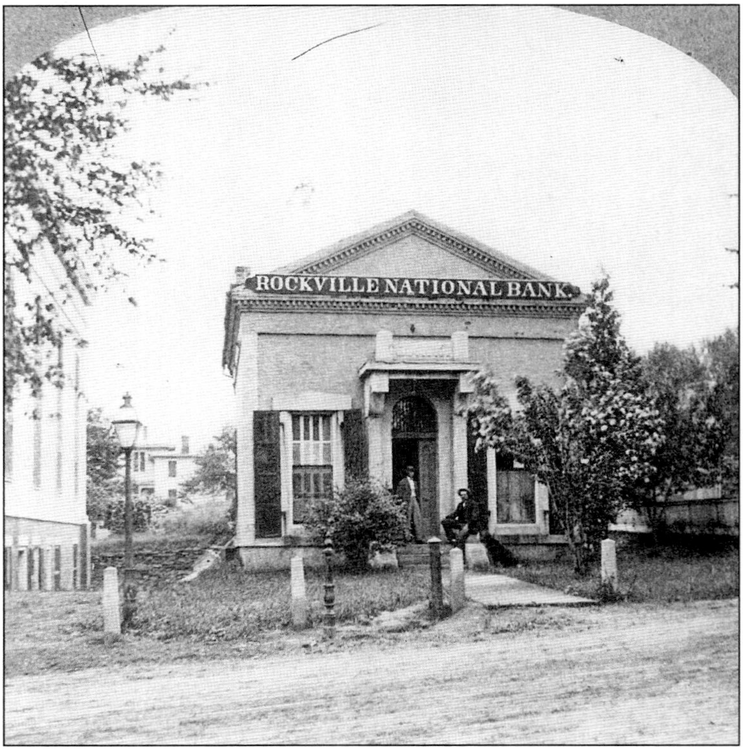

The Rockville National Bank, the first commercial bank in Rockville, was established in 1855 by a group of leading businessmen. Located on Elm Street adjacent to the Second Congregational Church, the building was replaced following a fire in 1889. In the twentieth century the bank was merged with the Connecticut Bank and Trust Company.

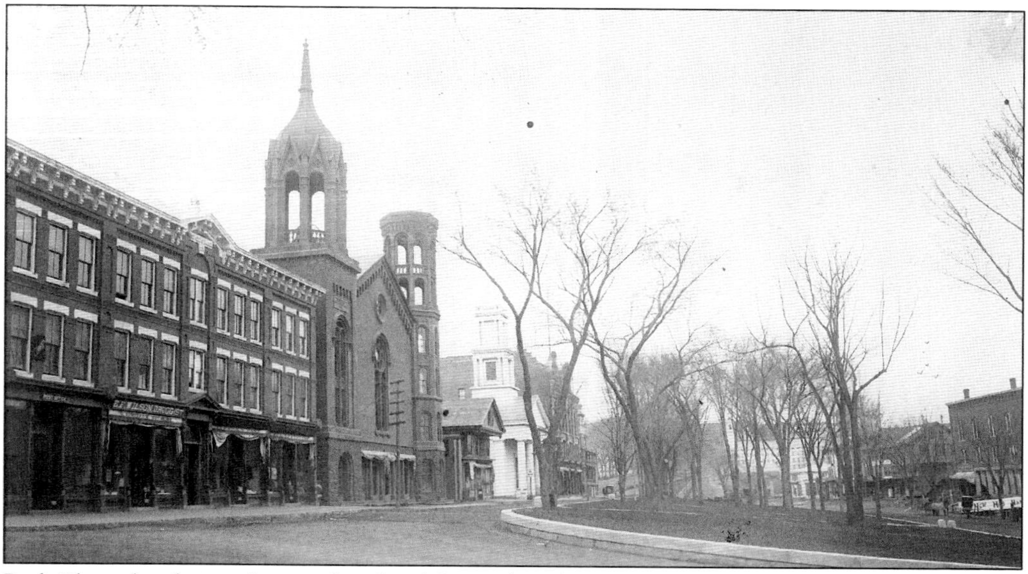

Park Place, bordering the north side of Central Park, was improved in 1879 with the building of the Citizen's Block (shown on the left). To the right of it is the Methodist church, a small store, and the First Congregational Church, built in 1837. In the center of the photograph is a glimpse of the Rockville Hotel. Commercial buildings line Main Street on the south side of the park.

Looking east on Main Street, St. Bernard's Terrace is on the upper left. The American mill can be seen in the center, and in the right foreground are several wood-framed commercial buildings. The streets were still unpaved and pedestrians had to endure clouds of dust in summer and ice, snow, and mud in the winter.

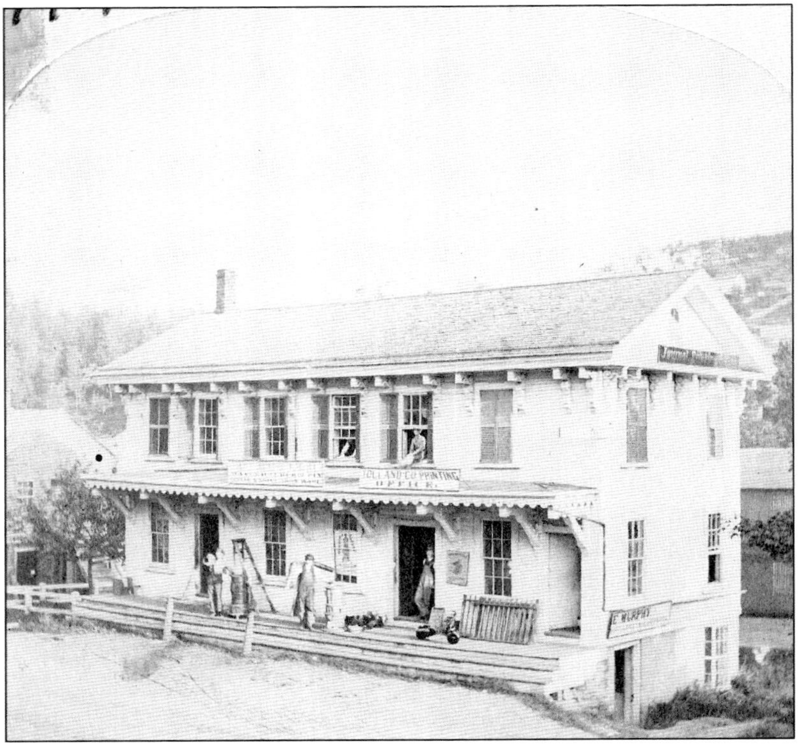

One of Rockville's early local papers, *The Rockville Journal*, had its office in the Butler Block on Main Street, as shown in this 1868 stereograph. A second local paper, the *Rockville Leader*, was later located on this same site.

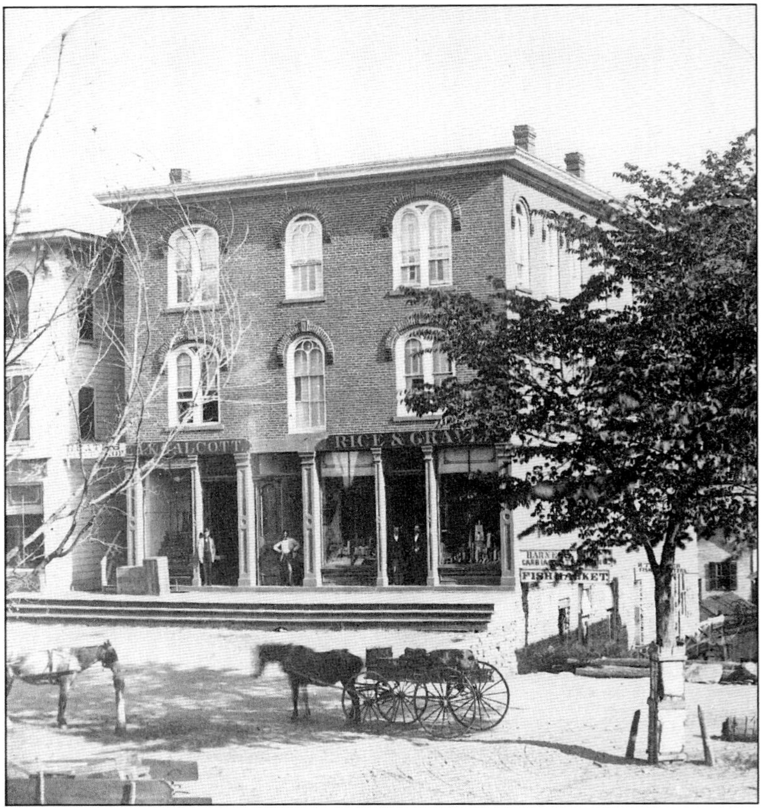

The Talcott Brothers store, shown here in a 1870s stereograph, was located in the Orcutt Block on Main Street. It sold "crockery and glassware." This Italianate-style structure was torn down during the 1960s urban renewal project.

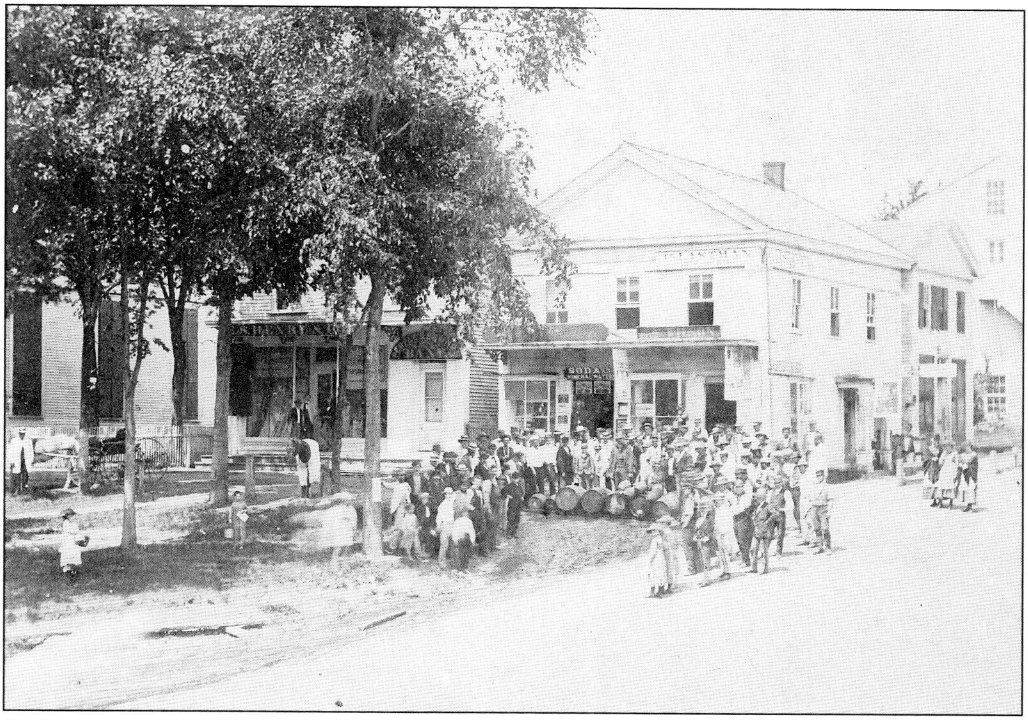

During the 1860s a vigorous temperance movement advocated the banning of "spirituous liquors" and Rockville briefly became a "dry" town. One summer day in 1871, a band of Rockville temperance advocates gathered in Central Park, near the corner of Park Place and Park Streets, and watched as town officials poured out several barrels of confiscated liquor into a nearby gutter.

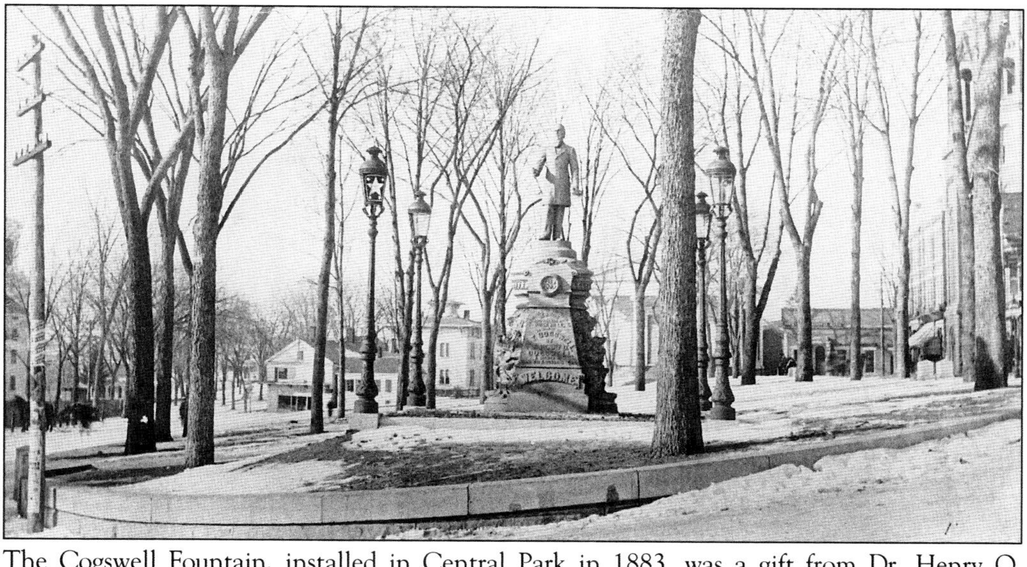

The Cogswell Fountain, installed in Central Park in 1883, was a gift from Dr. Henry O. Cogswell, an enthusiastic supporter of temperance. The statue on top represented Dr. Cogswell holding a glass of water in one hand and a temperance pledge in the other. In 1885 the statue mysteriously disappeared. It was eventually recovered but not replaced and eventually became part of a World War II scrap drive.

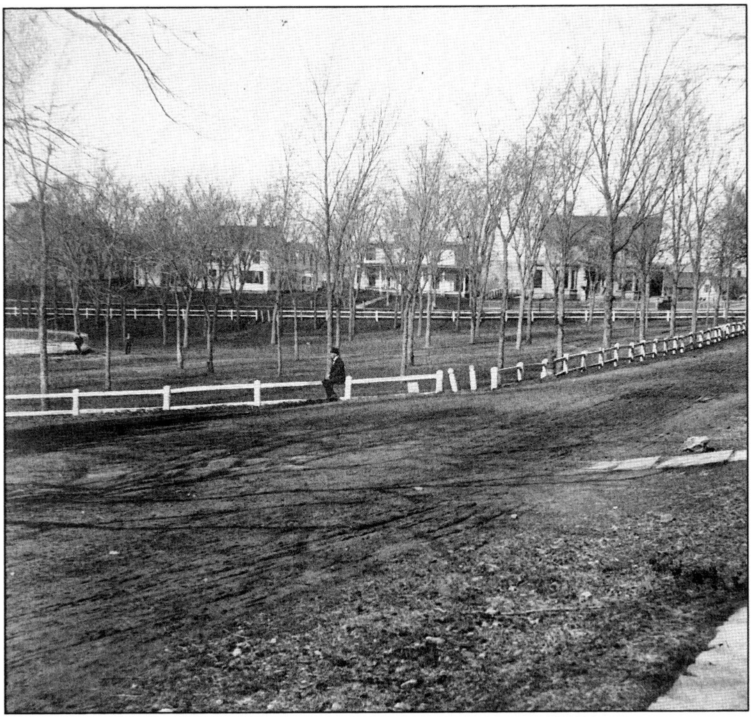

Originally used as a cow pasture, Talcott Park developed in the 1860s and 1870s as a small city park with many fine houses along its perimeter. Local residents, led by Mrs. Hudson Kellogg, formed a Park Association, and planted elm trees and marked the boundaries with a rail fence. In 1895 the Park Association gave the park to the city. Later, a fountain and bandstand were added.

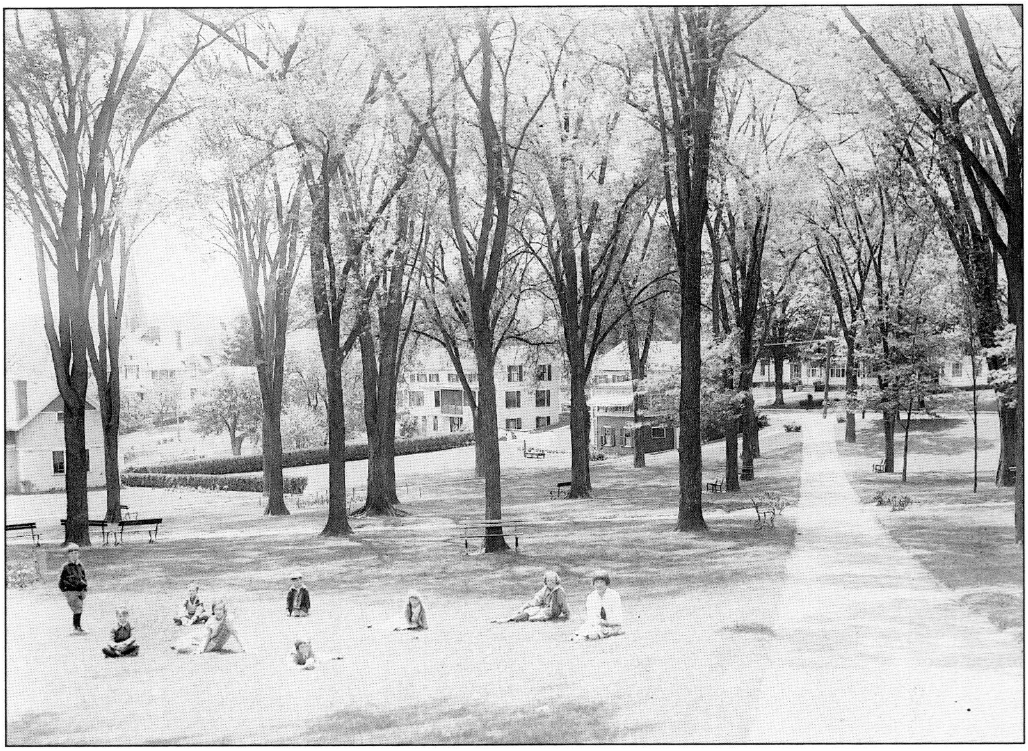

A photograph of Talcott Park taken in the 1930s shows the stately elms full grown. Soon after, the Hurricane of 1938 toppled them all. They were replaced by maple trees, which continue to provide a shady, restful spot for pedestrians.

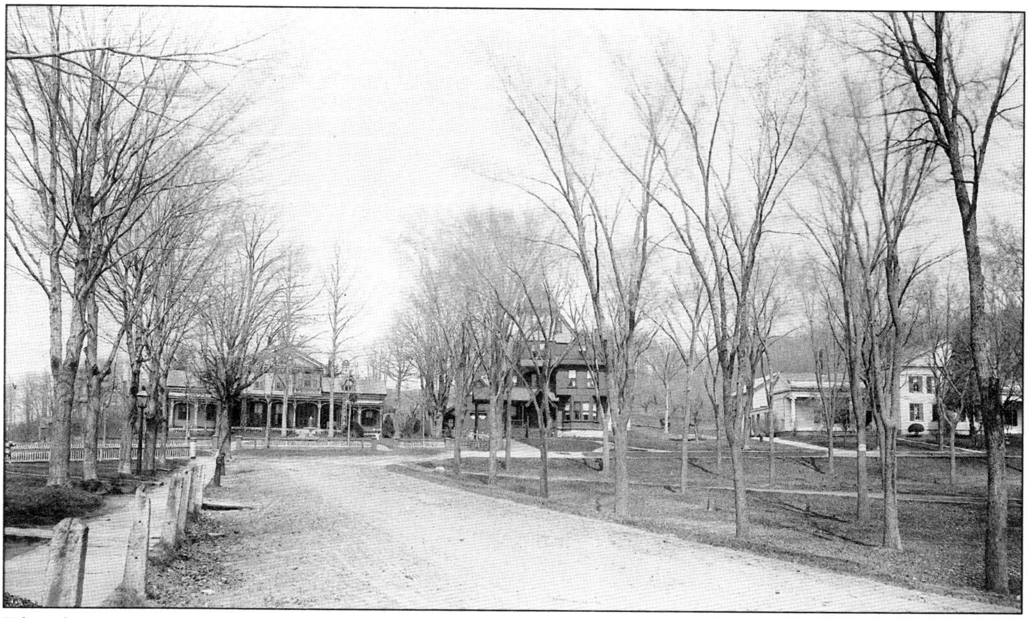

The homes of prominent citizens made the neighborhood near Talcott Park the most architecturally significant neighborhood in the historic district. This 1870s view shows the c. 1850 Dwight Loomis House (on the left), the 1881 Arthur T. Bissell House (in the center), and the 1847 Phineas Talcott House (on the right). Judge Loomis was Rockville's first lawyer, Bissell was a prominent businessman, and Talcott was a shareholder and agent of the American Mills Company.

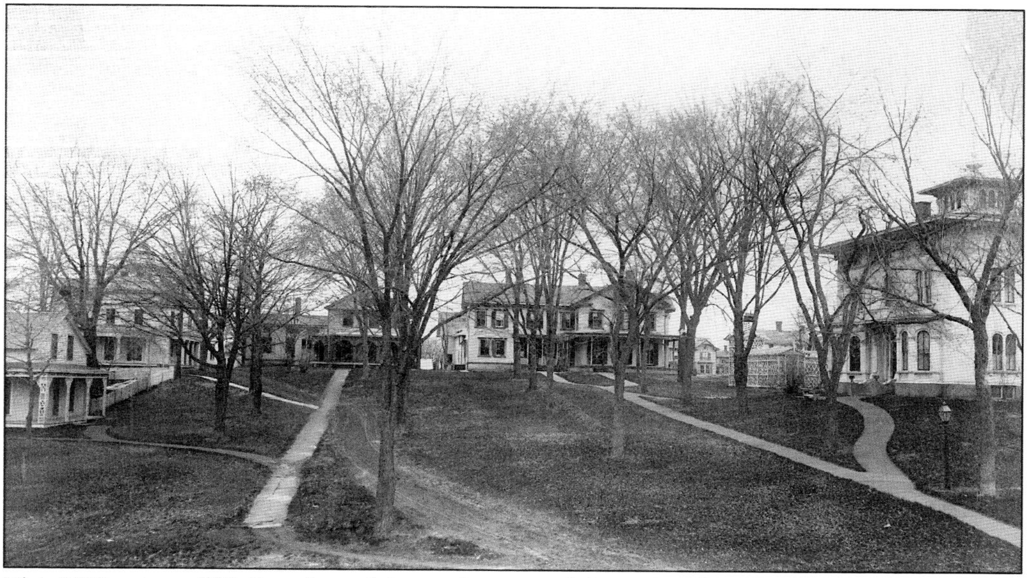

This 1880s view of "Kellogg Lawn" shows the original George Kellogg home (in the center). To the left were two boarding houses operated respectively by Mrs. Rose and Mrs. Talcott. To the extreme right is the George Kellogg Jr. House. These houses were moved or demolished when the Maxwell House (now part of Rockville General Hospital) was built in 1905.

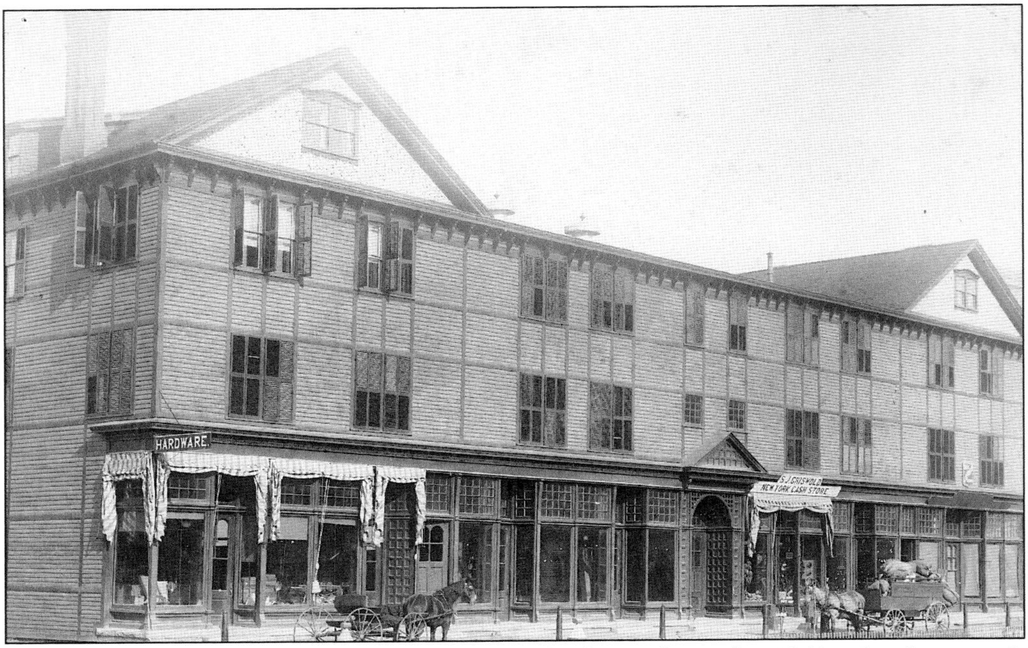

Built by Samuel Fitch during Rockville's period of growth in the 1860s, the first wood-framed Fitch Building featured several stores on the first floor, with apartments and a popular roller-skating rink on the upper floors. It was located on Union Street next to the Second Congregational Church.

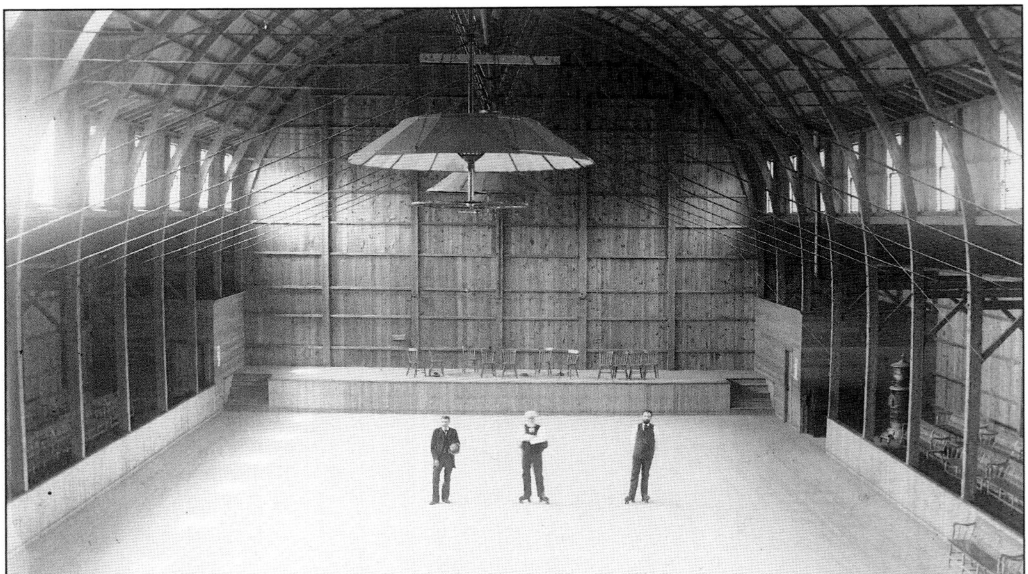

When Samuel Fitch built his business block, he included the skating rink shown in this interior view. Some businessmen objected to the rink, fearing it presented a fire hazard. In fact, the building did go up in smoke, but the fire that destroyed it originated elsewhere.

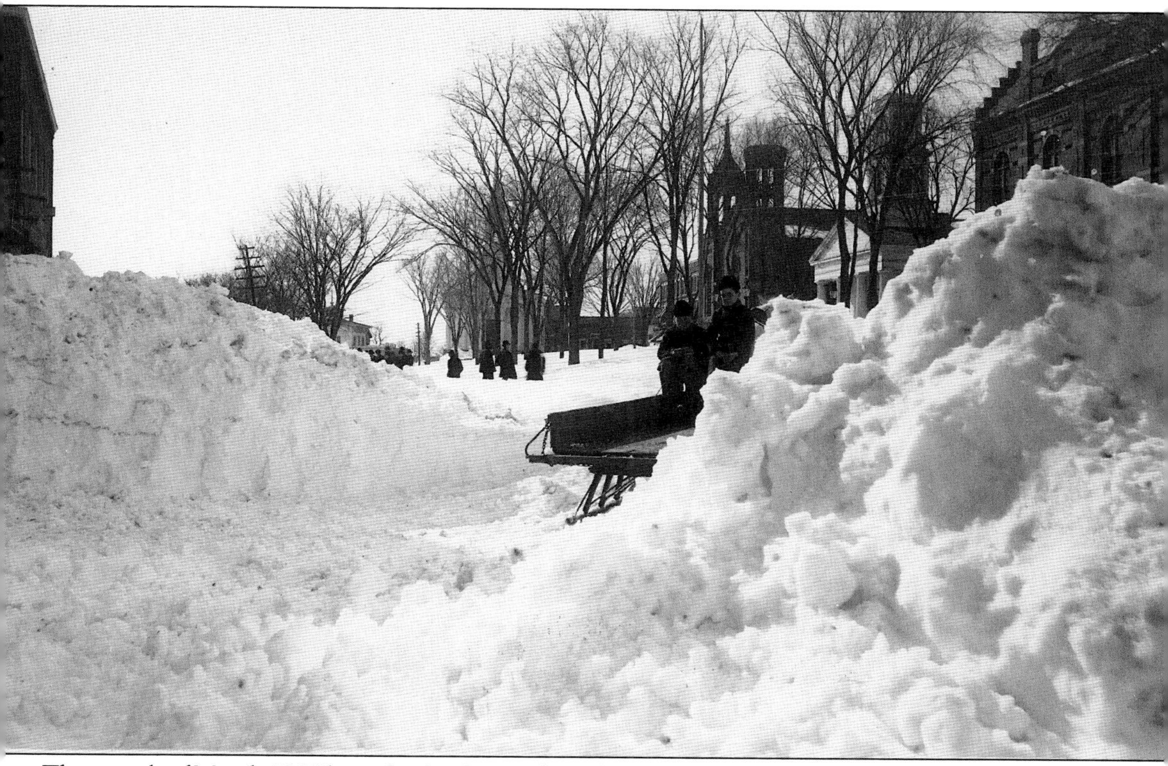

The month of March 1888 brought the Great Blizzard to New England. Three days of heavy snow and wind created drifts 12 to 18 feet high. One hundred and forty travelers were snowbound at Vernon Depot, and in the city, residents tunneled through snow to reach the streets. This view of Park Place gives some idea of the blizzard's impact on city streets.

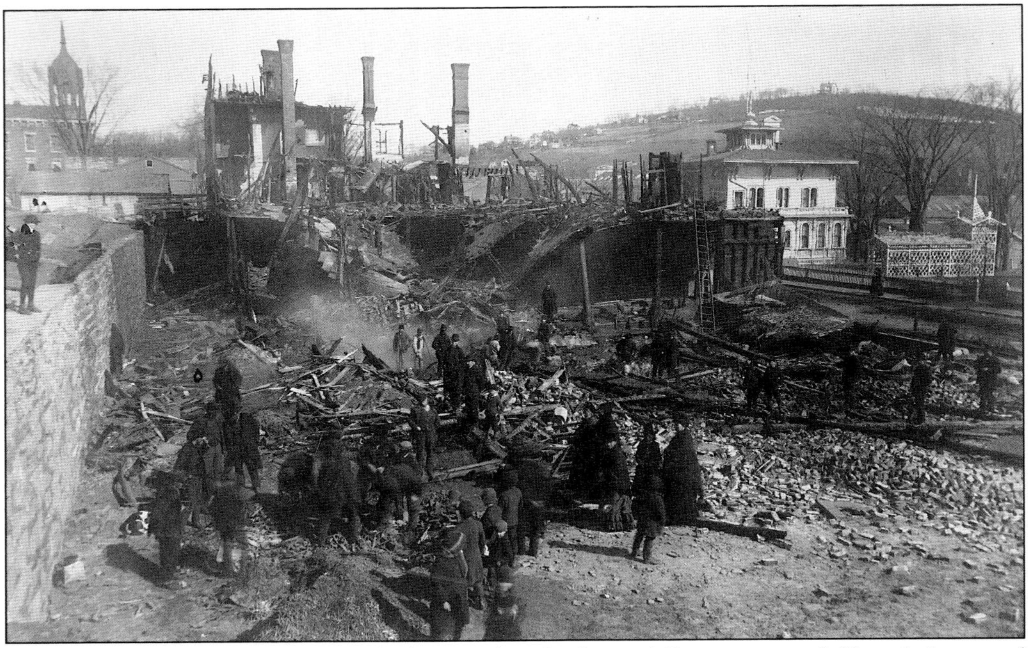

On an April night in 1888, a fire which started in the Second Congregational Church destroyed the church, the adjacent Fitch Building, and the Rockville National Bank building. In this view, stunned citizens survey the devastation in the village center.

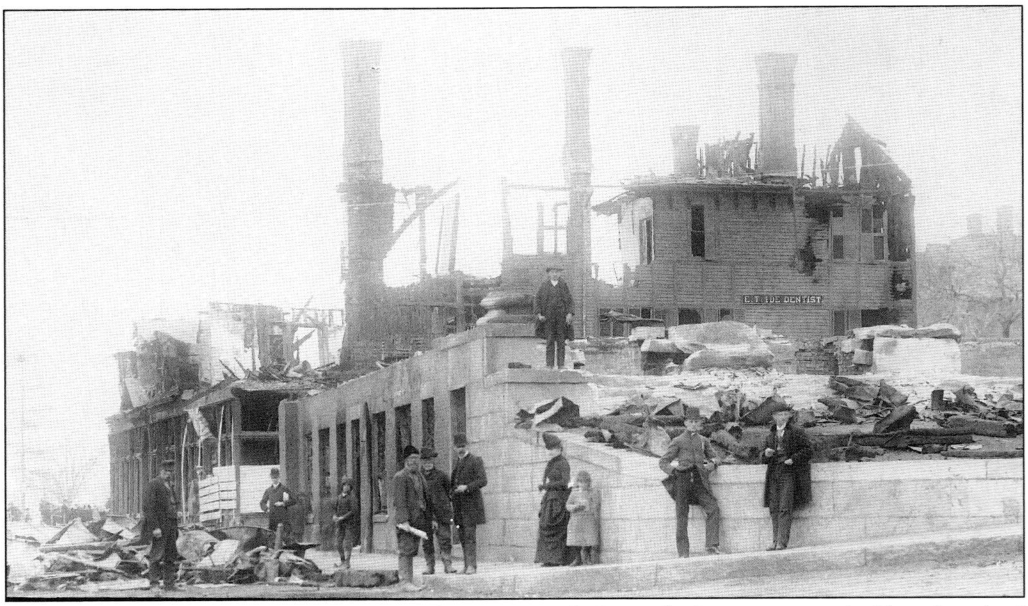

Previous to the April fire of 1888, the First and Second Congregational Churches had considered consolidation, and the First Congregational Church congregation, planning to build a larger building, had sold its lot to the town for a new town hall. Now both congregations were homeless. Rockville had just recovered from the record-setting Blizzard of 1888. Now the village confronted the financial and spiritual losses of the fire. What would 1889 bring?

Five

The City of Rockville

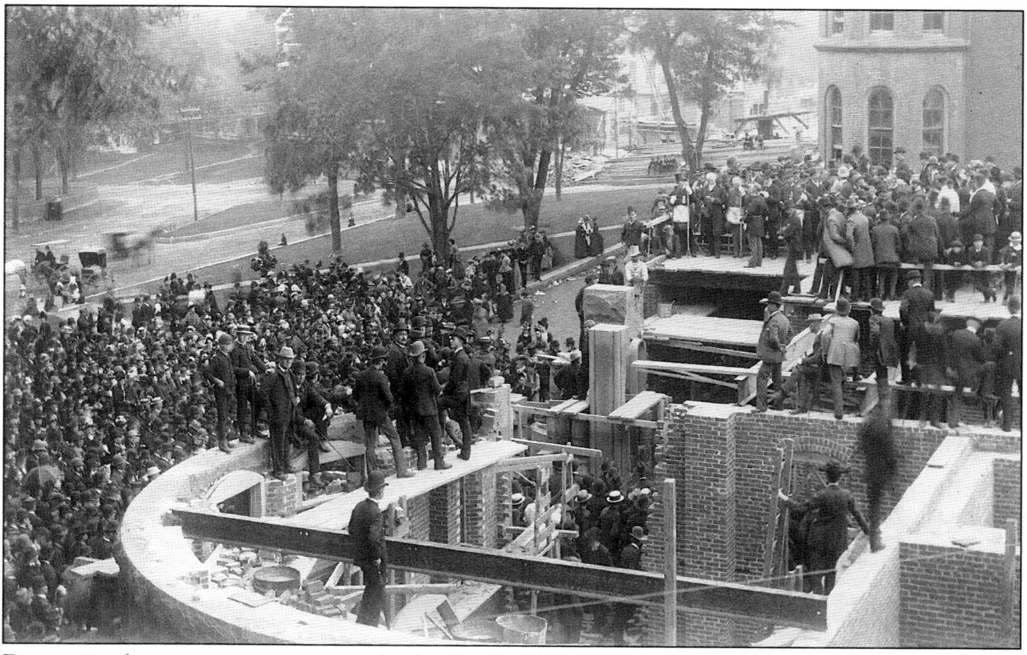

Determined to overcome recent setbacks, Rockville officials continued with their plans to build a town hall that would also be a memorial to local men who had served in the Civil War. On Memorial Day, 1889, the cornerstone was laid to what would become the Memorial Building. In the distance on the right is scaffolding for the new Union Congregational Church.

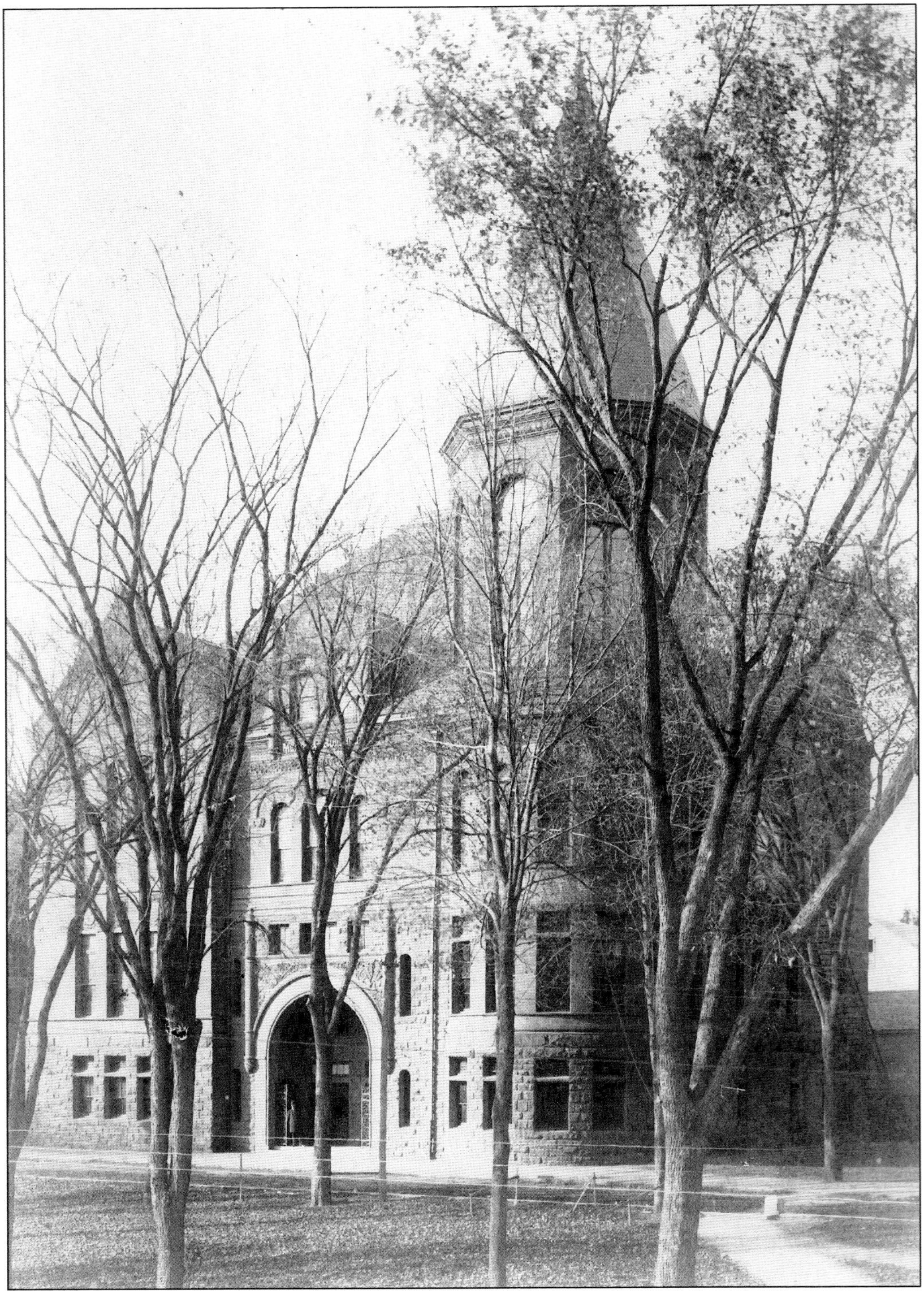

By September 1890, the Memorial Building was completed and open to the public. Over the doorway are carvings of guns, drums, flags, and other military symbols. The Grand Army of the Republic, a Civil War veterans group, had a meeting hall on the second floor which is still maintained today by the Sons of Union Veterans as the New England Civil War Museum.

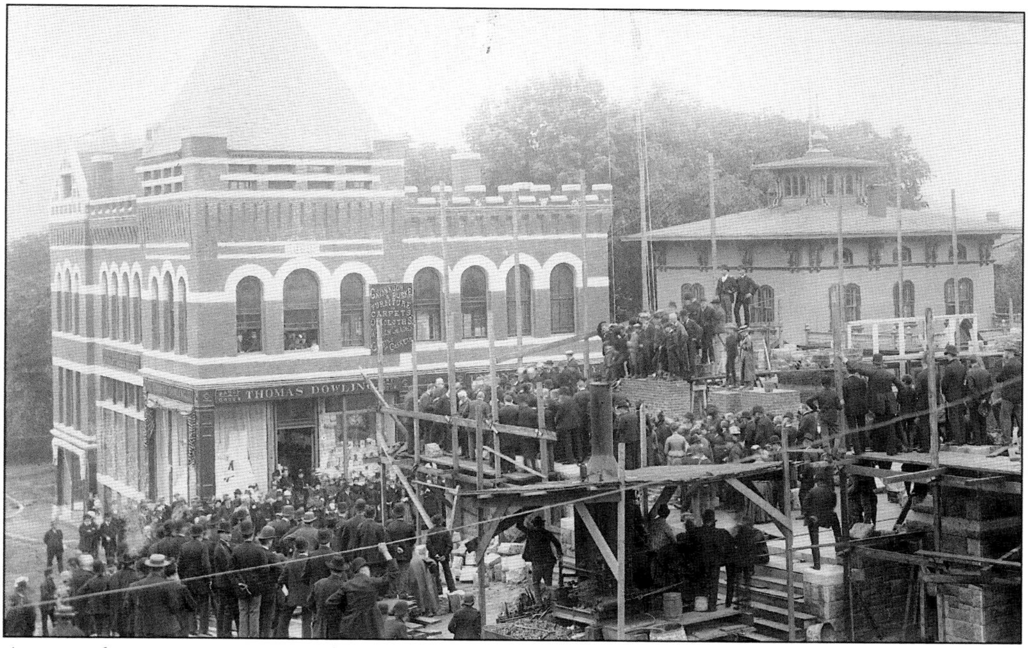

A year of resurrection, 1889 also saw the cornerstone laid for the new Union Congregational Church building. In the background is the Dowling Block, also built in 1889 following a fire in the Doane Building further up Main Street.

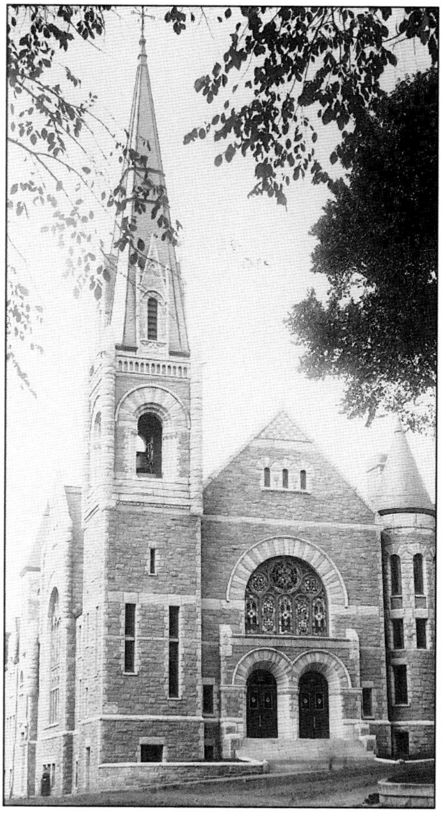

In September of 1890, the completed Union Congregational Church was dedicated. Representing the union of the First and Second Congregational Churches, it was reputed to be "the most beautiful modern church building in all the region." Constructed of granite, it featured a spire which towered 168 feet high.

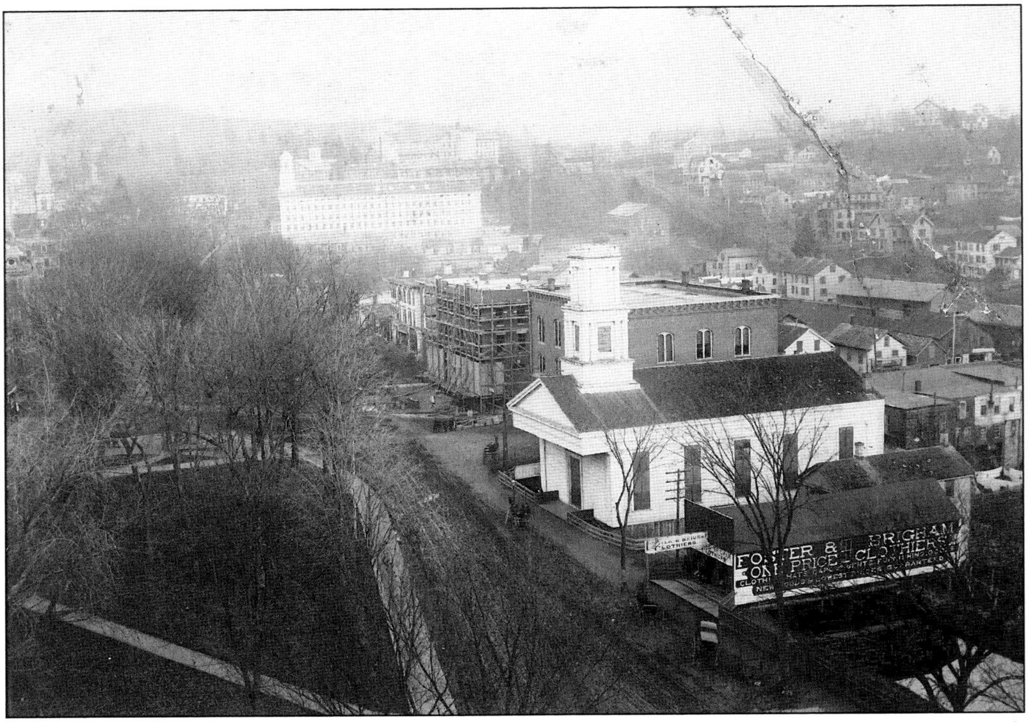

While the Memorial Building and Union Congregational Church were being constructed, the old First Congregational Church was moved to the south side of Main Street and used for services by the combined congregations until Union Church was finished. The scaffolding on the nearby Doane Building gives further evidence of Rockville's rise from the ashes of the previous year's fires.

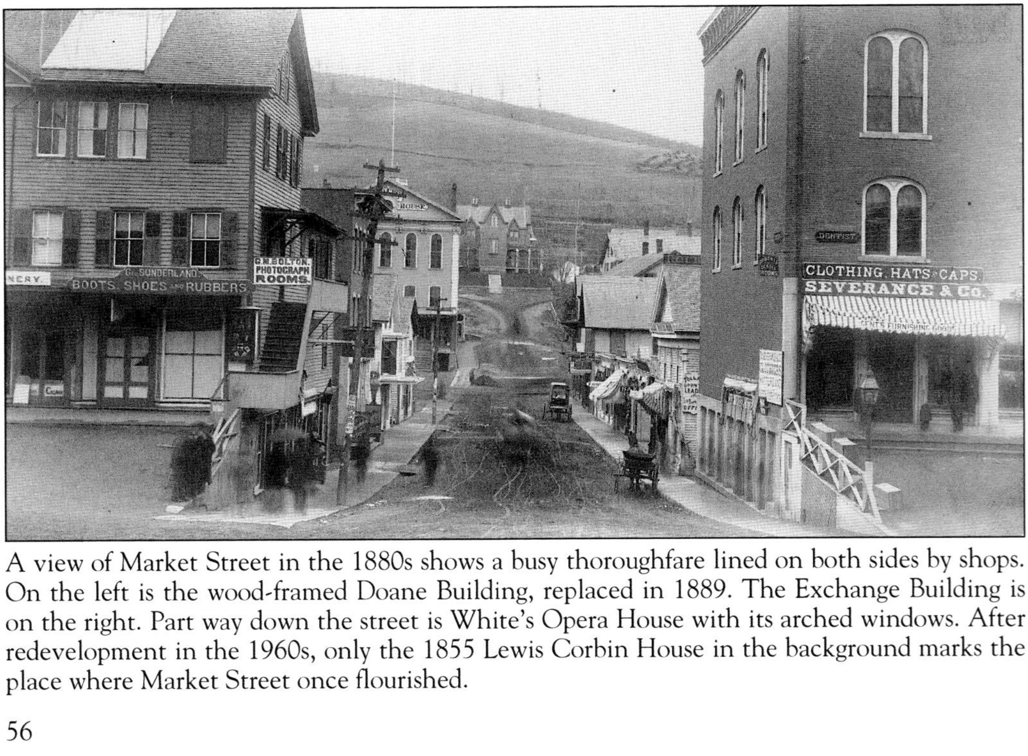

A view of Market Street in the 1880s shows a busy thoroughfare lined on both sides by shops. On the left is the wood-framed Doane Building, replaced in 1889. The Exchange Building is on the right. Part way down the street is White's Opera House with its arched windows. After redevelopment in the 1960s, only the 1855 Lewis Corbin House in the background marks the place where Market Street once flourished.

In 1851 an earlier hotel was replaced with the Rockville House, which was renovated in the 1880s to its appearance in this photograph. A center for social and business affairs, the hotel had a billiard parlor and a telegraph office. The hotel was located at the corner of Park Street and St. Bernard's Terrace. It was razed during the 1960s redevelopment.

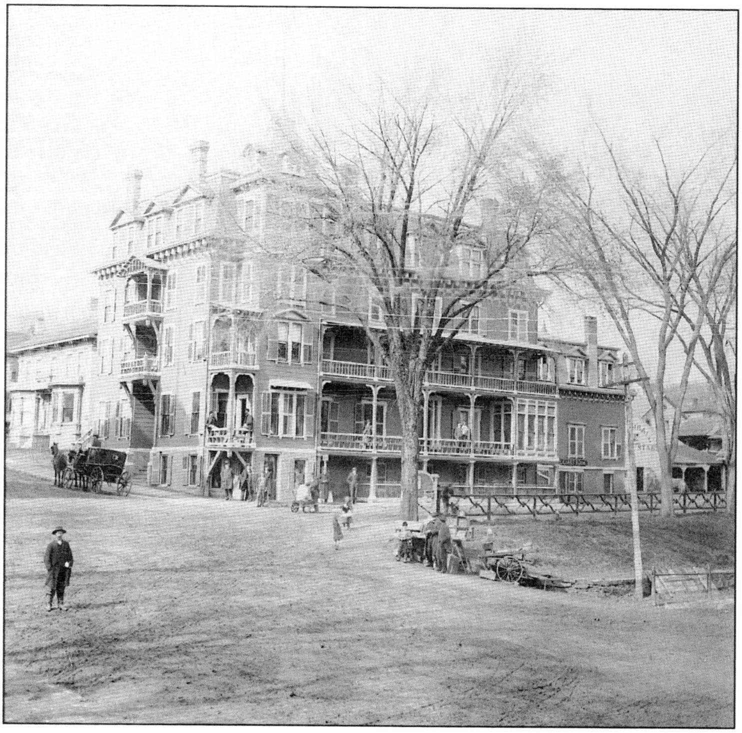

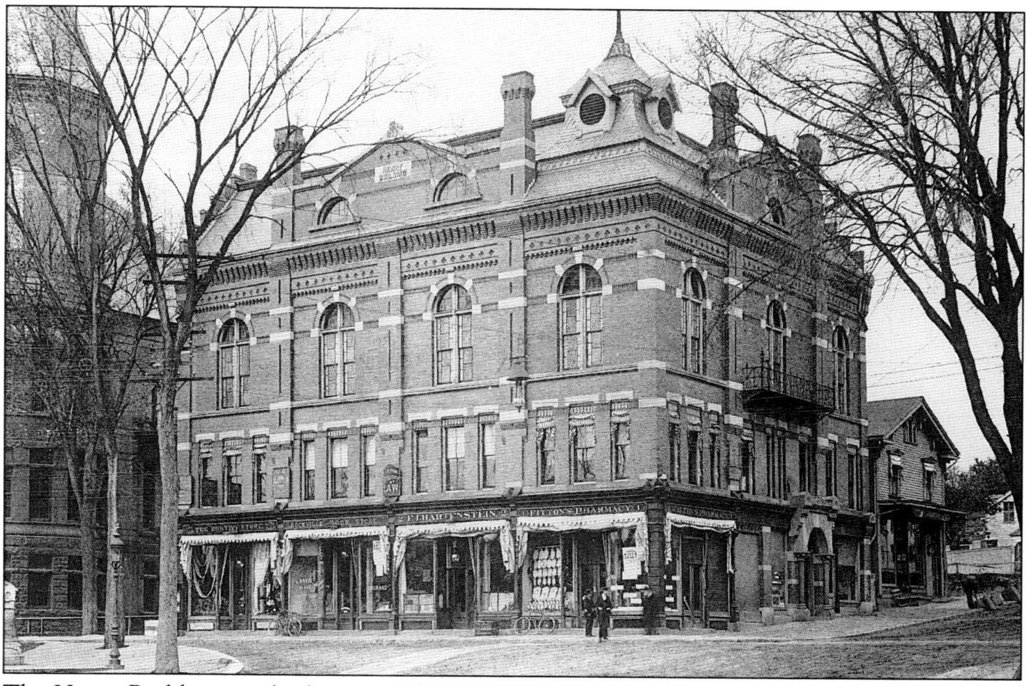

The Henry Building was built in 1880 by E. Stevens Henry, a prominent businessman. Located on the third floor of the building was the Henry Opera House, a splendid auditorium which could seat up to one thousand people. The Opera House was the scene of many fine theatrical and musical entertainments. With the advent of movie theaters, it fell into disuse and was razed in the 1960s.

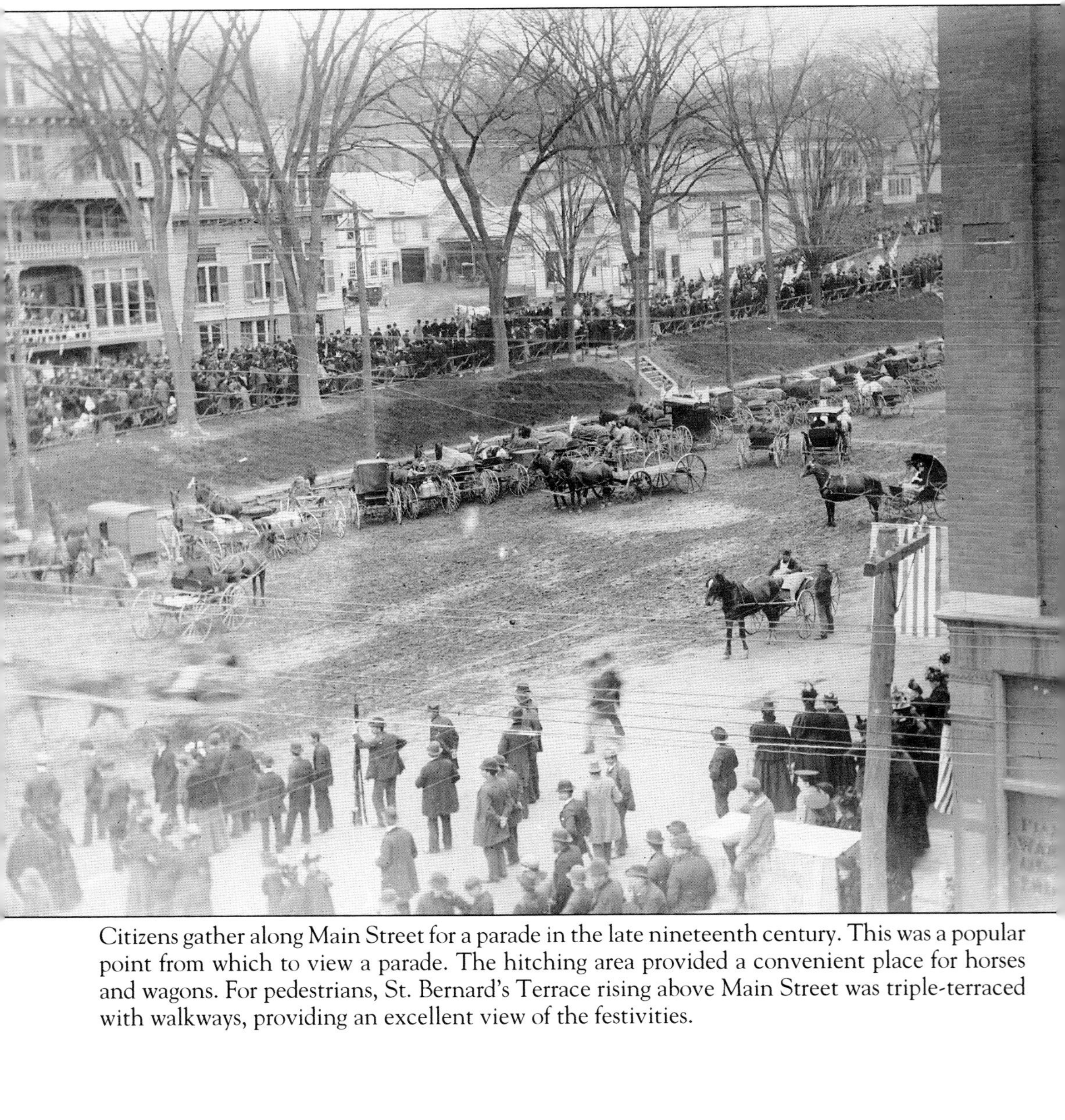

Citizens gather along Main Street for a parade in the late nineteenth century. This was a popular point from which to view a parade. The hitching area provided a convenient place for horses and wagons. For pedestrians, St. Bernard's Terrace rising above Main Street was triple-terraced with walkways, providing an excellent view of the festivities.

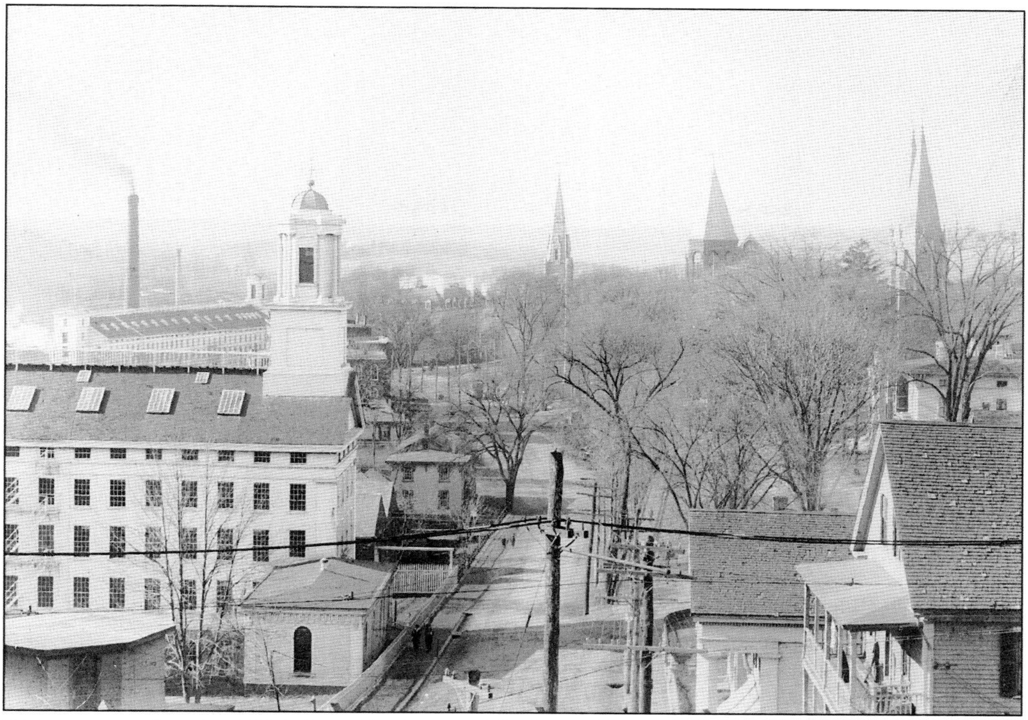

This view, taken in 1914 from Stickney Hill above Prospect Street and East Main Street, shows the American mill on the left. Important elements of community life in Rockville are represented in the skyline: the smokestack for industry, steeples for churches, and the Memorial Building spire for government.

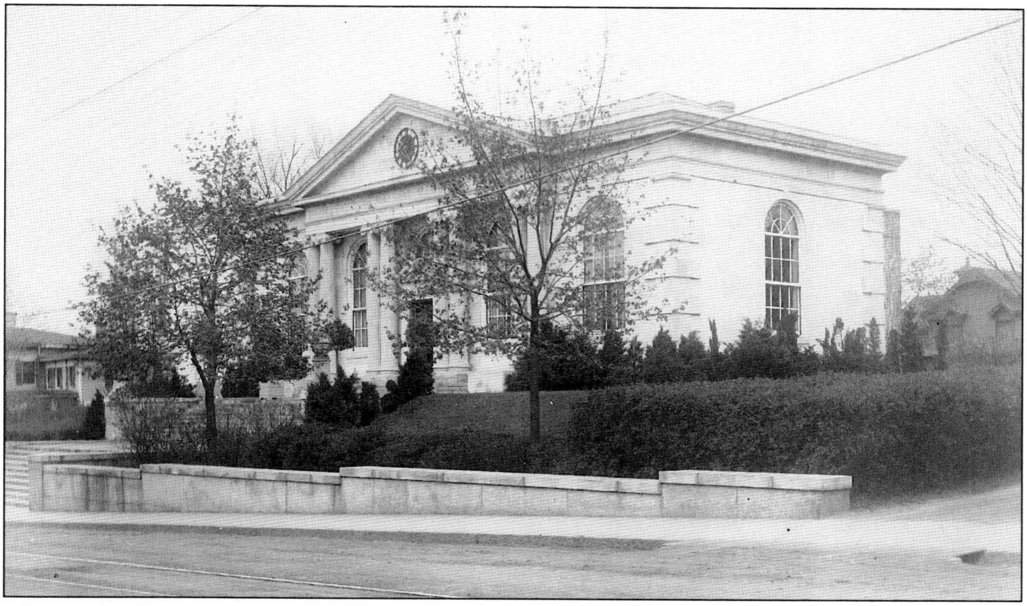

The Rockville Public Library building was built in 1904. Designed by prominent architect Charles A. Platt, the building was given to the town by the Maxwell family in honor of the late George Maxwell, a staunch supporter of public libraries.

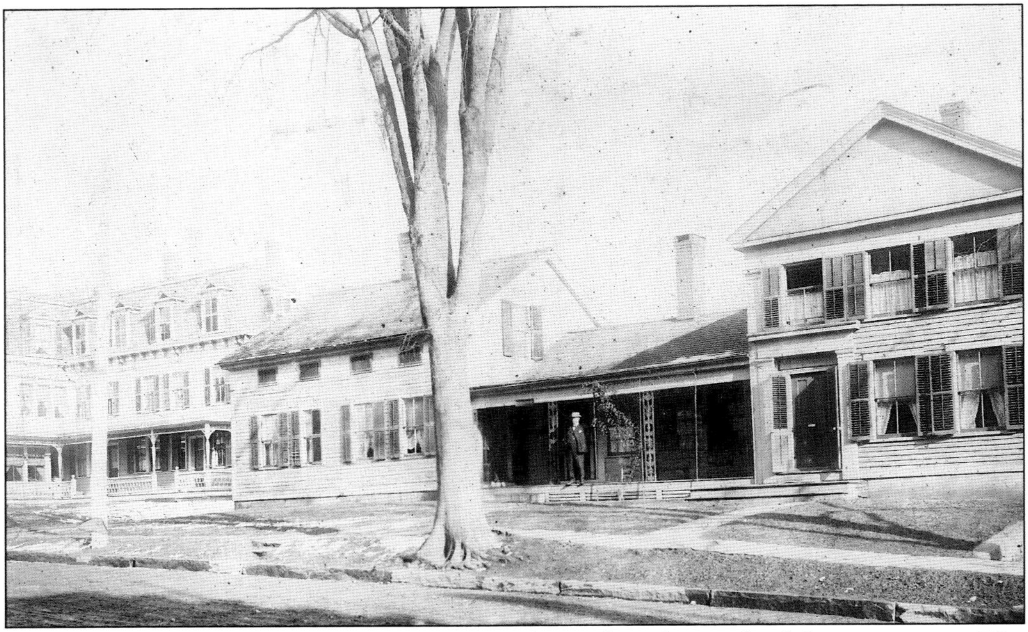

As Rockville expanded, neighborhoods changed to reflect the needs of the community. The lower end of Park Street was originally residential, as shown here. The Yost House (on the left) was replaced by the post office in 1918. The next two attached houses belonged to Frank Skinner, the town clerk. They were replaced in 1925 by the Sykes school building.

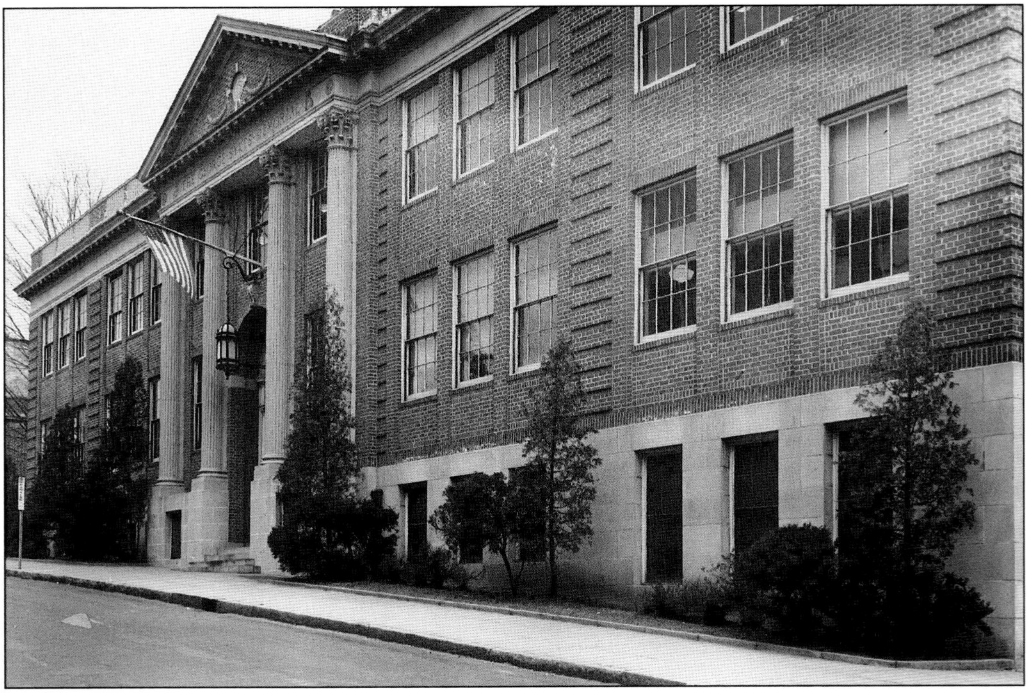

The George Sykes Manual Training and High School originated with a bequest of $100,000 from Sykes in 1903. In the ensuing years, the town found it needed a new high school. Through the collaborative efforts of the town and the Sykes trust fund, the new high school was dedicated in February of 1925.

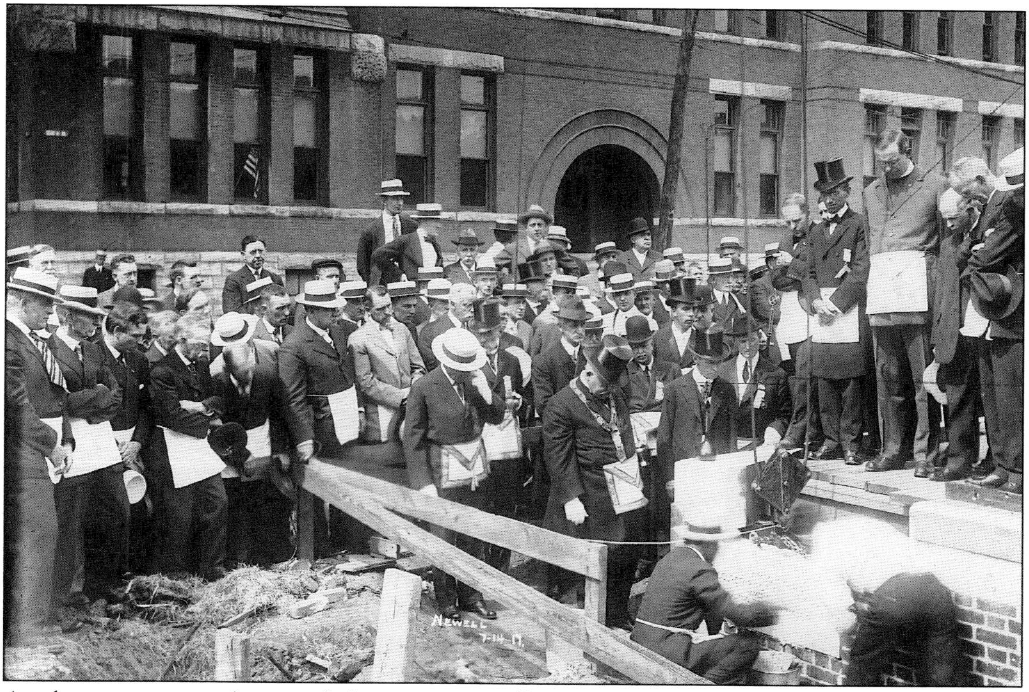

At the cornerstone laying of the new post office in 1917, the crowd pauses for a solemn moment. The men wearing aprons represent the Most Worshipful Grand Lodge of Masons, who participated in the ceremony. The 1892 Rockville High School is visible in the background.

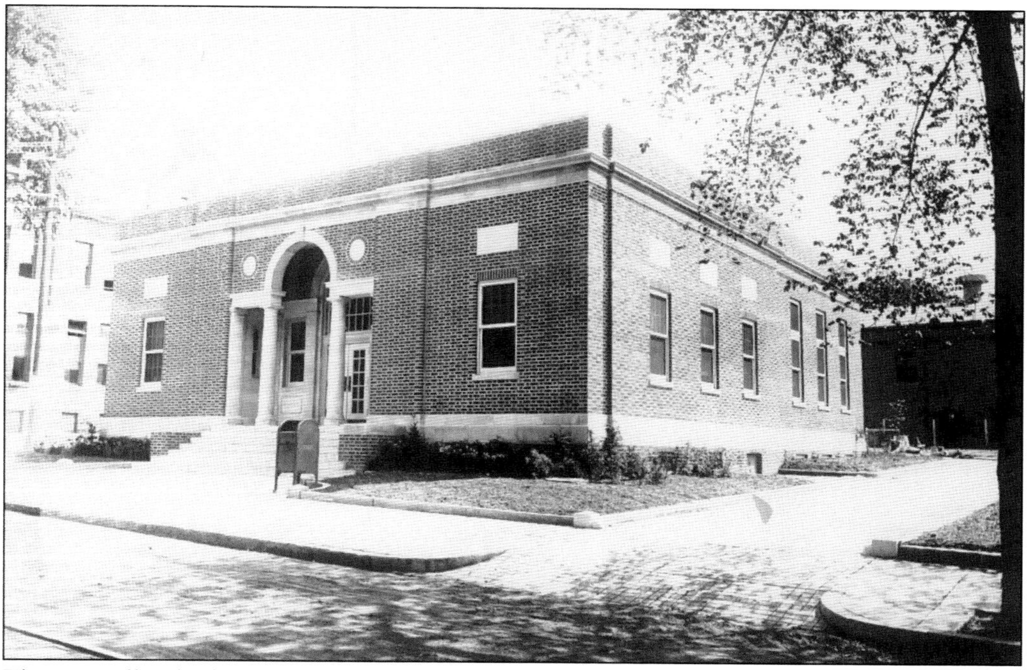

The post office building was used until the 1970s, when a new building was opened. Located conveniently near downtown when built, the lack of parking space limited its use in later years. The building is awaiting redevelopment at the present time.

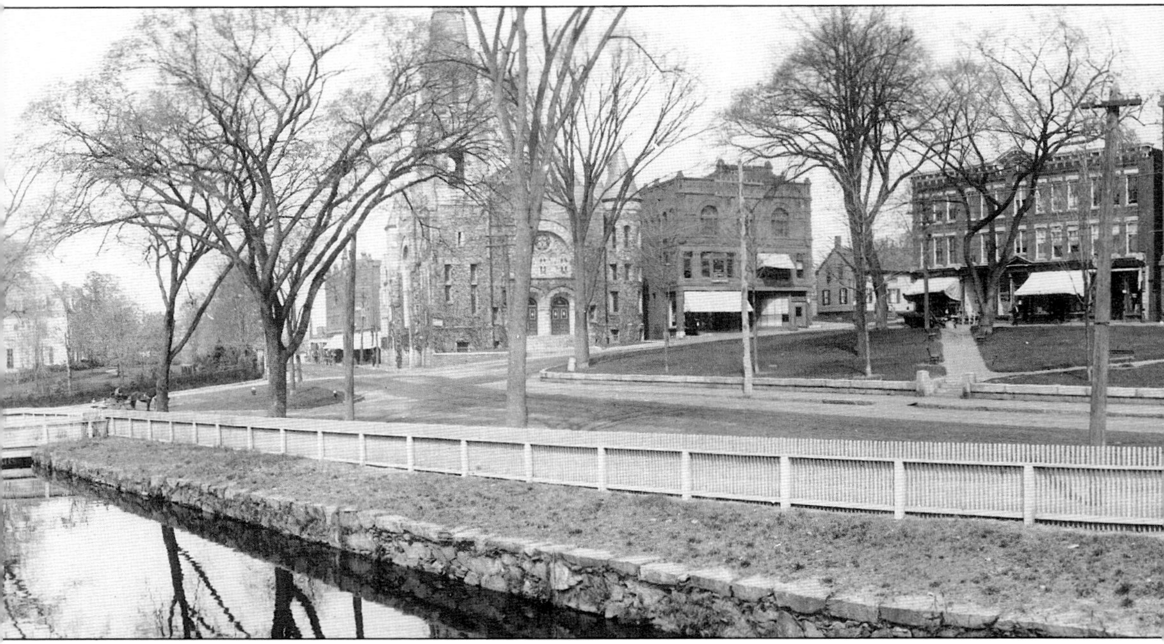

At the dawn of the twentieth century, the citizens of Rockville were proud of their attractively rebuilt city center, appealing residential neighborhoods, and thriving mills. Rockville was the center of economic and social activities for the surrounding rural community. In 1911 a local photographer. standing on a bridge over the Rock mill canal, took a panoramic view of Park

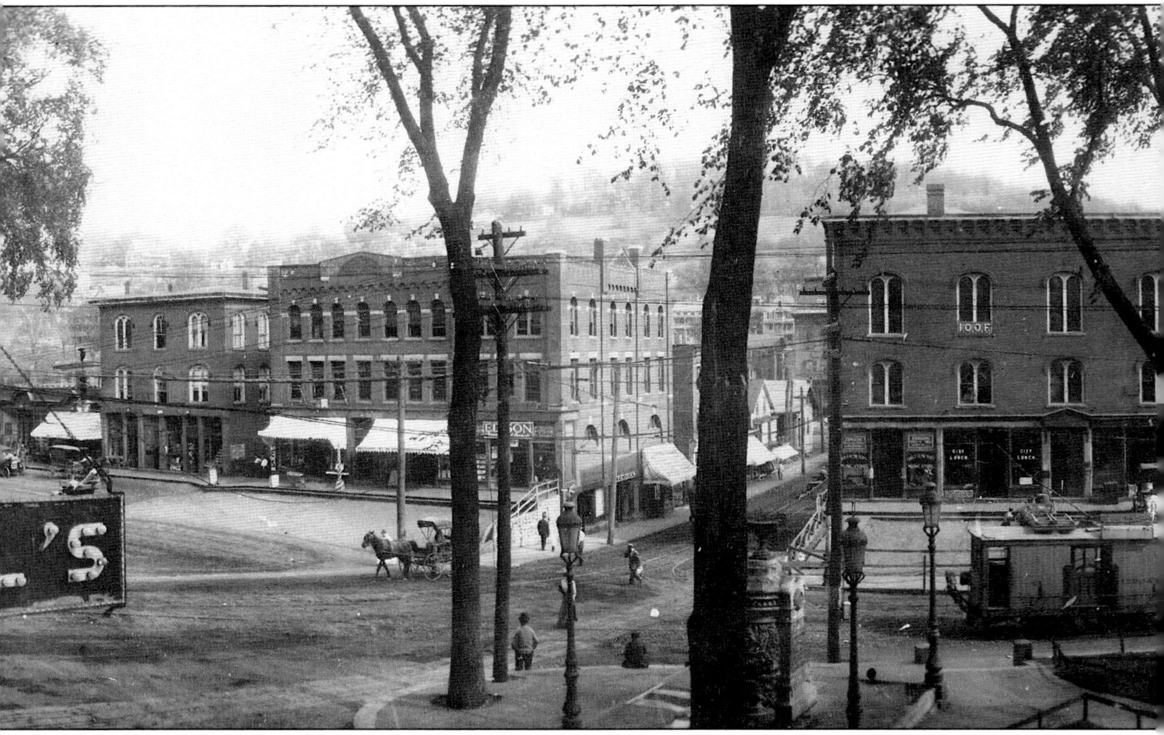

The commercial blocks along the south side of East Main Street were photographed from an upper floor of the Henry Building. Captured in this view, from left to right, are the Orcutt

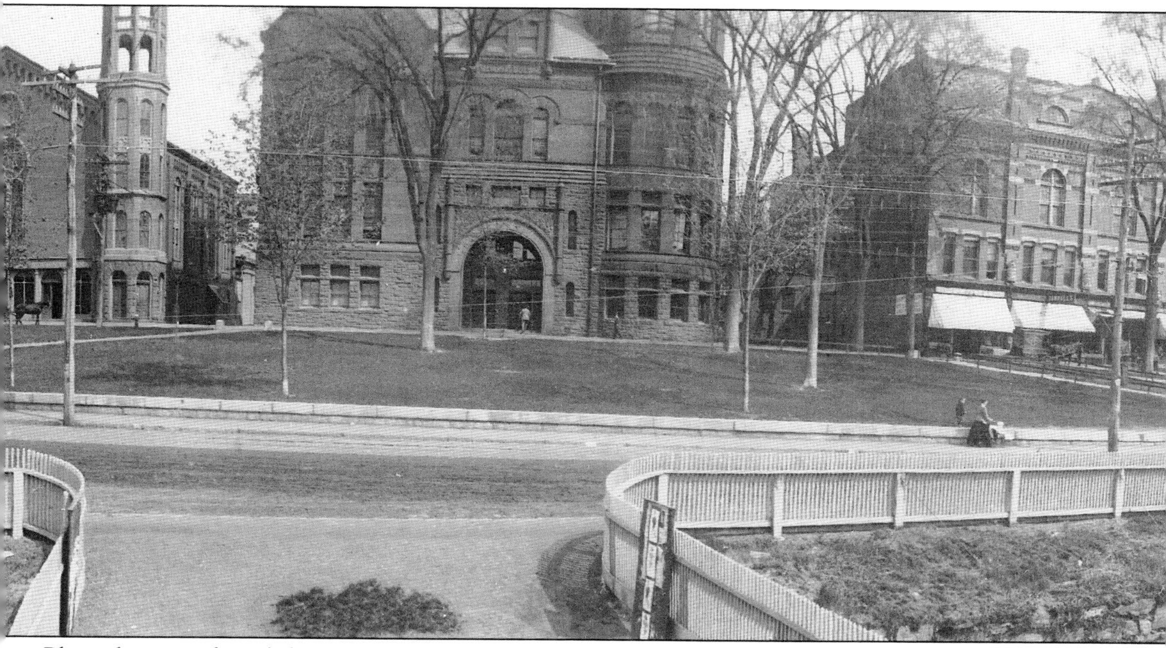

Place showing, from left to right, Union Congregational Church, the Rockville National Bank, the Citizen's Block, the Rockville Methodist Episcopal Church, the Memorial Building, and the Henry Building.

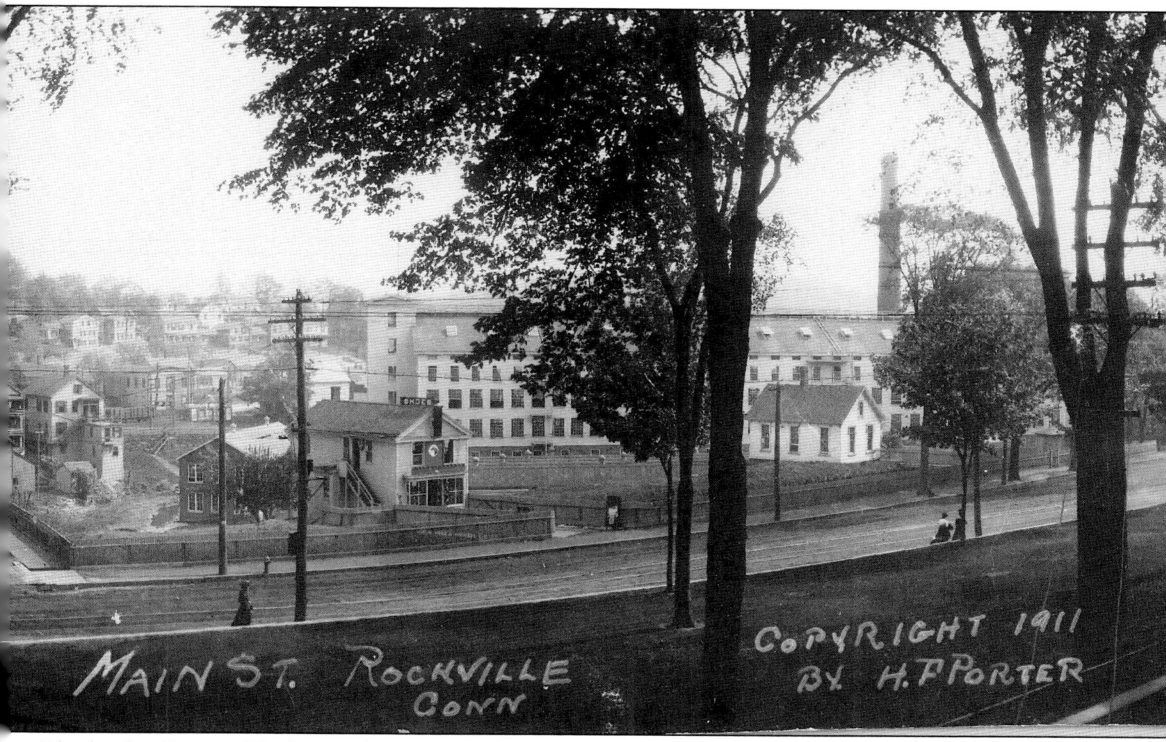

Block, the Doane Block, Market Street, the Exchange Block, and the Rock mill buildings as they appeared in 1911.

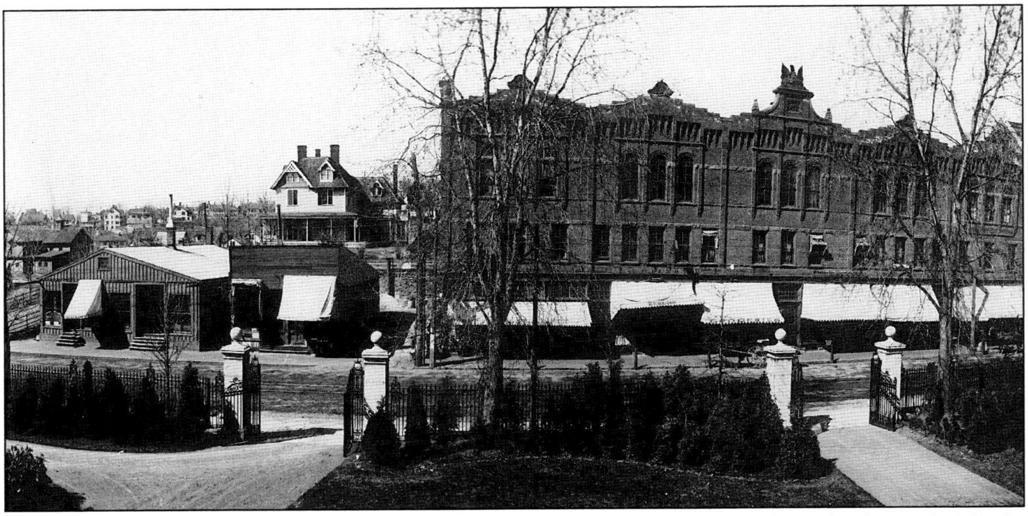

Taken from an upper story of the Maxwell House, this view shows the rebuilt Fitch Block. Along the roof line, the carved stone phoenix symbolizing rebirth is visible. Rising above the buildings to the left was the home of Samuel Fitch, owner of the Fitch Block (he was also the first mayor of Rockville). The iron fence and stone gateposts in the foreground that bordered the Maxwell property are still standing.

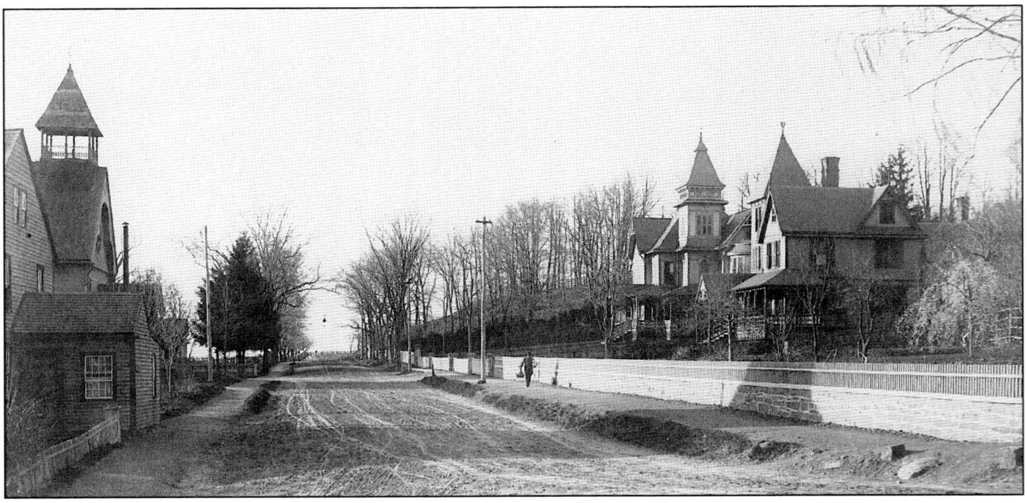

Affluent residential neighborhoods expanded as mill owners and businessmen built homes near Talcott Park. In this view of Ellington Avenue, St. John's Episcopal Church is on the left. Cyrus Winchell built the two houses on the right about 1885. At first Winchell rented the houses; later they were purchased by Rockville business men. The four-sided towers were a distinctive feature of the "stick-style" architecture popular at that time.

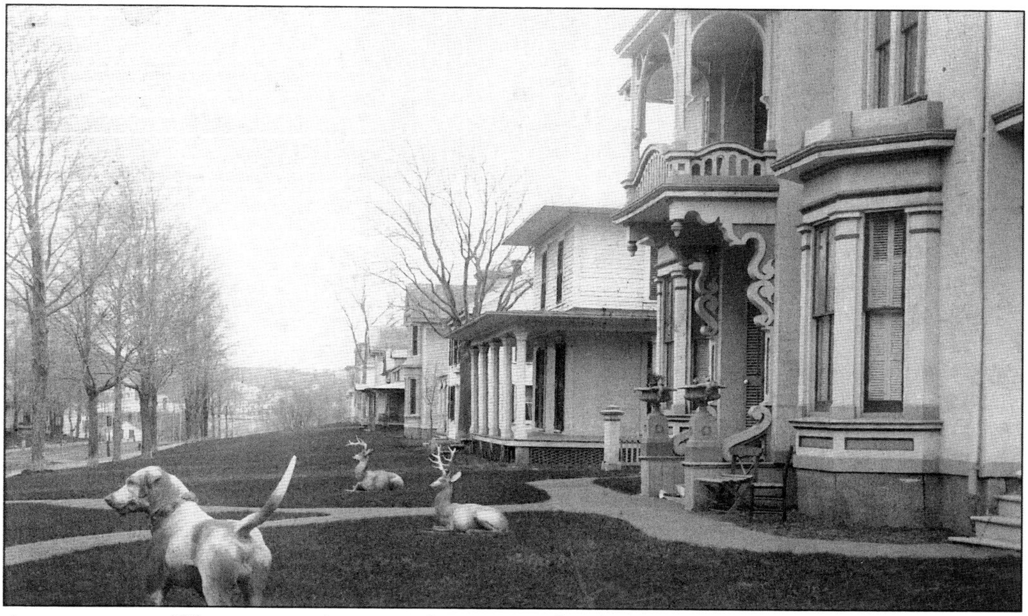

A streetscape of Victorian architecture lines one side of Elm Street. Most of these homes stand today. The dog and deer are lawn sculptures.

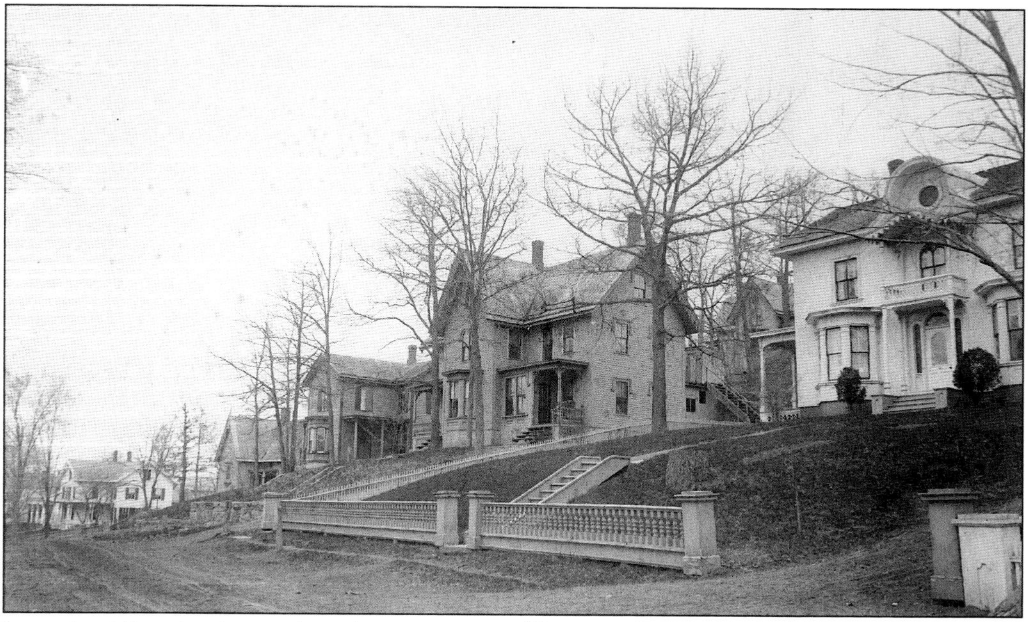

Imposing Victorian homes line the upper part of Prospect Street near Talcott Park. The house on the extreme right was built in 1863 by George M. Paulk, a contractor who participated in the building of many of Rockville's mills.

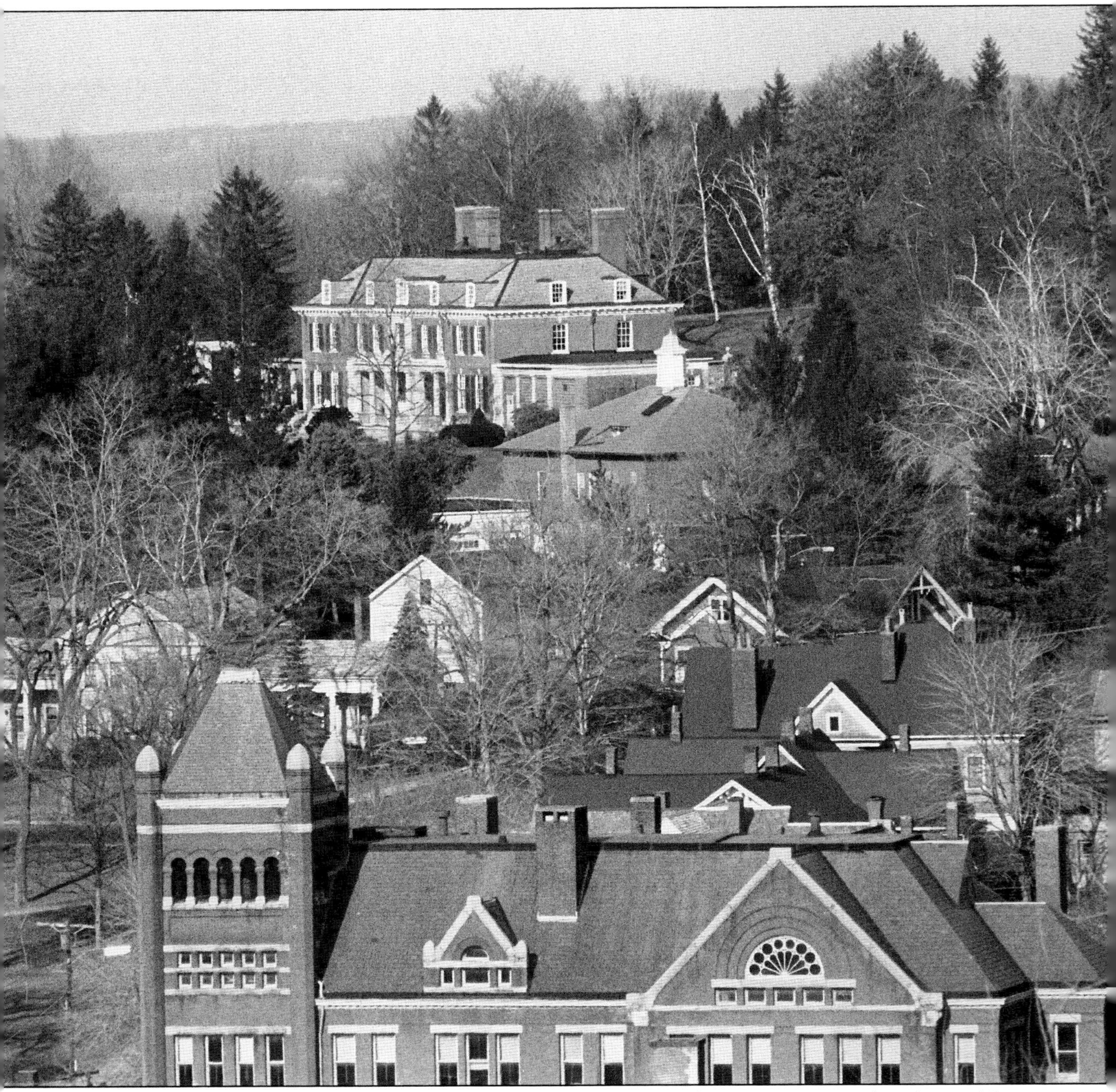

The economic and social prominence of the Maxwell family is apparent in the physical location of Maxwell Court, the home of mill owner Francis Maxwell. Designed by noted architect Charles A. Platt and built in 1902, this imposing building surveys the city from its elevated location on North Park Street. The 1892 Rockville High School is in the foreground.

Six

Public Services for a Growing Community

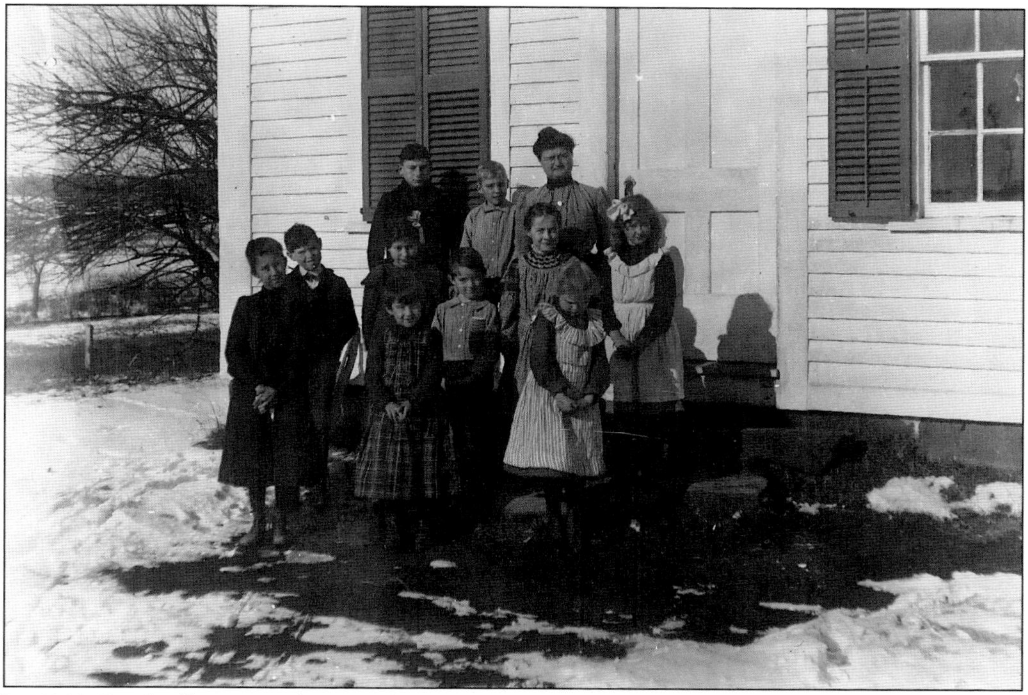

In 1889, Rockville received a city charter and with it the authority to lay a city tax. Within a decade, the city had street lights, improved fire and police protection, and better schools. In this view, children pose with their teacher on the steps of the new West District School. The school, located on Maple Street, was built in 1893.

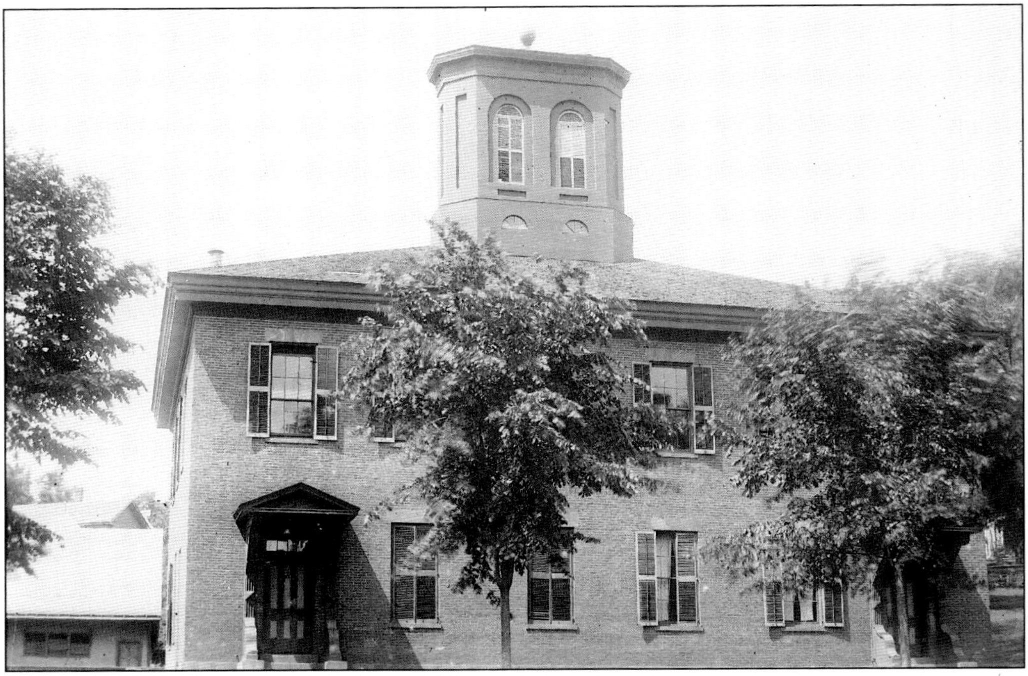

A commitment to education was demonstrated early in Rockville's development. Since the 1820s small country schools had existed in several locations. In 1849 the Brick School on School Street was opened. Only grammar-school levels were taught until 1870, when the town recognized the need to add a high school program. The first high school class of two students graduated from the program in 1872.

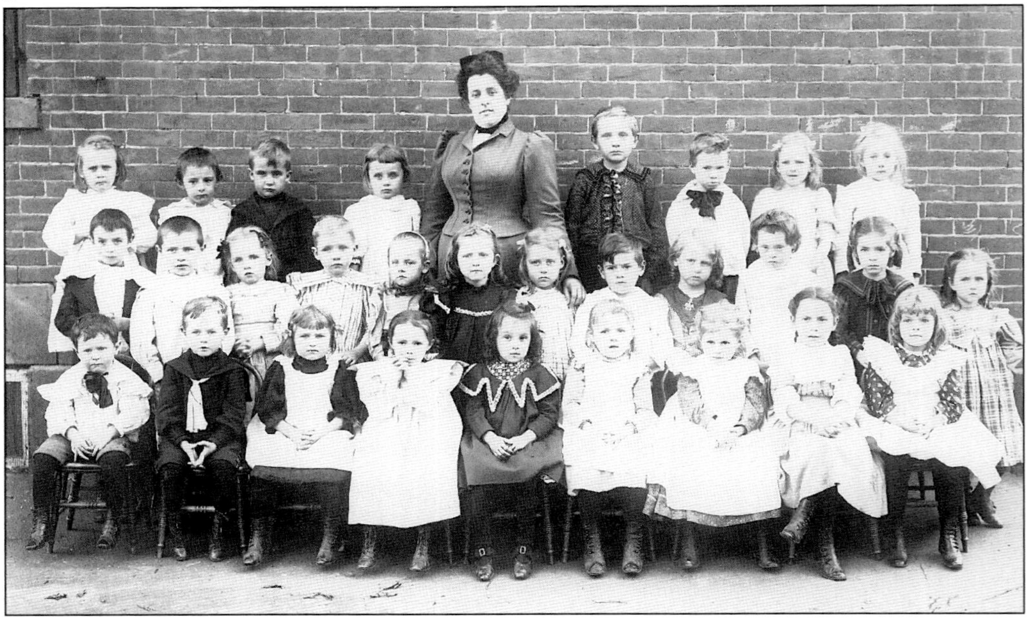

Miss Bessie Durfee's kindergarten class poses for their class picture in September 1900. A teacher for 50 years in the Rockville schools, Bessie Durfee cared about her students. In her will she set up a trust fund to provide health care for needy students. The trust fund is used today for preventive health care for schoolchildren.

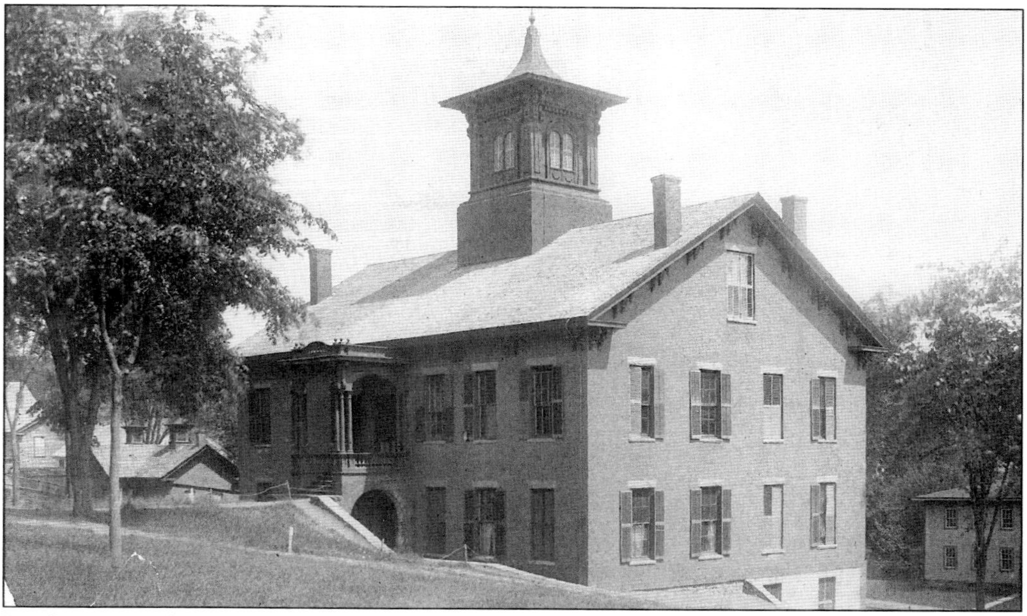

By the 1860s the school population in Rockville had grown so much that another building was necessary. The East School building on School Street opened in 1870 and served as an elementary school until 1974. The cupola and roof were blown off in the Hurricane of 1938. After being vacant for several years, the building was recently renovated and is used by the Tolland Judicial District for juvenile matters.

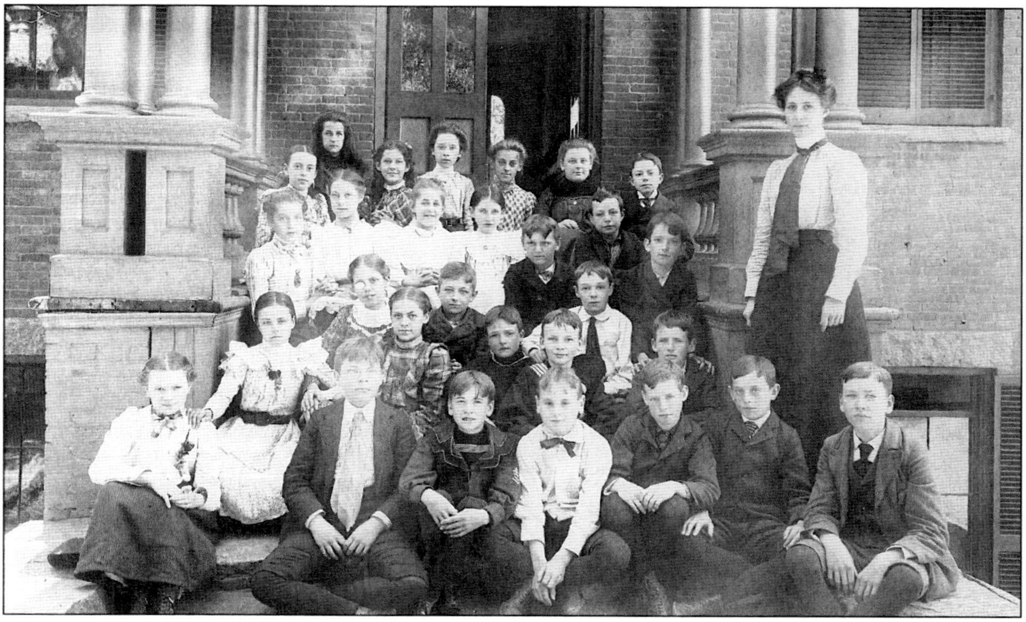

Miss Florence Whitlock and her sixth-grade class are shown here outside the East School in 1900. Miss Whitlock taught the middle grades for many years. To encourage scholarship, she established an endowment for a cash prize in four subject areas to be awarded each year to the top students in grades six, seven, and eight.

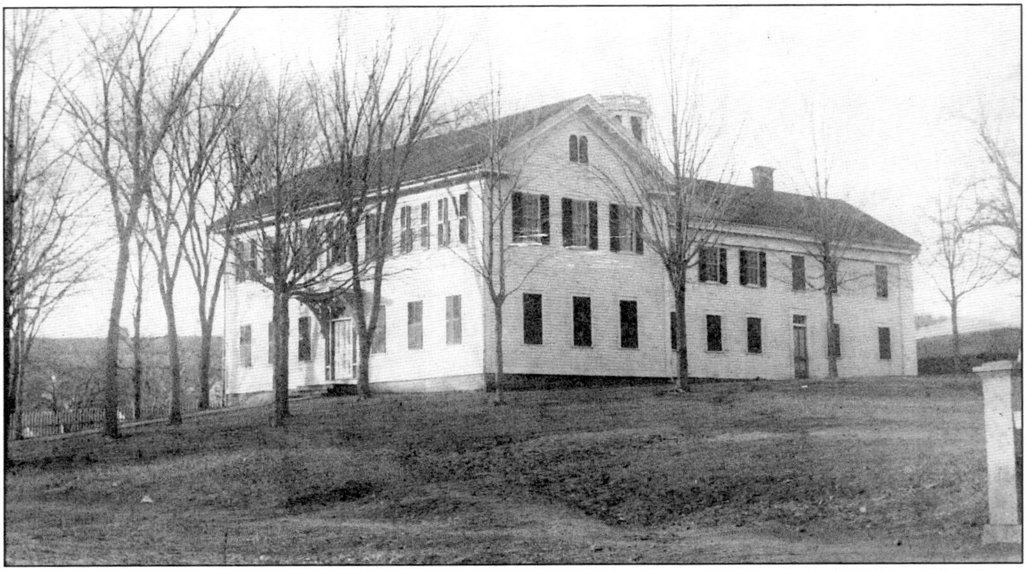

To accommodate the increasing number of students, the West District School was built in 1893, replacing an 1849 structure. The school, which stood where the present Maple Street school playground is located, was replaced in 1924.

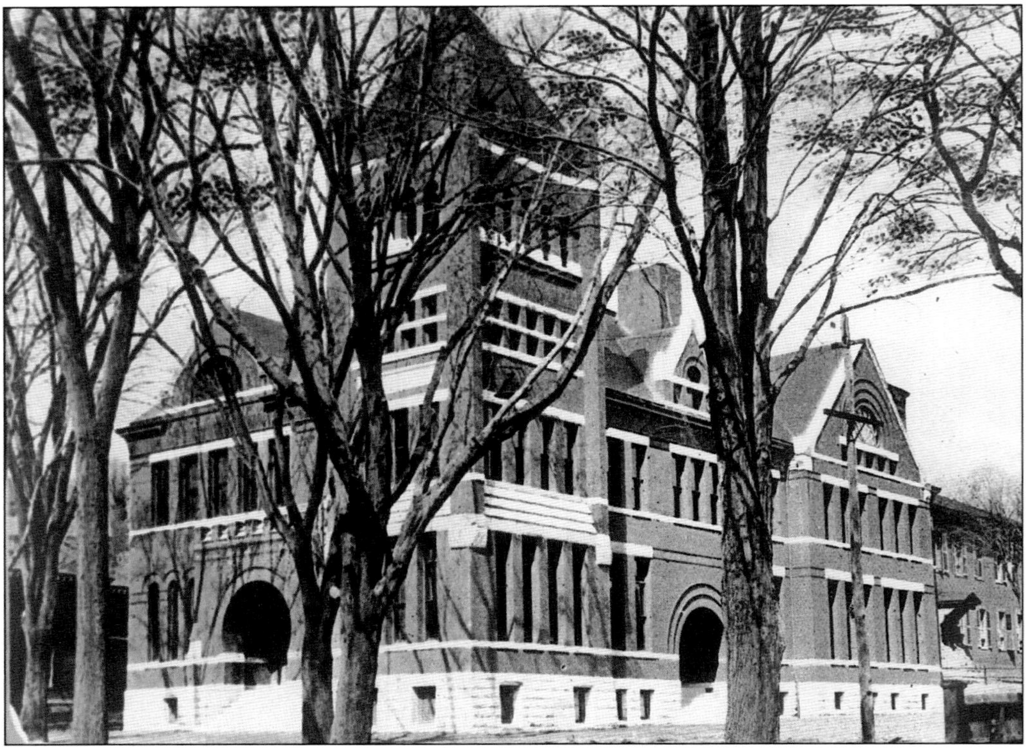

The growing number of students wishing to continue their education through high school resulted in the construction of a new high school building on the corner of School and Park Streets in 1892. The Romanesque-style building accommodated Rockville High School until 1925, when a larger school, the George Sykes Manual Training and High School, was opened. The old high school building now houses the offices of Vernon's education department.

George Sykes was an English immigrant, a descendant of generations of Yorkshire wool workers. In 1866, at the age of 26, he came to Rockville to serve as superintendent of the Hockanum mill. Eventually he became president of the combined Hockanum, Springville, and New England Companies.

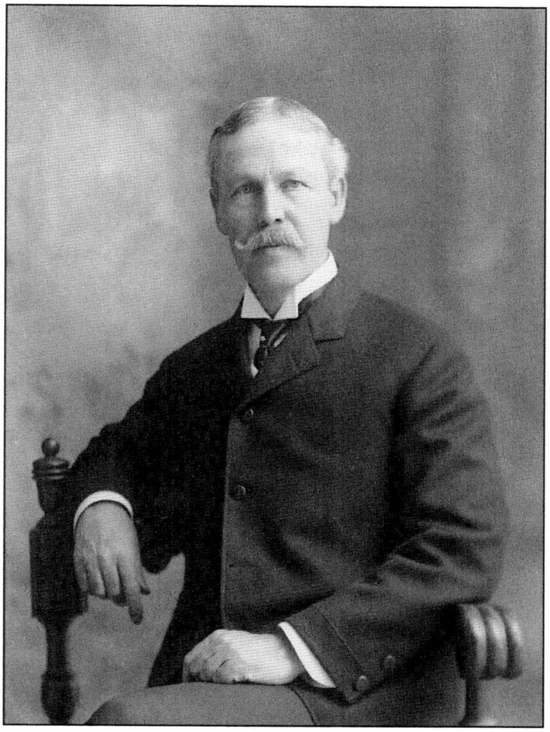

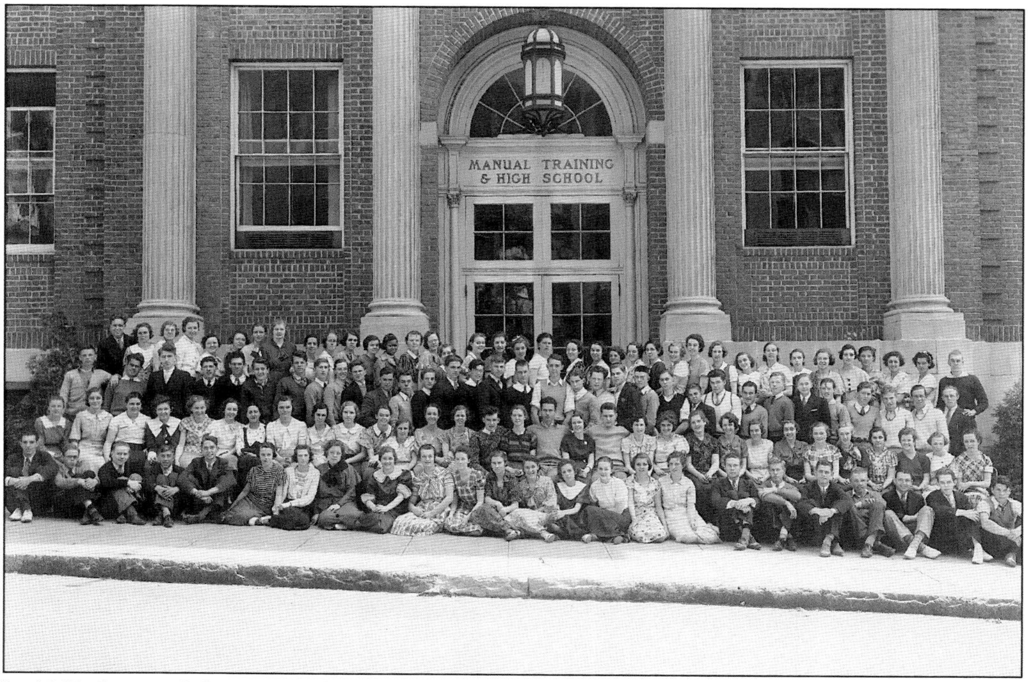

In 1903 George Sykes, remembering his struggle to achieve an education, bequeathed $100,000 to establish a manual training school for boys, most of whom, at the time, left school and went to work at the age of 14. He would have been pleased to see the class shown here graduating from the school which bore his name and incorporated industrial arts in the high school curriculum.

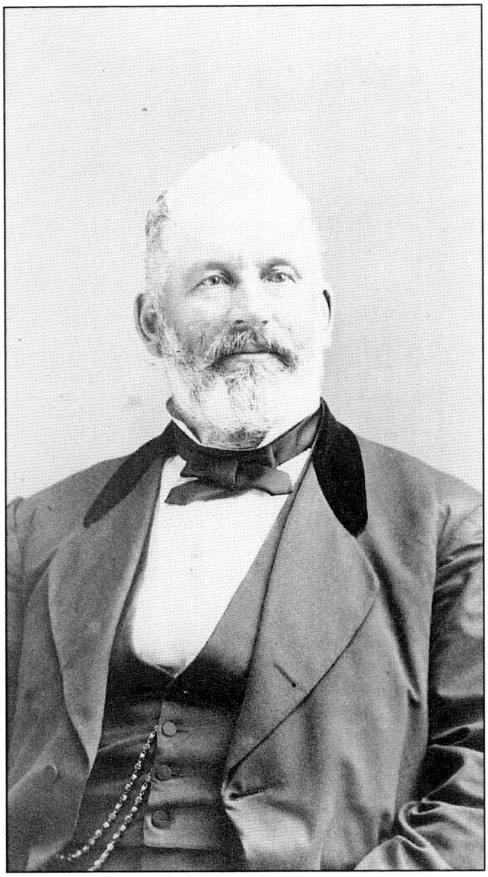

Dr. Francis L. Dickinson practiced medicine in Rockville from 1863 until his death in 1897. As was customary at the time, he made house calls and conducted his practice from his home, which still stands on Prospect Street.

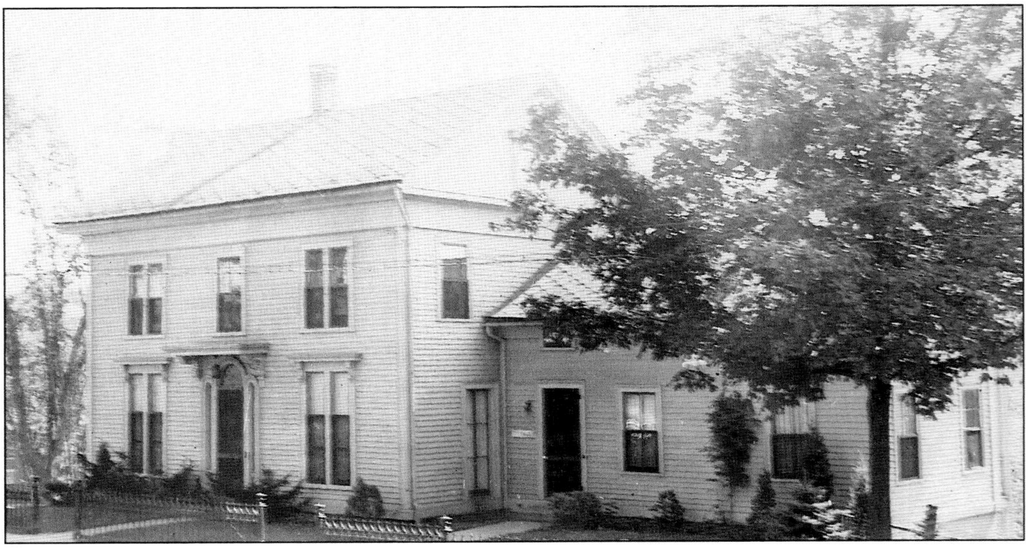

The former Dickinson Home was converted to a nurses' home when the Rockville City Hospital opened across the street. Today, the house is once more a private residence.

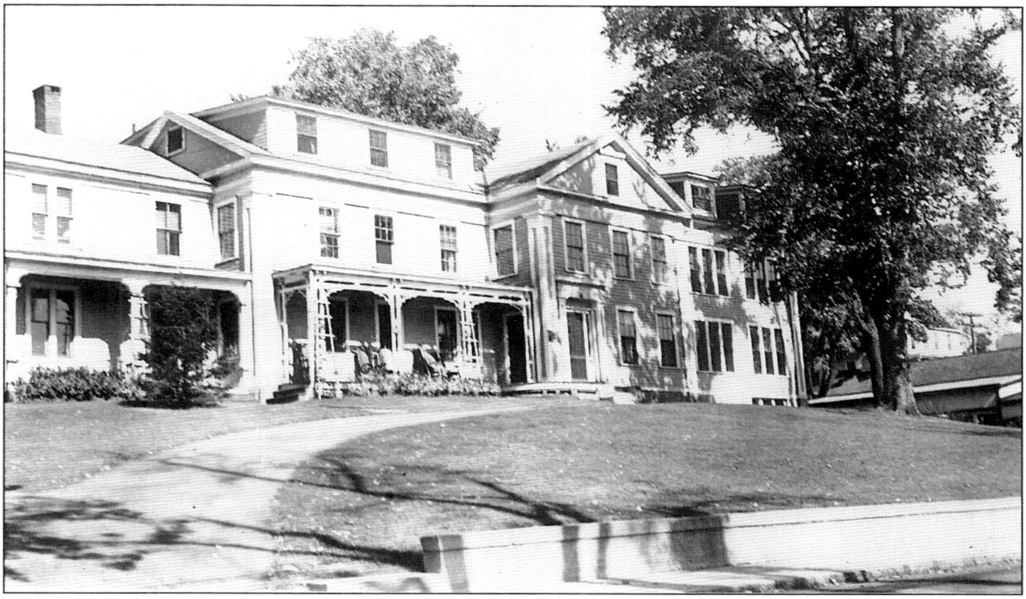

Until 1921, Rockville had no hospital and patients were necessarily treated at home. The outbreak of influenza in 1918 persuaded the community that a hospital was needed, and the Rockville City Hospital was opened three years later. It was located on Prospect Street in the Gaynor House, a former boarding house. The building was used as a hospital until 1945, and subsequently became an apartment house.

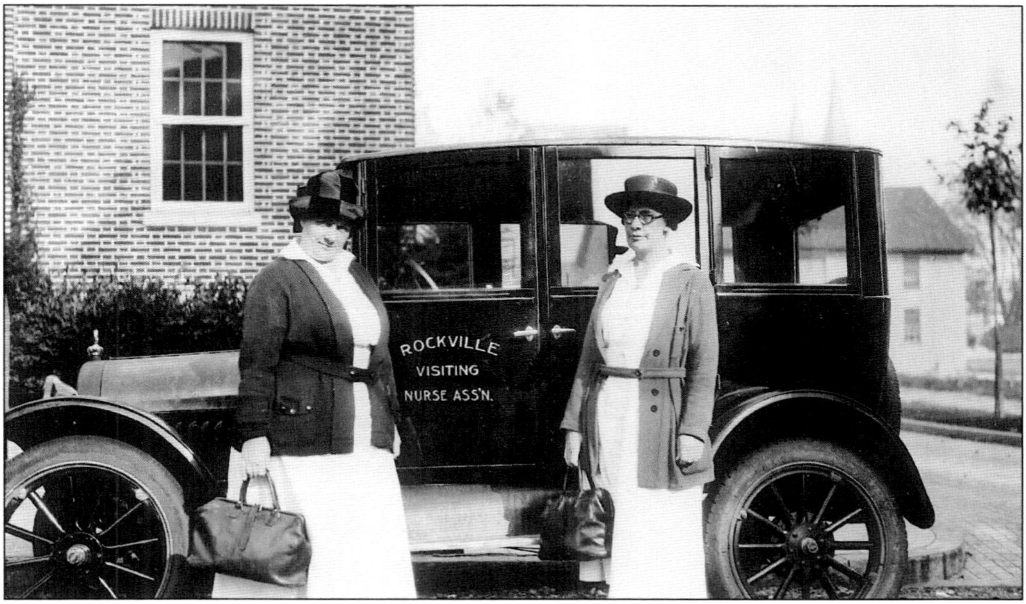

Before the hospital opened, Rockville relied on home care provided by visiting nurses. The Rockville Visiting Nurses Association was established in 1913. At first the nurses walked, but they were later given a horse-drawn buggy. The acquisition of an automobile in the 1920s was a great step forward. Margaret Dornheim (left) and Helen Regan (right) proudly pose in front of their car.

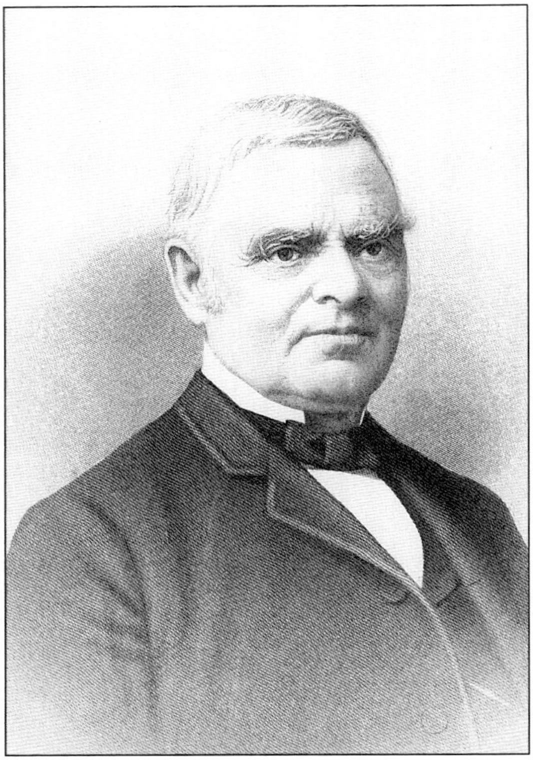

George Maxwell came to Rockville in 1847 as a partner in the Rock Company store. Later he invested in the Hockanum Company and, in association with George Sykes, reorganized the New England and Springville Companies. He served as president of the three companies until his death in 1891. He was also involved in other Rockville businesses and was undoubtedly Rockville's most successful businessman.

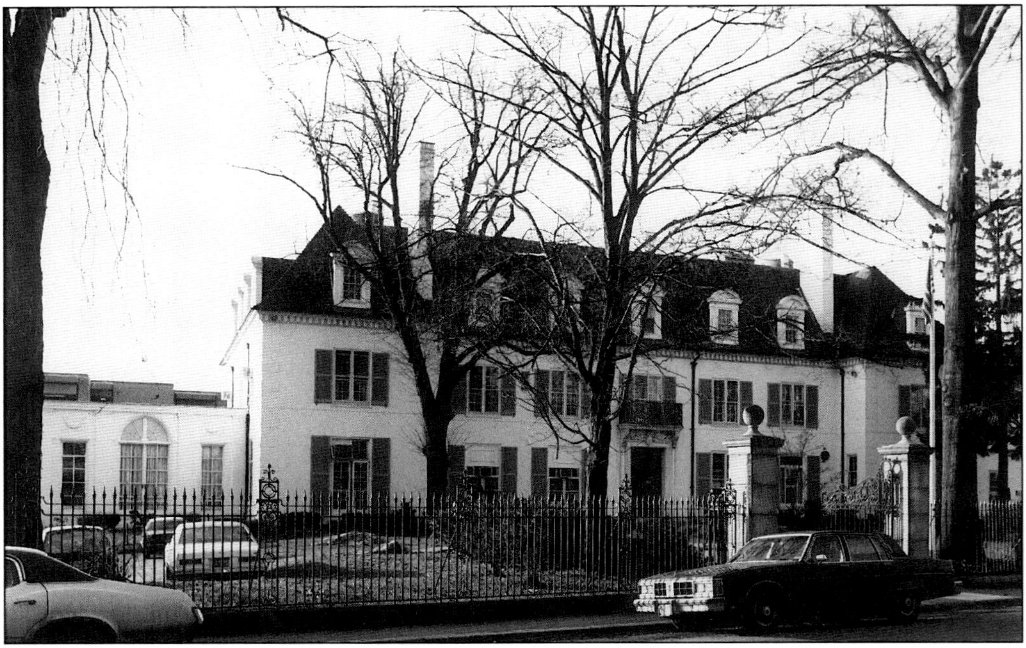

In 1905 the Maxwell family moved the family homestead to make way for the imposing Classical Revival-style house shown here. The house is an early example of the work of noted architect Charles A. Platt. In 1945 it was purchased and rehabilitated to accommodate the Rockville City Hospital (later Rockville General Hospital). Today it remains as the administrative wing of the hospital.

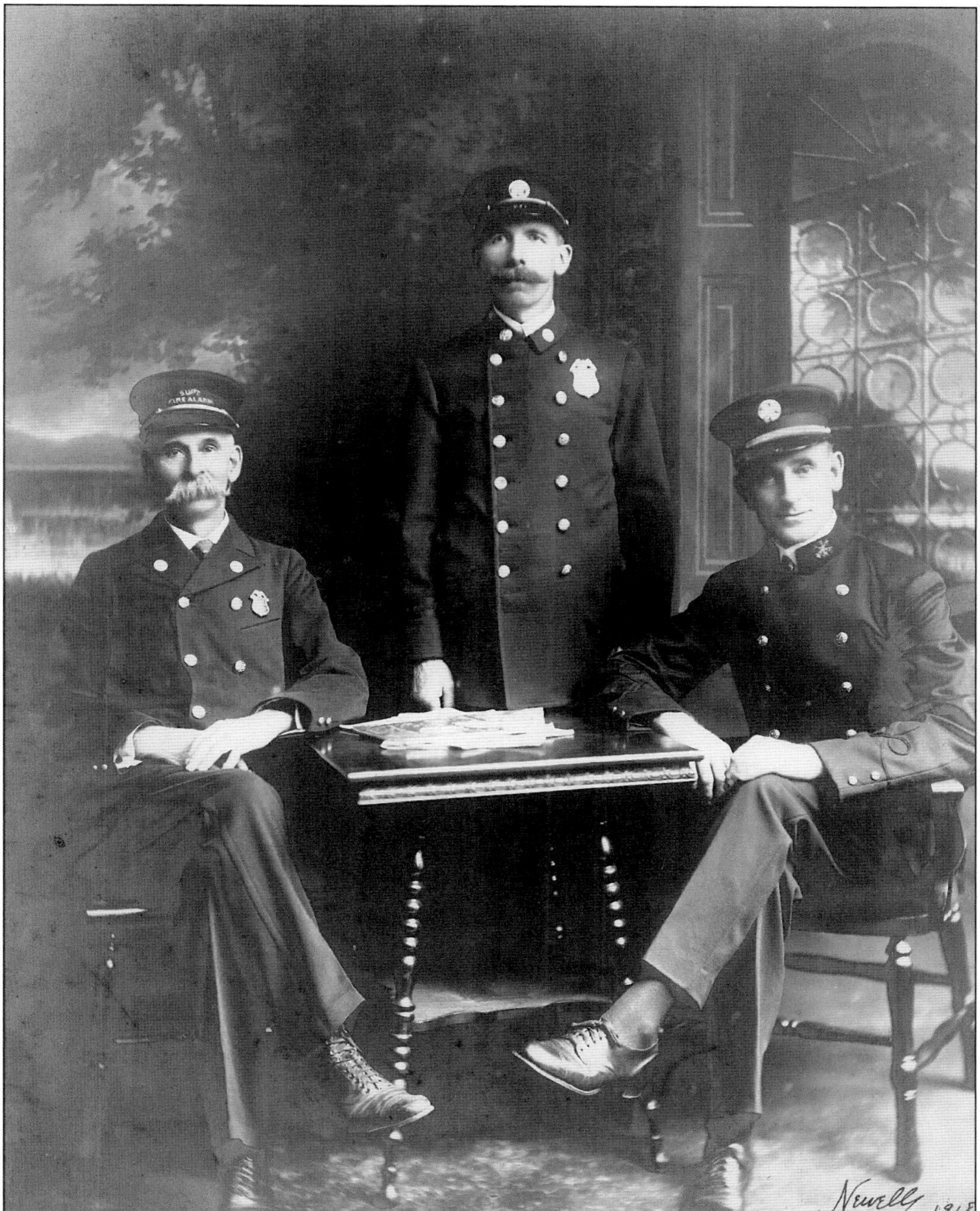

Rockville Fire Department officials—from left to right are Superintendent A.T. Dickerson, Captain Bernard F. Shea, and Chief George Milne—sit for a portrait in 1918. Volunteer fire companies had existed since 1855, but it was not until 1880 that an official town fire department was established—still volunteer, as it remains today.

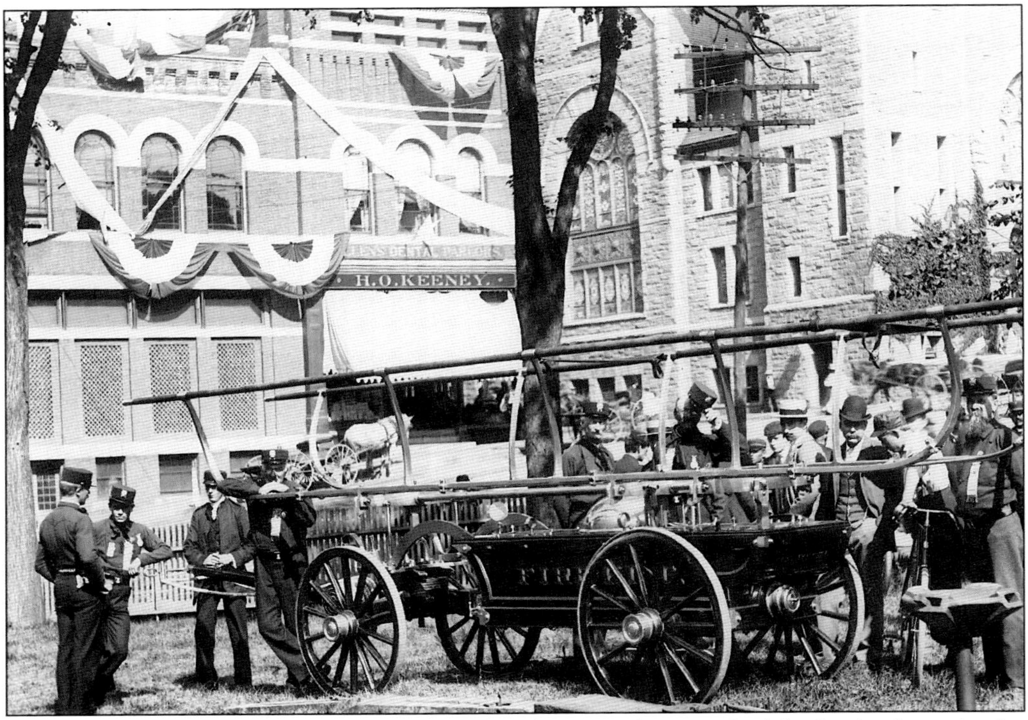

The first fire companies used the Fire King, a hand-operated pump which had to be drawn by the firemen to the scene of the fire. By 1897, when the Fire King was proudly displayed at a Firemen's Field Day, Rockville had two companies, two firehouses, and more modern equipment.

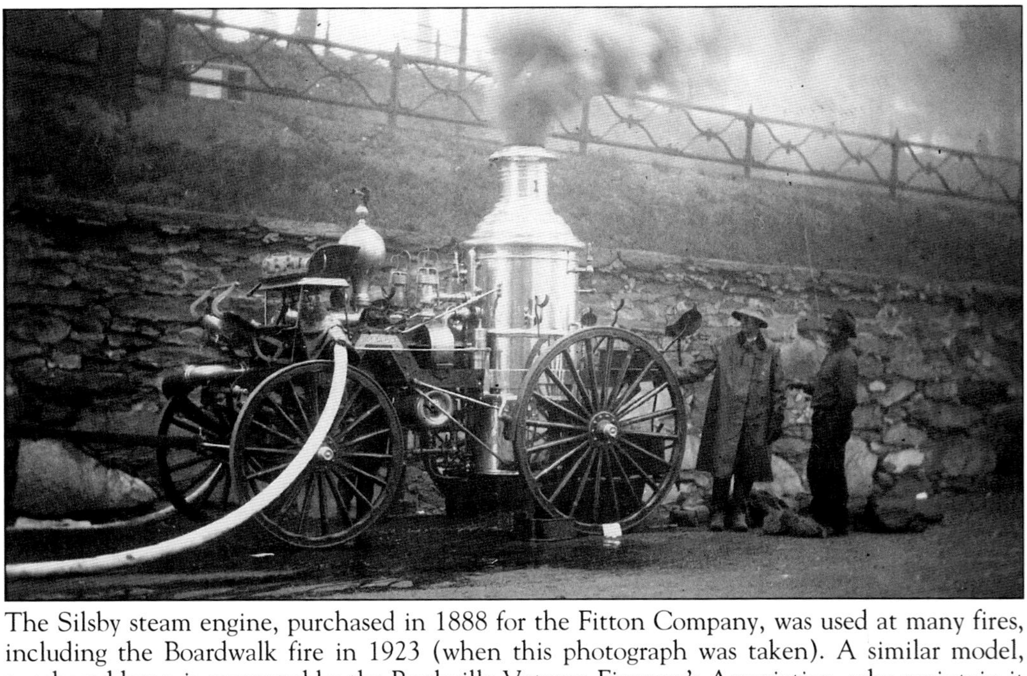

The Silsby steam engine, purchased in 1888 for the Fitton Company, was used at many fires, including the Boardwalk fire in 1923 (when this photograph was taken). A similar model, purchased later, is preserved by the Rockville Veteran Firemen's Association, who maintain it in operating condition and provide demonstrations from time to time.

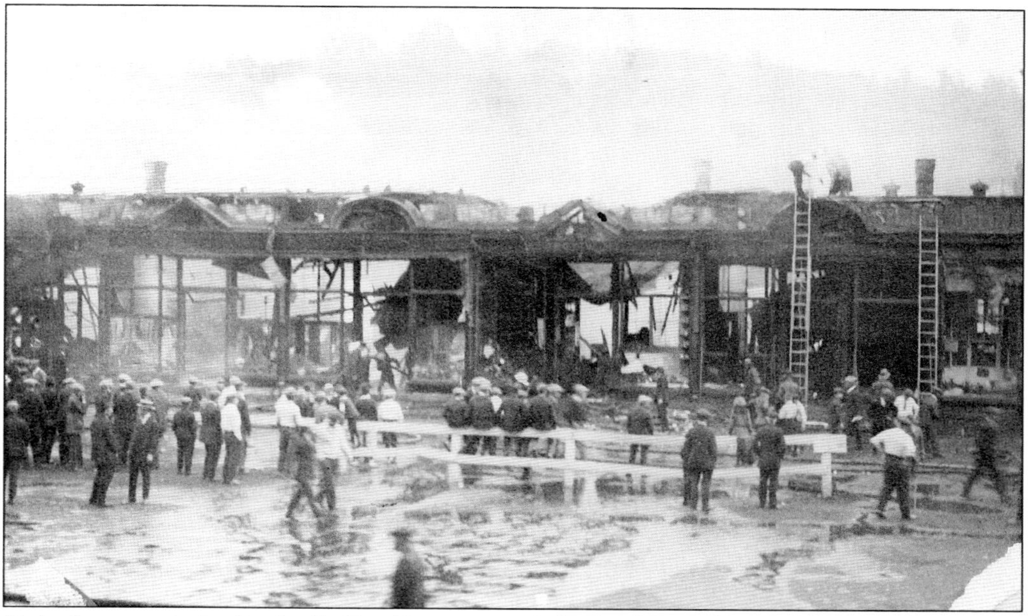

Onlookers watch the Rockville Fire Department fight the flames that engulfed the stores along the Boardwalk on May 28, 1923.

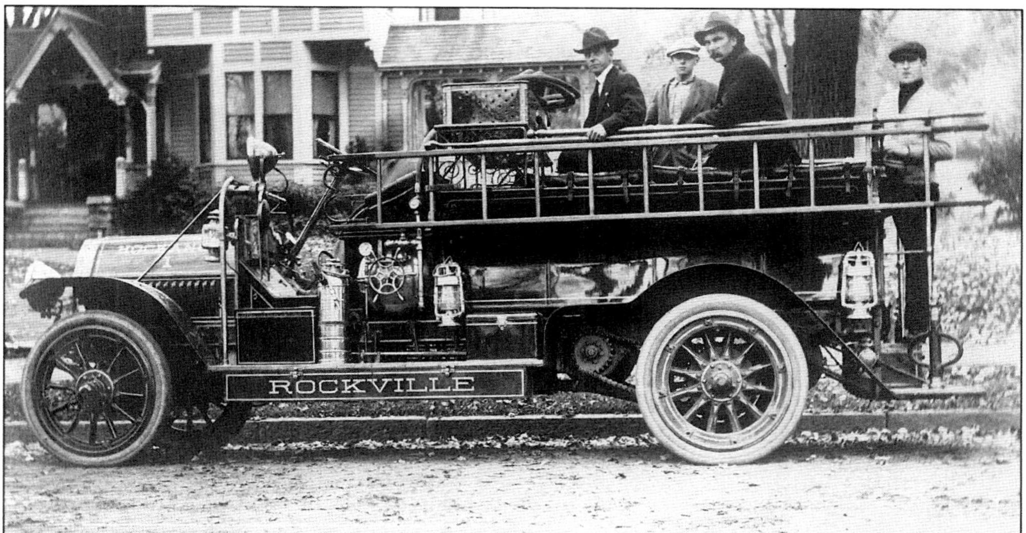

The first motorized apparatus, the Knox Chemical Wagon, c. 1923, considerably improved fire fighting in Rockville. Firemen could arrive at the scene of the fire more quickly and chemicals, similar to those in a hand-held extinguisher, could be used to bring fires under control.

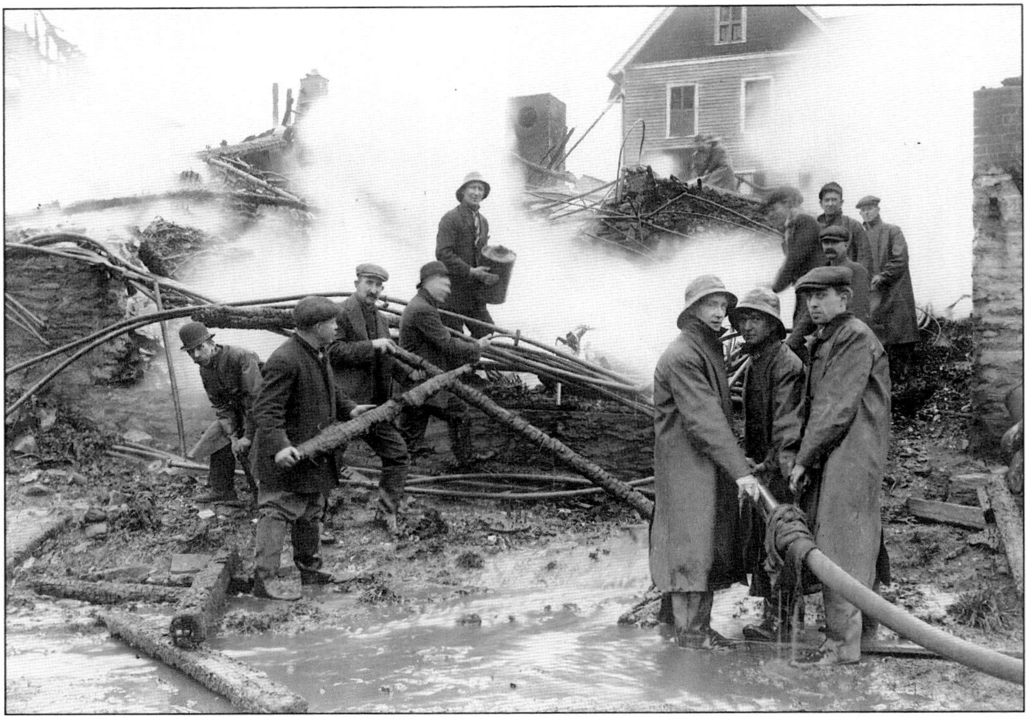

Firemen battle the still smoldering ruins of E.J. Martin's Kingfisher Fishline factory in May 1916.

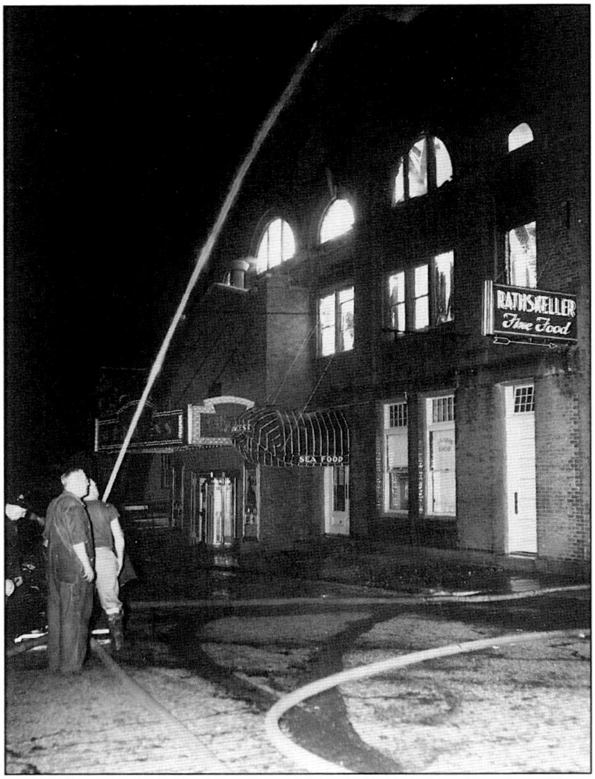

The Princess Theater fire lit up the dark night in a spectacular blaze in 1949. The movie theater was located in the Turn Hall, built by a German gymnastic society in 1897. Fortunately the building was saved and serves today as the meeting place of the Polish-American Citizens Club.

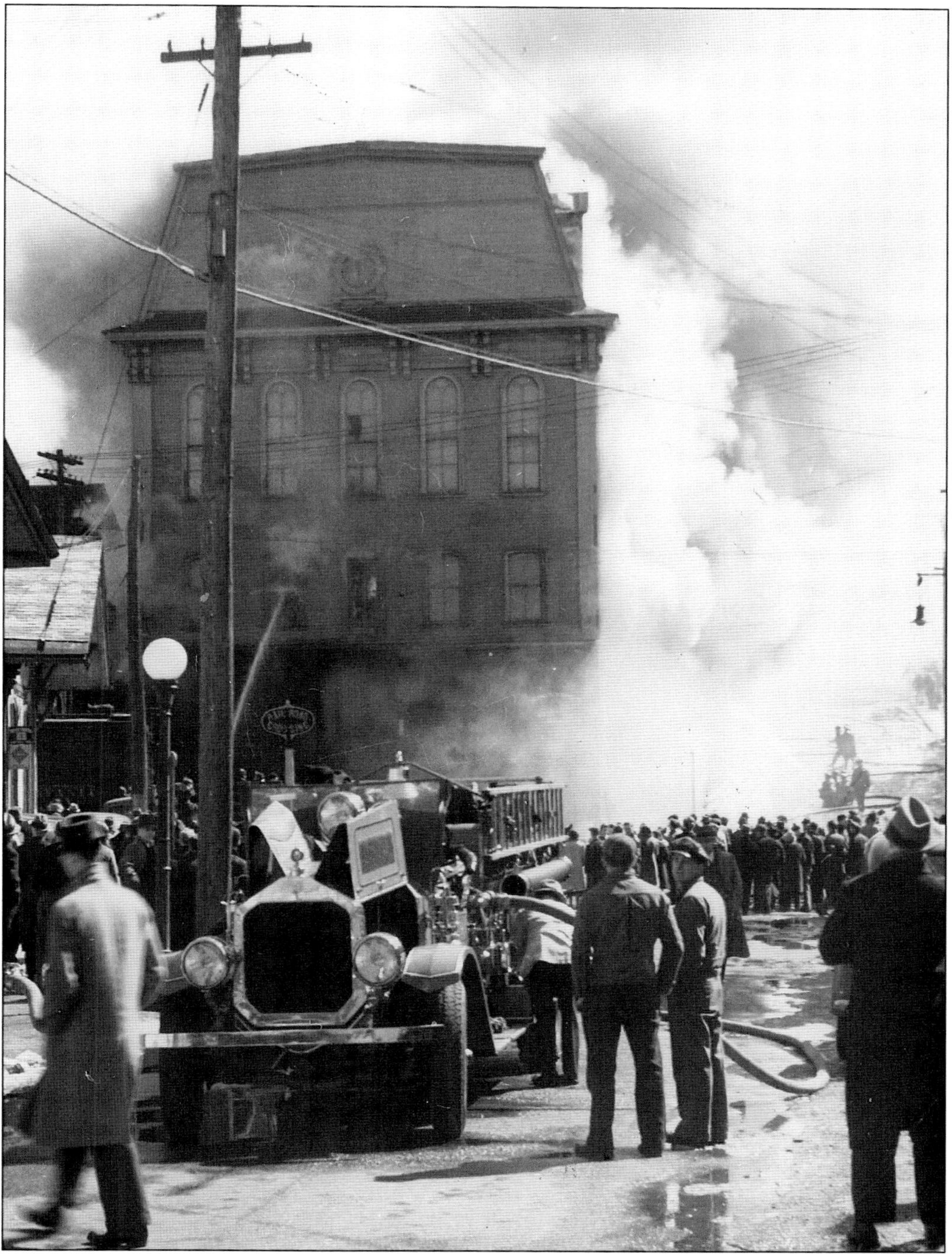

The White's Opera House is engulfed in smoke during the March 1941 fire that destroyed the building. Originally a church, the building was moved from Ellington to Rockville, where Cyrus White converted it to a theater in 1869. In later years the Opera House occupied the top two floors and the *Rockville Journal* was located on the ground floor.

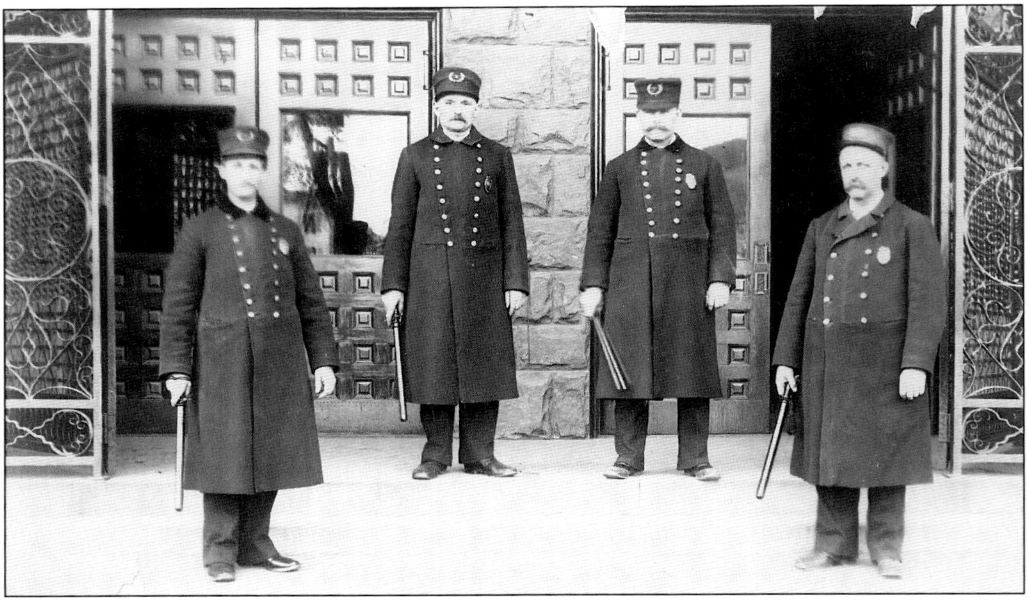

In uniform and carrying night sticks, Rockville's first policemen stand in front of the Memorial Building. One of the first acts of the new city government in 1890 was to establish a police force. The four officers shown here served from 1890 to 1898. They are, from left to right, Dennis W. Delaney, Fred Einsiedel, James Lynch, and Captain William H. Cady.

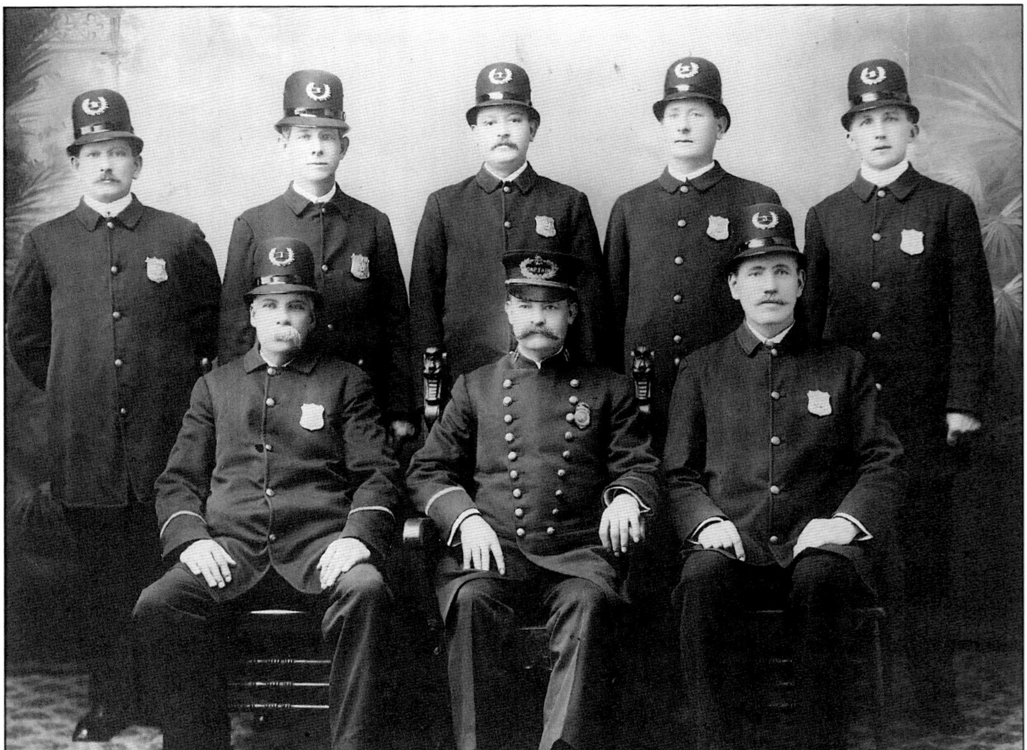

By 1916 the police department had grown, as shown in this studio portrait, to a force of four officers and four supernumeraries. Occupying the center chair is Captain Leopold Krause.

Seven

Vernon Goes to War

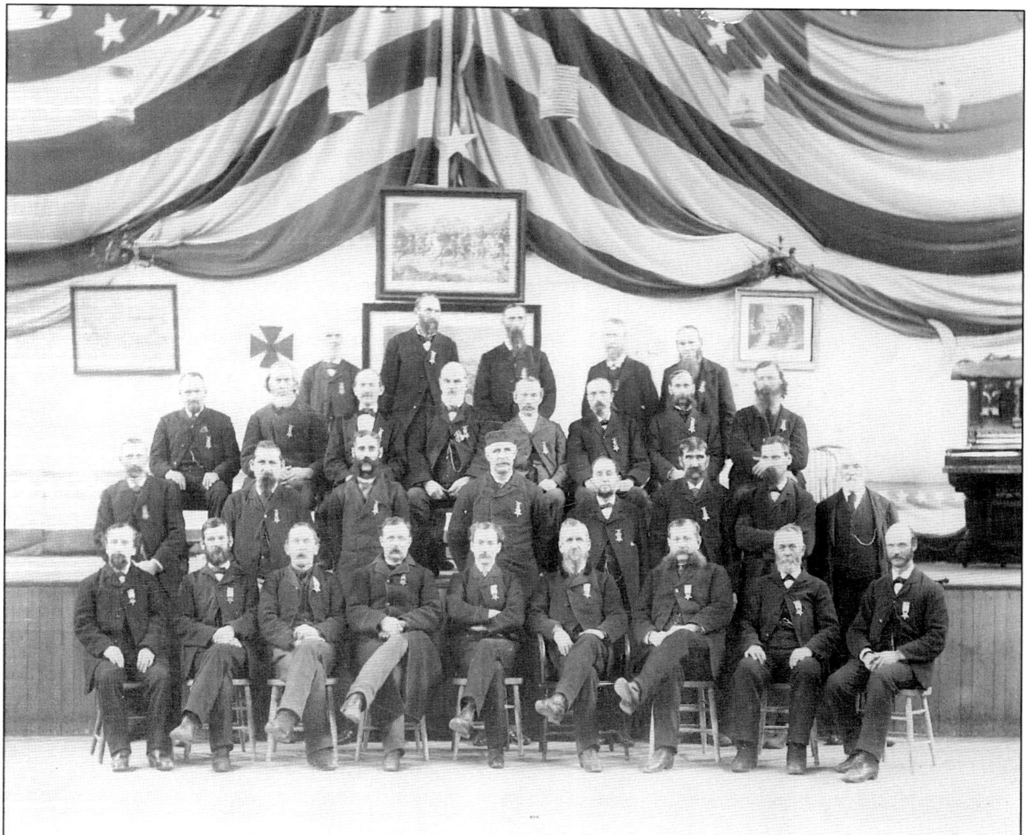

When the Civil War started in 1861, three hundred men from Vernon answered the call to arms. In 1885, the Civil War veterans established a local chapter of the Grand Army of the Republic. Gathered together in their meeting hall in the Memorial Building, Civil War veterans pose for a photograph. The New England Civil War Museum is now located here and is maintained by their descendants, the Sons of Union Veterans..

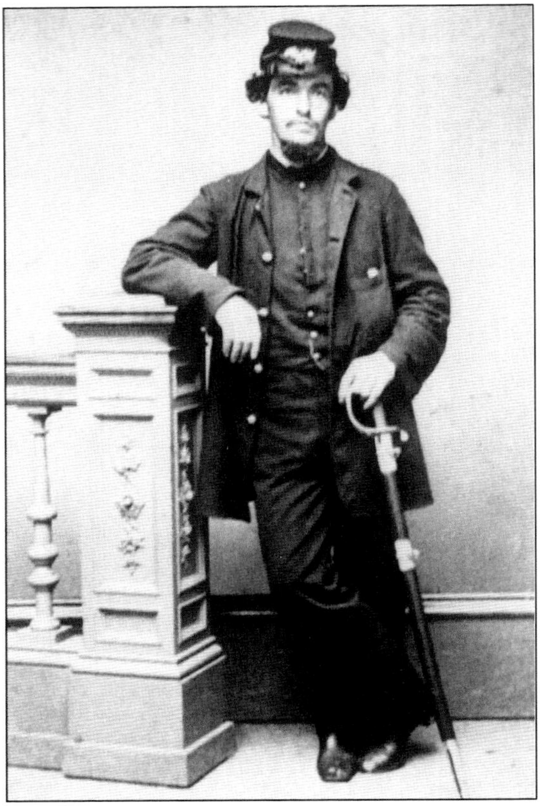

Col. Thomas F. Burpee of Vernon, commander of the 21st Volunteer Infantry, was fatally wounded in the Battle of Cold Harbor, VA, and died June 9, 1864. Burpee Post, GAR No. 71, chartered April 18, 1885, honors his name.

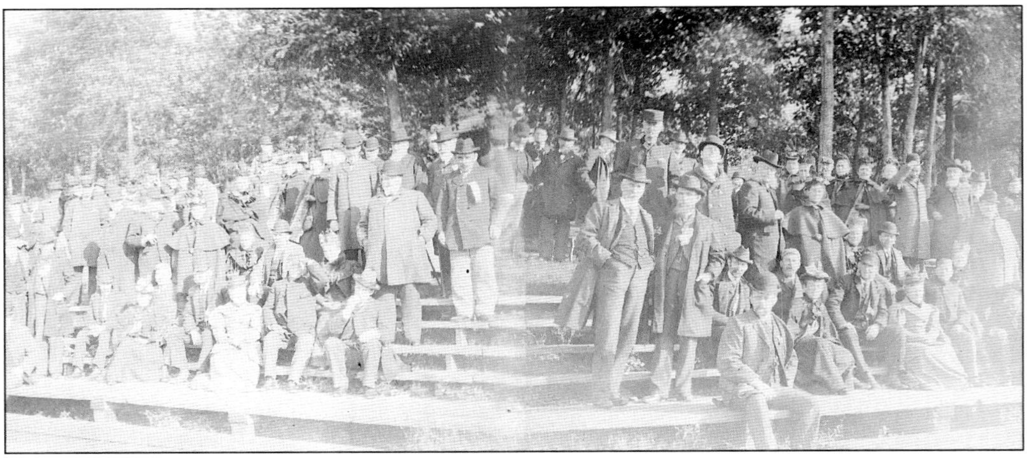

In 1894 Civil War veterans from Rockville traveled with their families to Gettysburg, where this photograph was taken. The purpose of the trip was to witness the unveiling of a monument to the 14th Regiment, Connecticut Volunteers, who participated in the Battle of Antietam.

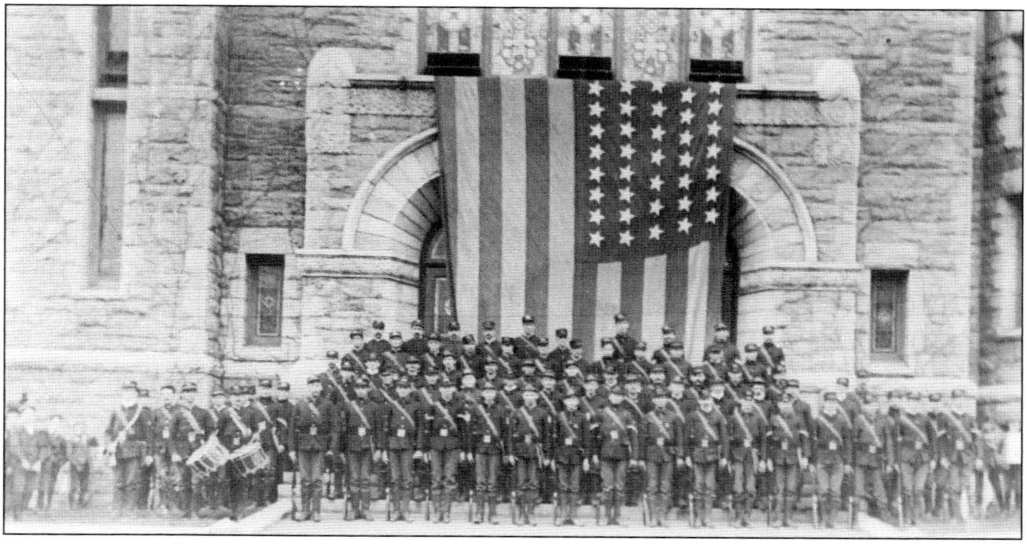

In May 1898, volunteers from Vernon responded yet again to the nation's call to arms. Company C, First Regiment, gathered on the steps of Union Congregational Church for a photograph before leaving to fight in the Spanish-American War.

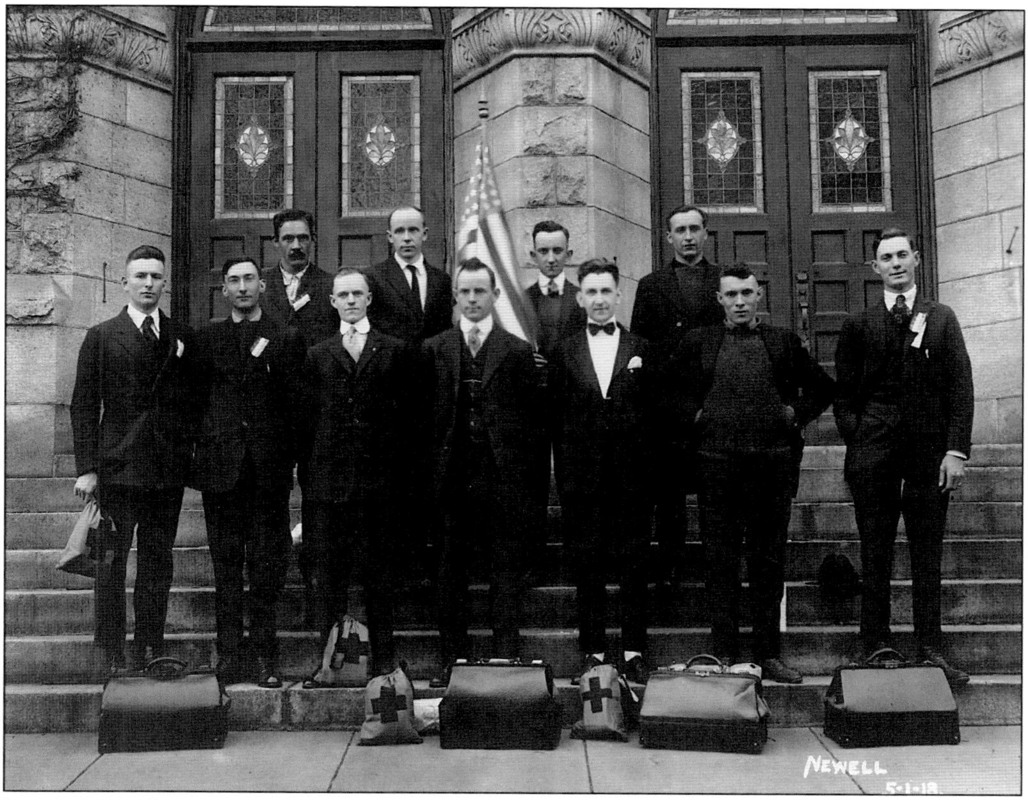

In 1918 another group of young men posed on the steps of Union Congregational Church before leaving to join the military after the United States declared war on Germany.

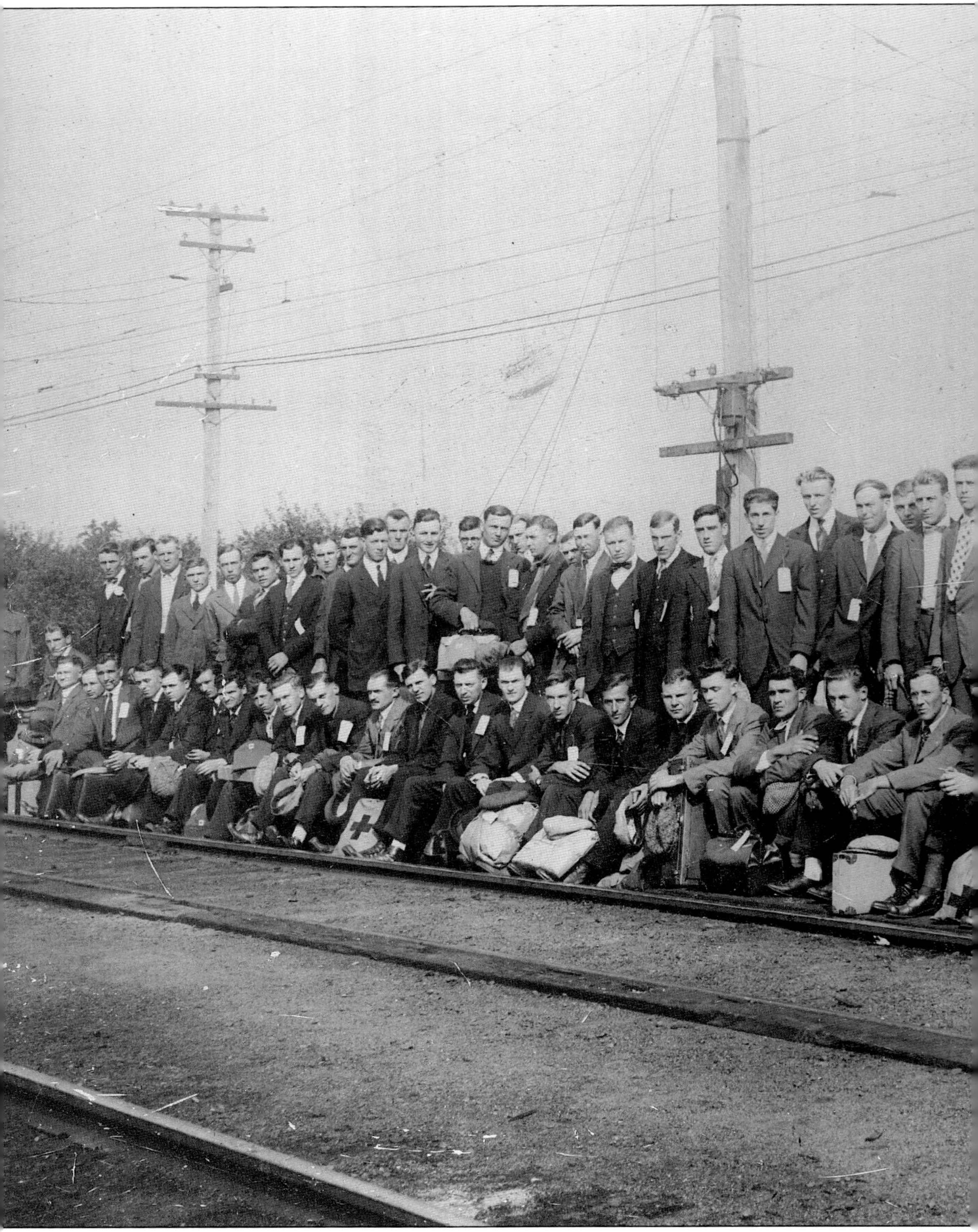

With a mixture of pride and apprehension, young men wait at the Vernon Depot station for the train to carry them to the battlefields of World War I. For many this trip would be the first time away from their home town. In addition to a suitcase, each man carries a "Comfort Kit"

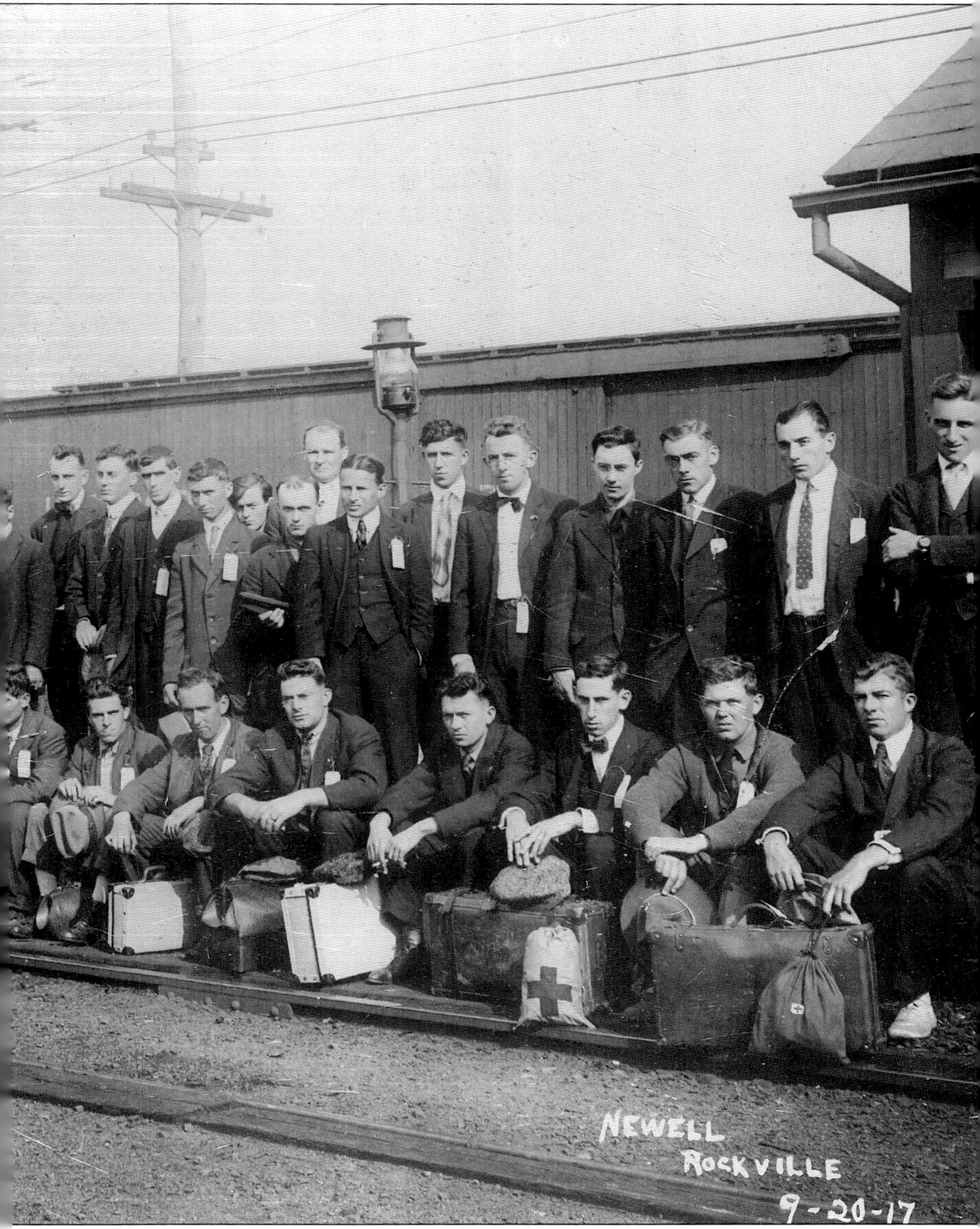

presented to him by the Red Cross. Perhaps it was these "kit bags" that inspired the popular World War I song, "Pack up your troubles in your old kit bag."

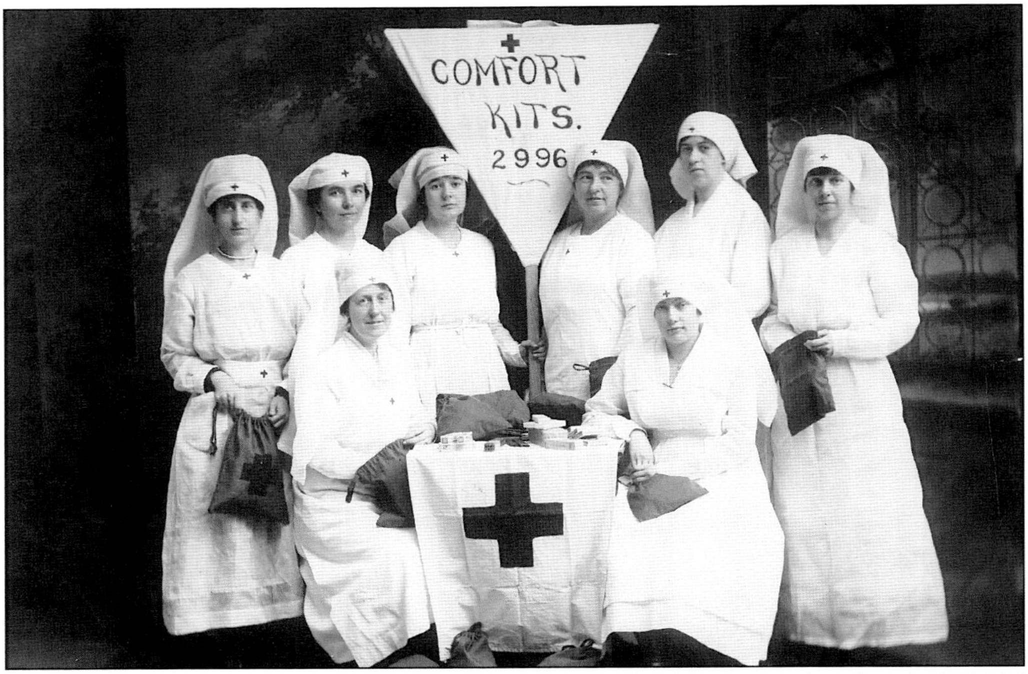

On the home front, Red Cross volunteers in the Rockville chapter sewed and packed "2,996 comfort kits," and provided support for many other services.

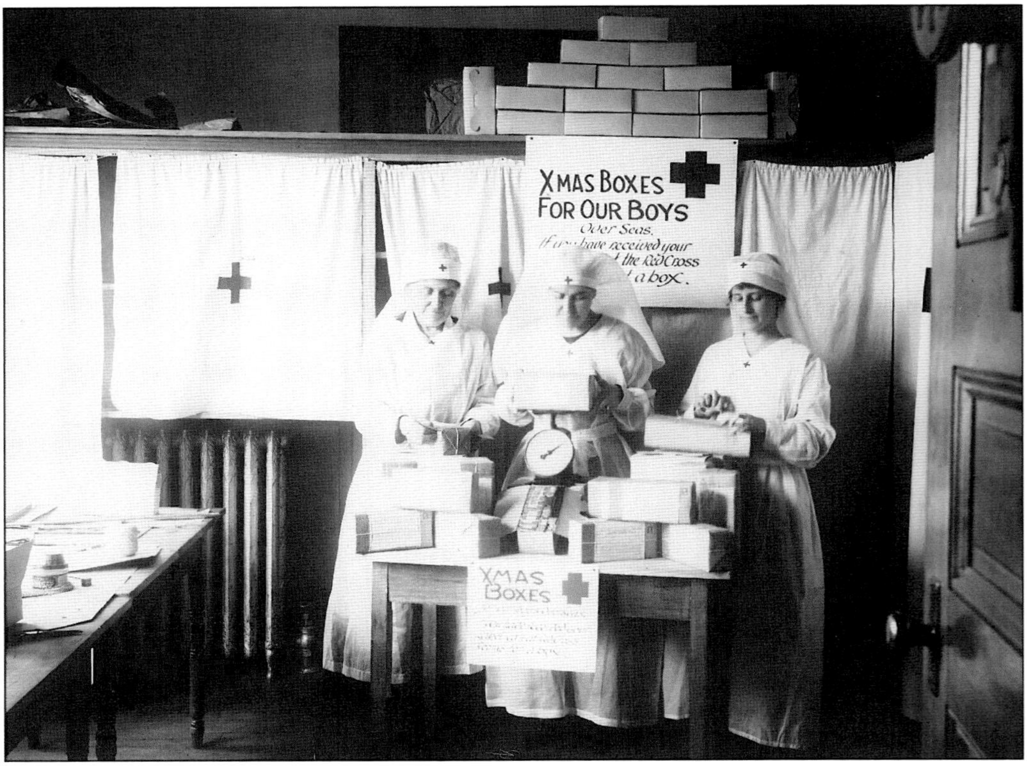

Christmas boxes, prepared by local Red Cross chapters like the one pictured here in Rockville, were greatly appreciated by the soldiers.

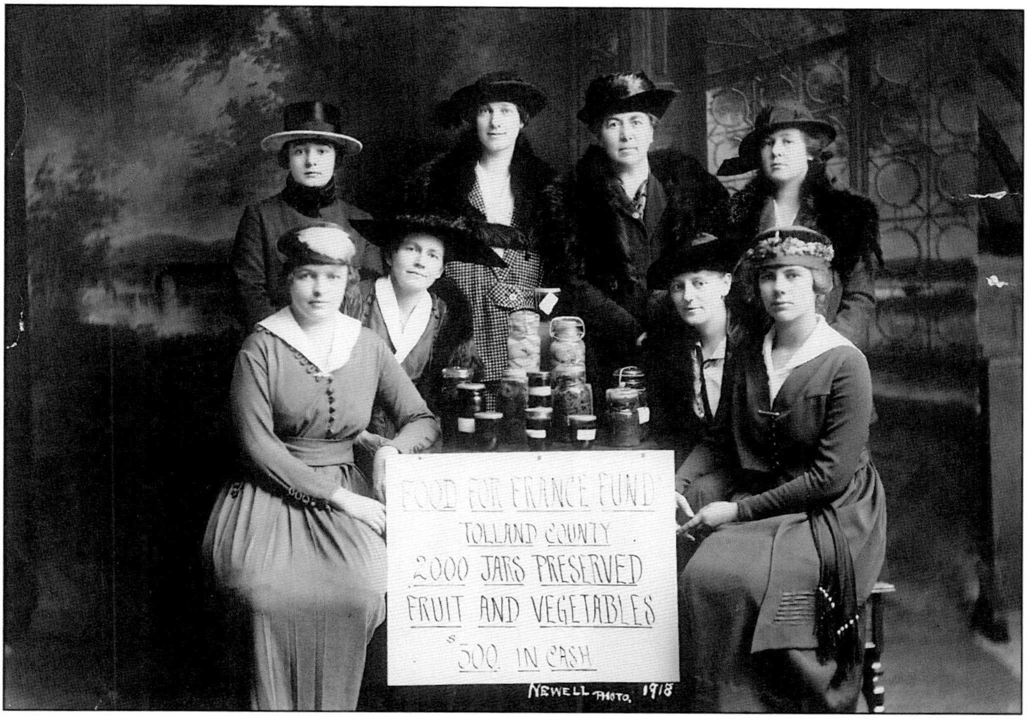

Vernon citizens participated in many other home front activities in support of the war. The group of women pictured here are justly proud of their efforts to help alleviate suffering in war-torn France.

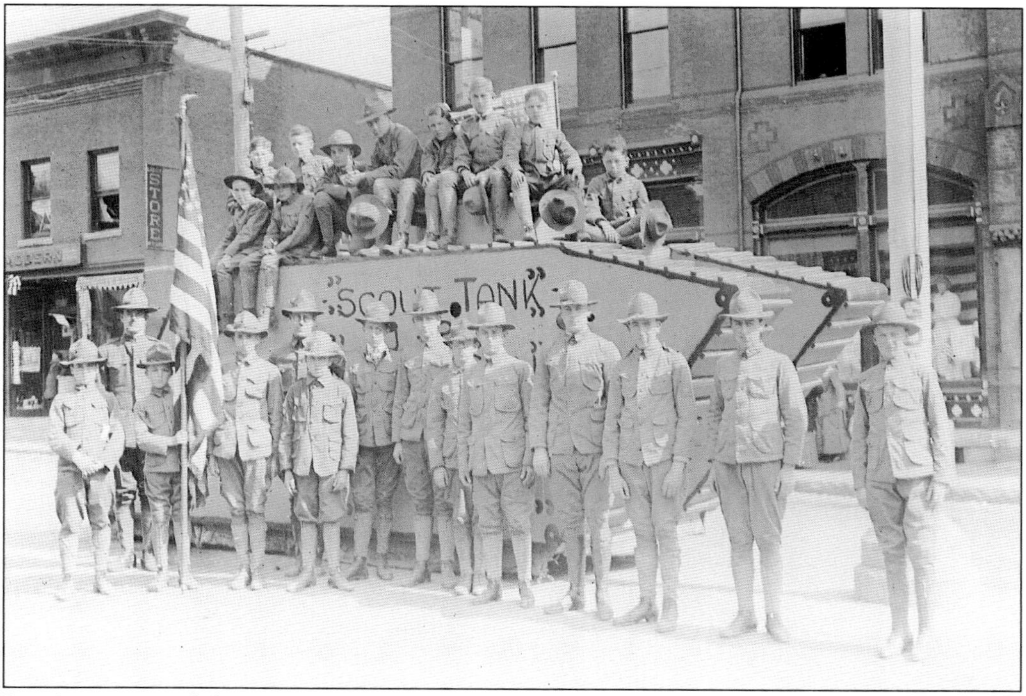

Boy Scouts joined the war effort by constructing this replica of a tank, which they named "U-2 Buy a Bond," encouraging the sale of war bonds.

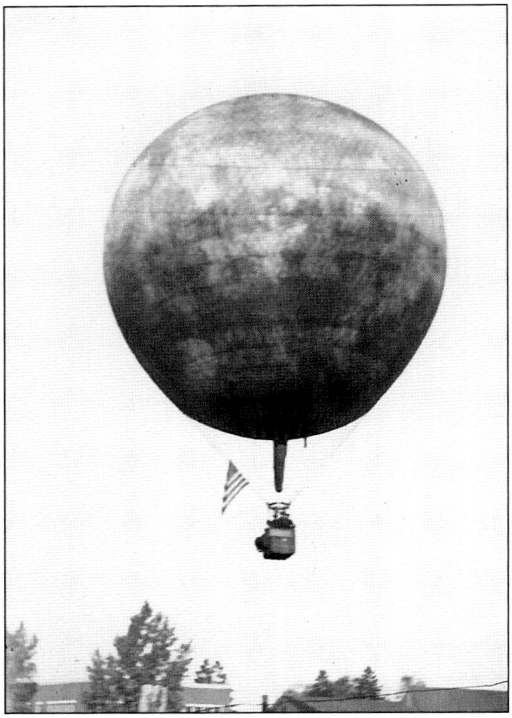

Successfully aloft, a balloon floats over St. Joseph's School in Rockville in September 1917. During World War I, the Maxwell brothers and others established the Collegiate Balloon School at the Windermere factory in nearby Ellington, where they proposed to manufacture balloons and train pilots for the United States Army.

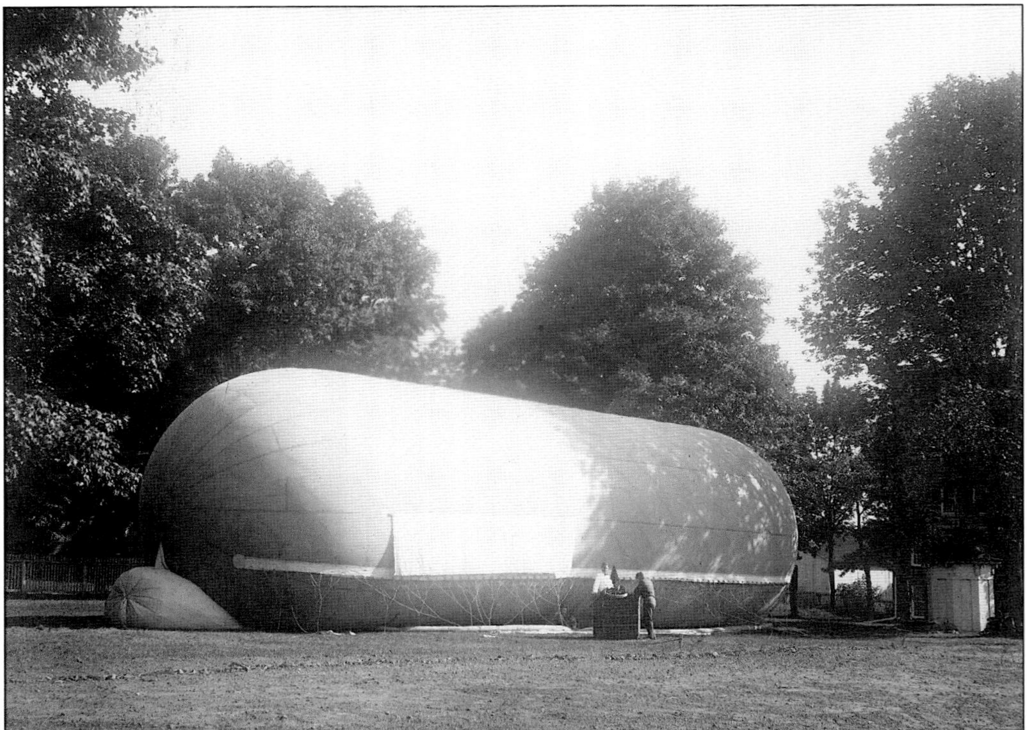

On view in this photograph is a small dirigible balloon, one of nine balloons the school planned to use to instruct U.S. Army officers in the operation of free and captive balloons. When the weather grew cold, the school was moved to Georgia. It does not appear to have returned.

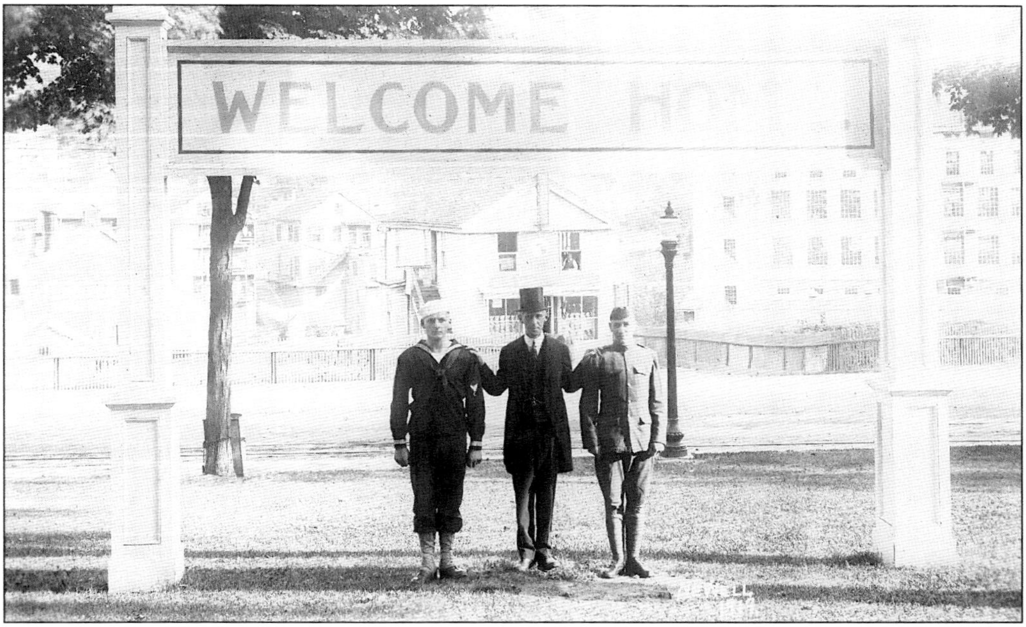

With the war's end on November 11, 1918, Vernon prepared to welcome home its returning soldiers. "Welcome Home Day," a town-wide celebration, took place on May 3, 1919. Here Mayor John Cameron, standing under a ceremonial arch in Rockville's Central Park, greets representatives of the Army and Navy. The Rock mill can be seen in the background.

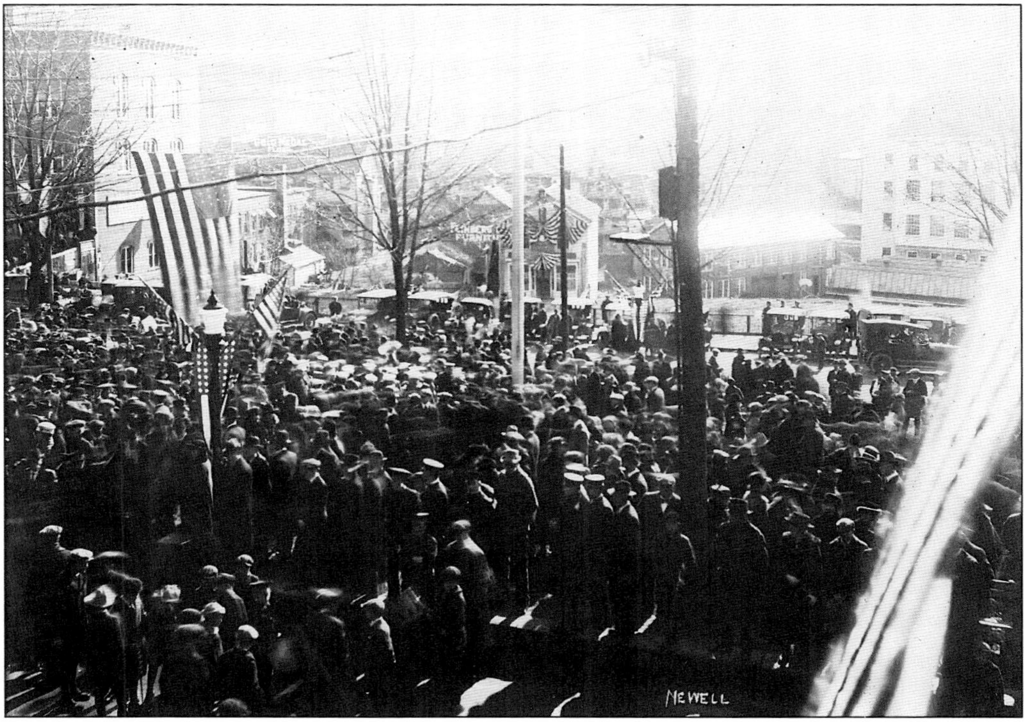

Armistice Day in 1920 was commemorated with a large parade through downtown Rockville. In this view, the camera captures a somber moment as participants gather in Central Park for the official ceremony of remembrance.

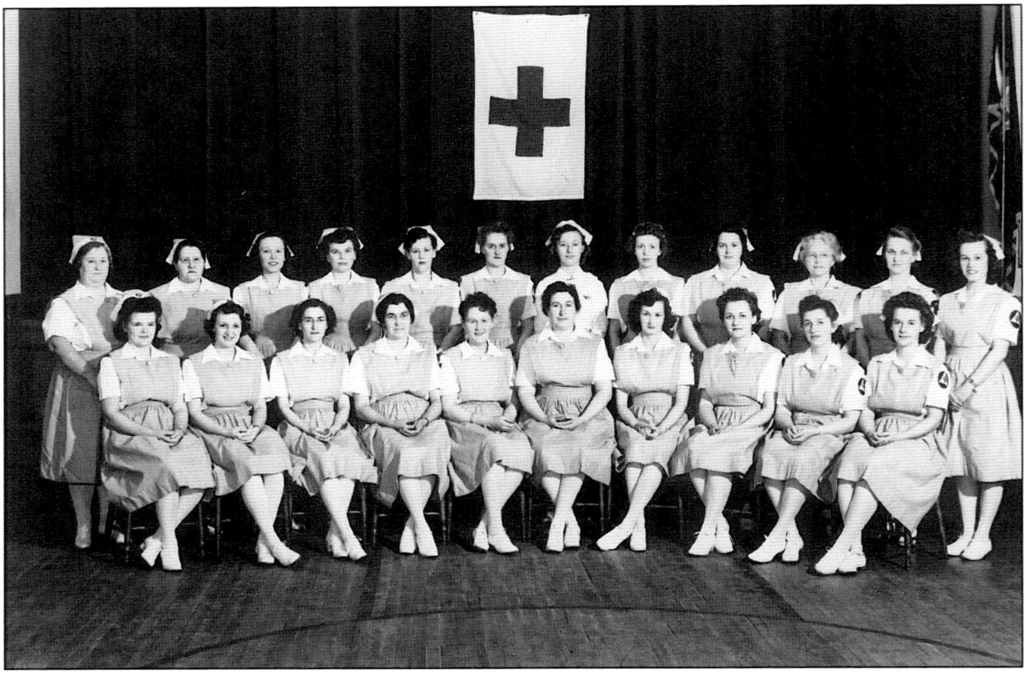

With the outbreak of World War II, the Red Cross was once more called upon to provide support services on the home front. To relieve the shortage of nurses in civilian hospitals, the Red Cross established a training program for volunteer nurses. Sponsored by the Rockville chapter, a class of volunteers poses for a photograph after receiving their caps and pins.

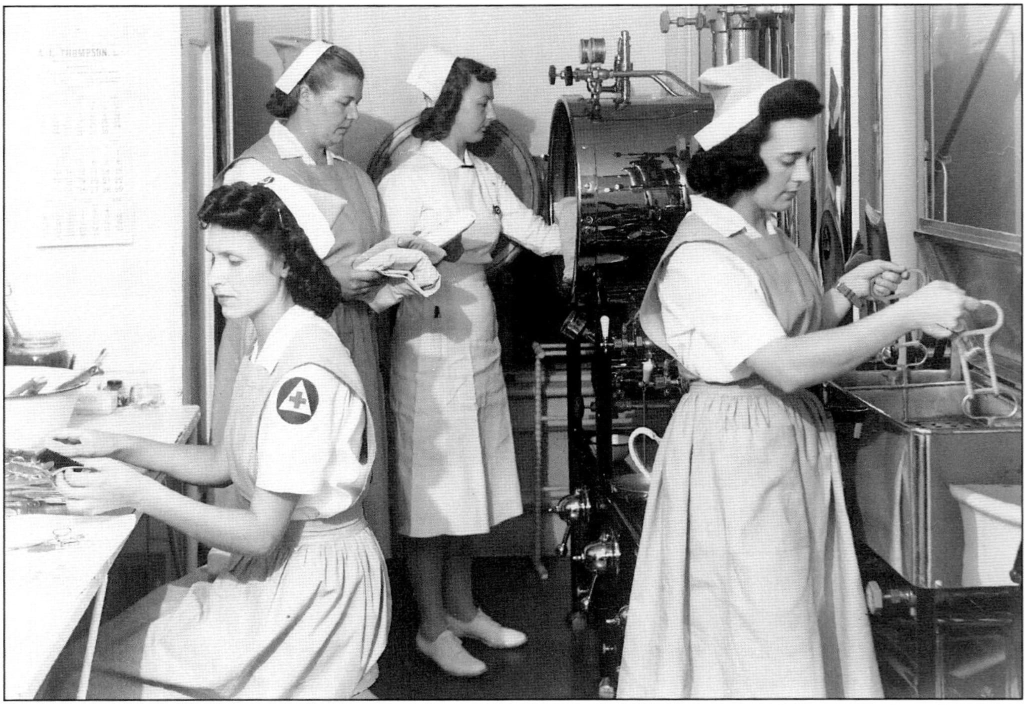

Volunteers performed many valuable services, such as sterilization. In this view, they learn to sterilize instruments by washing, wrapping, and then placing them in the autoclave.

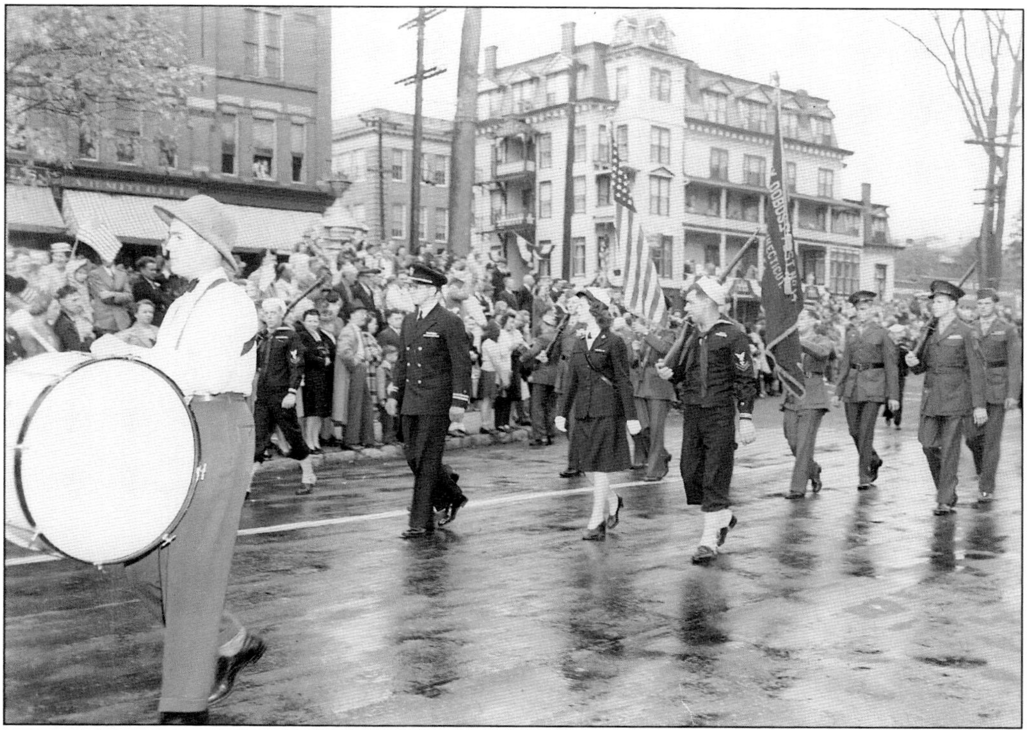

To celebrate the end of World War II in 1945, citizens turned out at a Welcome Home parade to honor the men and women who served. In this view, the color guard has passed the Rockville Hotel on Main Street.

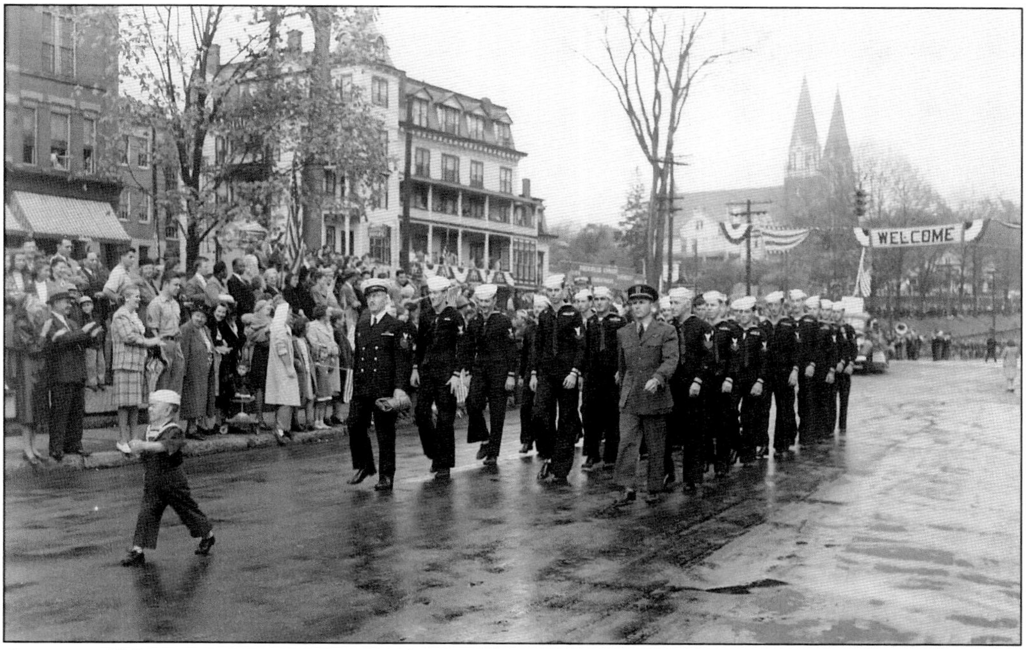

A unit of Navy veterans is given a hearty welcome as they march down Main Street. The Rockville Hotel and St. Bernard's Church can be seen in the background.

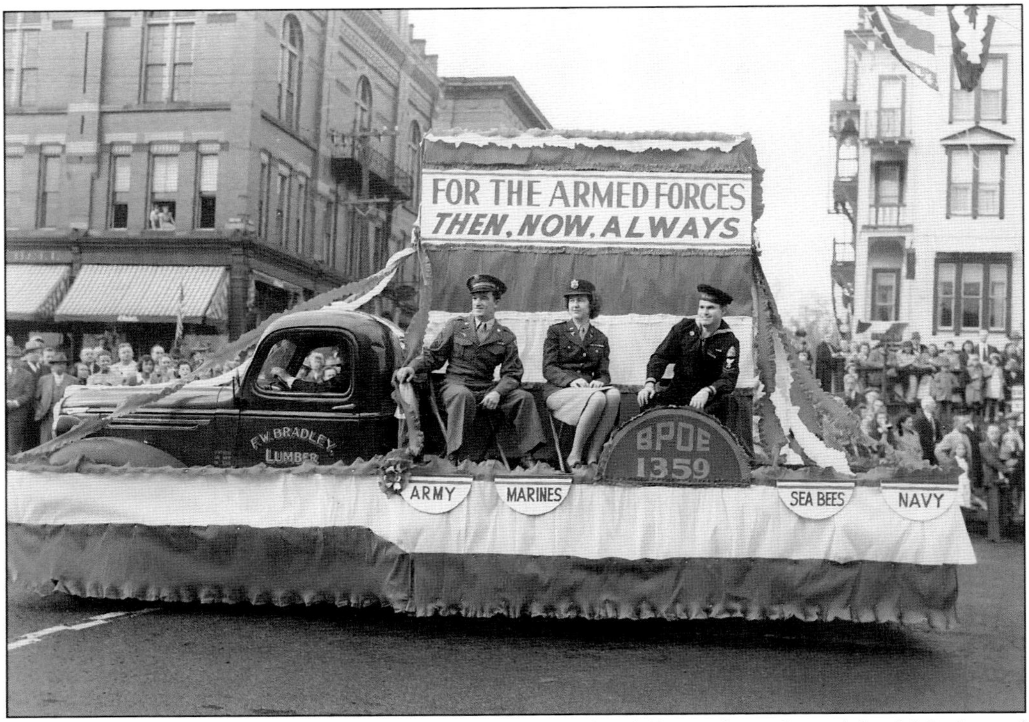

Sponsored by the Elks Club, this float pays tribute to the different branches of the U.S. Armed Forces. The float is just crossing the Park Street intersection. The Henry Building (on the left) and the Rockville Hotel (on the right) were razed during the 1960s redevelopment project.

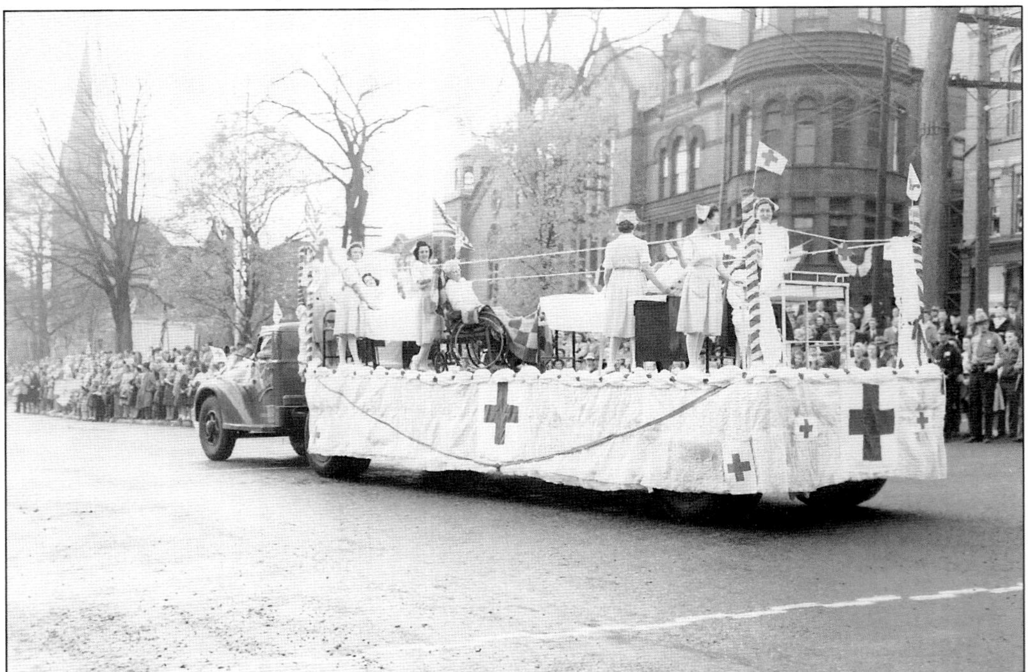

A float honoring the work of the Red Cross moves toward Central Park with the Memorial Building in the background.

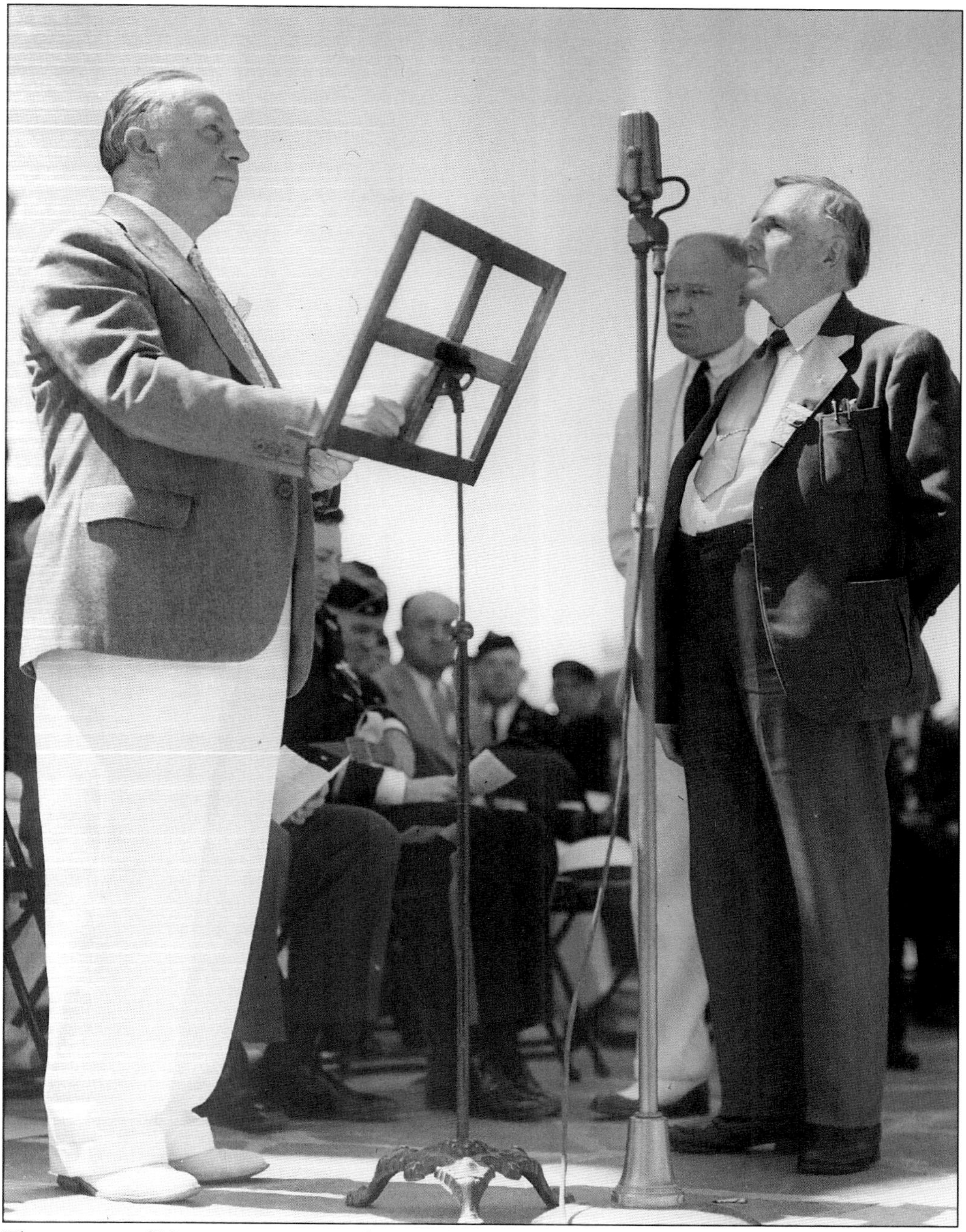

The citizens of Vernon, respecting the sacrifices of those who fought in our nation's wars, have honored their own through the years. The Memorial Building commemorates veterans of the Civil War. In 1939, the War Memorial Tower atop Fox Hill was dedicated in memory of those who fought in all wars. During the dedication ceremony for the War Memorial Tower, Rev. George S. Brookes (left) and Mayor Claude Mills (right) were featured speakers.

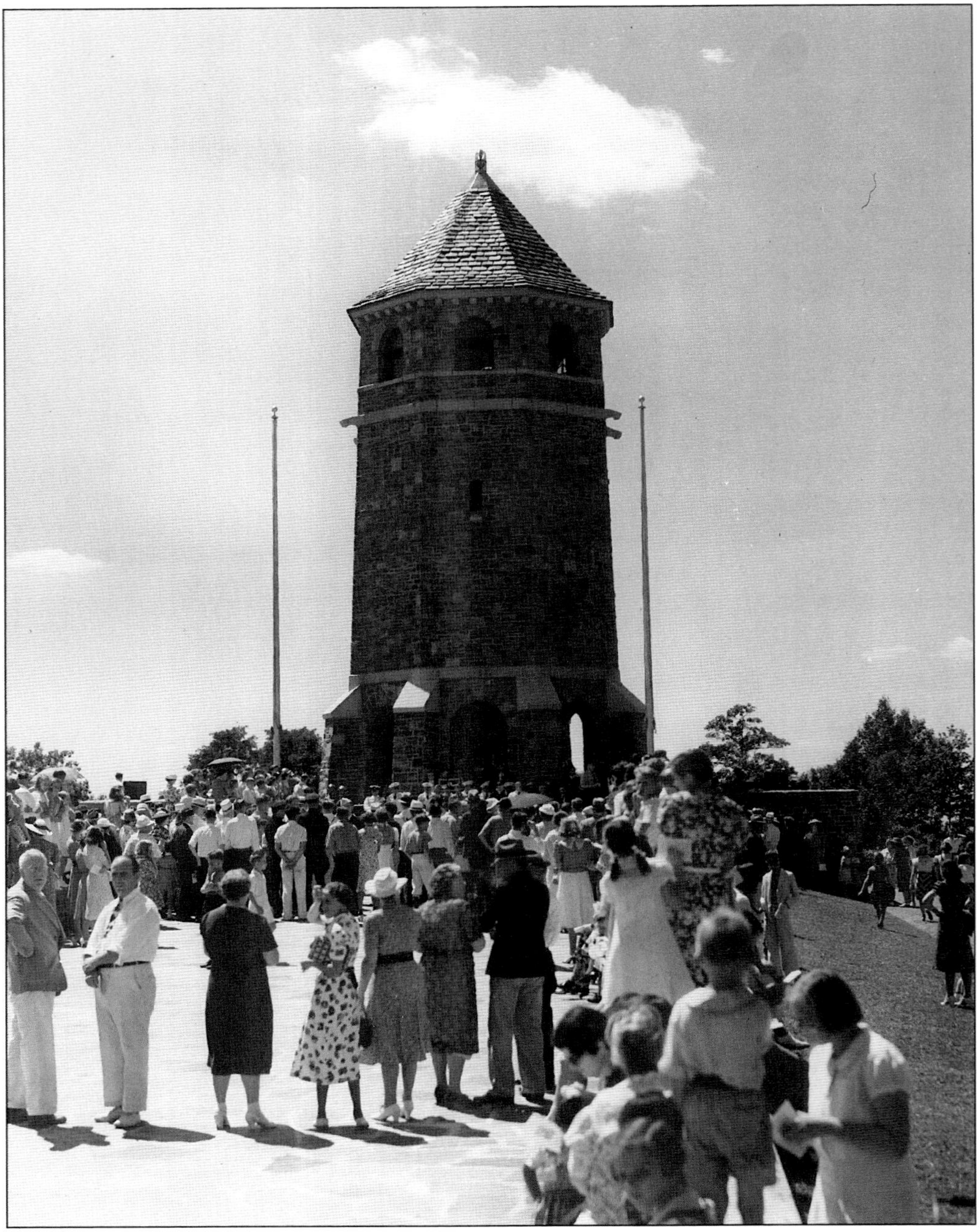

Onlookers gather in front of the newly dedicated War Memorial Tower on Fox Hill in August 1939. It was designed by New York architect Walter B. Chambers, who was inspired by an ancient Romanesque church in France. The tower was built by Works Project Administration workers using local stone. A spectacular view of the surrounding towns may be seen from the observation area.

Eight

Keeping Business Moving

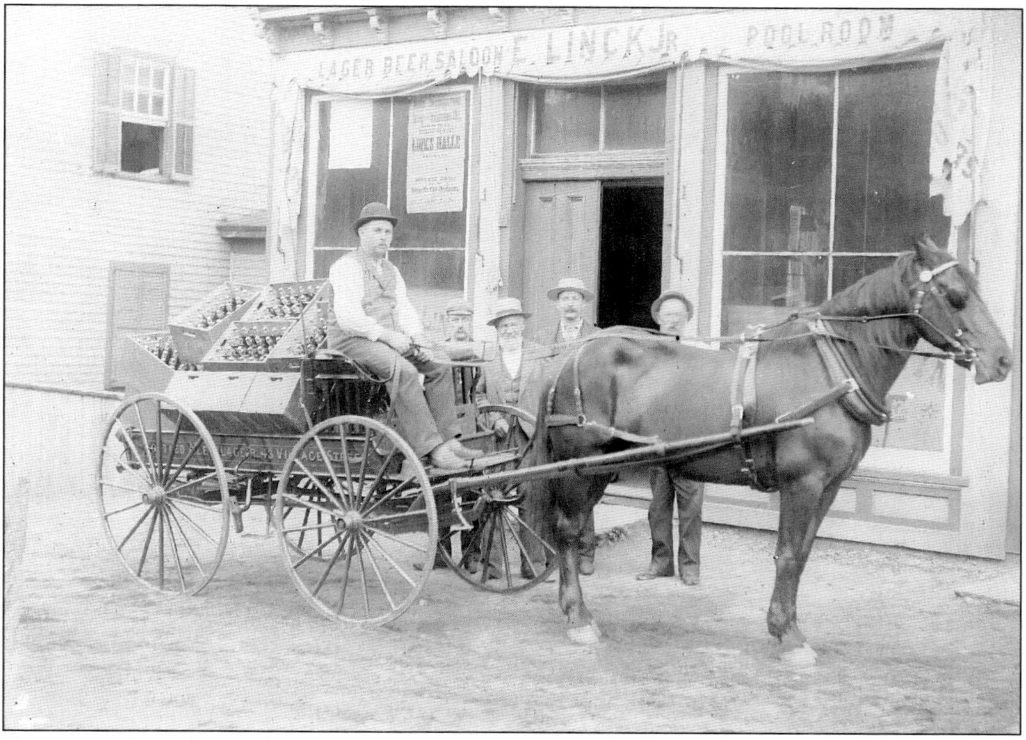

Commerce has always depended on fast and efficient transportation. In nineteenth-century Rockville, horse-drawn wagons were a practical way to keep business moving. Delivery wagons were a familiar sight on the Rockville's streets. The proprietor of Linck's Saloon used this wagon for deliveries of bottled beverages.

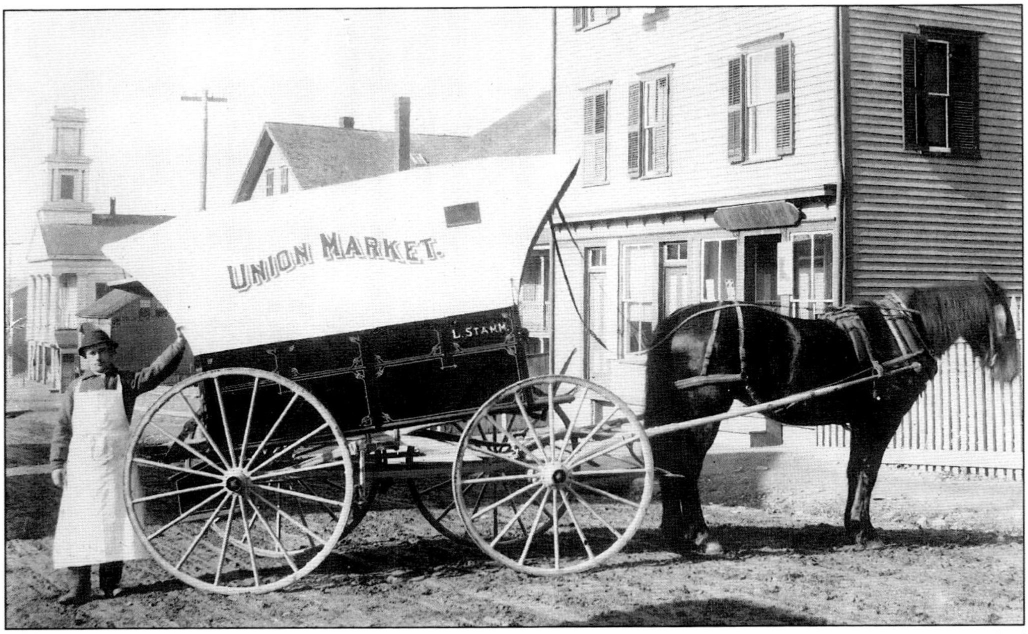

Housewives did not have to leave home to shop for food or other essentials. Most stores provided for delivery service. Louis Stamm's store, the Union Market, was located on the corner of Union and Ward Streets. The store sold meat and provisions, which may account for the white butcher's apron worn by the unidentified man standing next to the wagon.

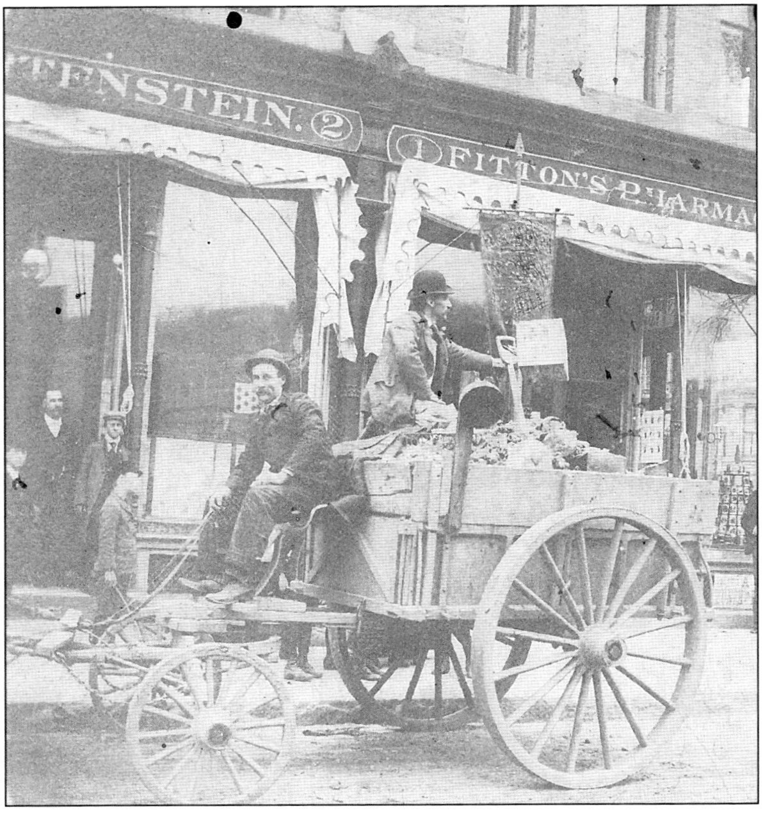

Peddlers also plied their trade in Rockville, selling their goods from house to house. This wagon and driver were photographed in front of Fitton's pharmacy in the Henry Building. This photograph probably dates from the last decades of the nineteenth century.

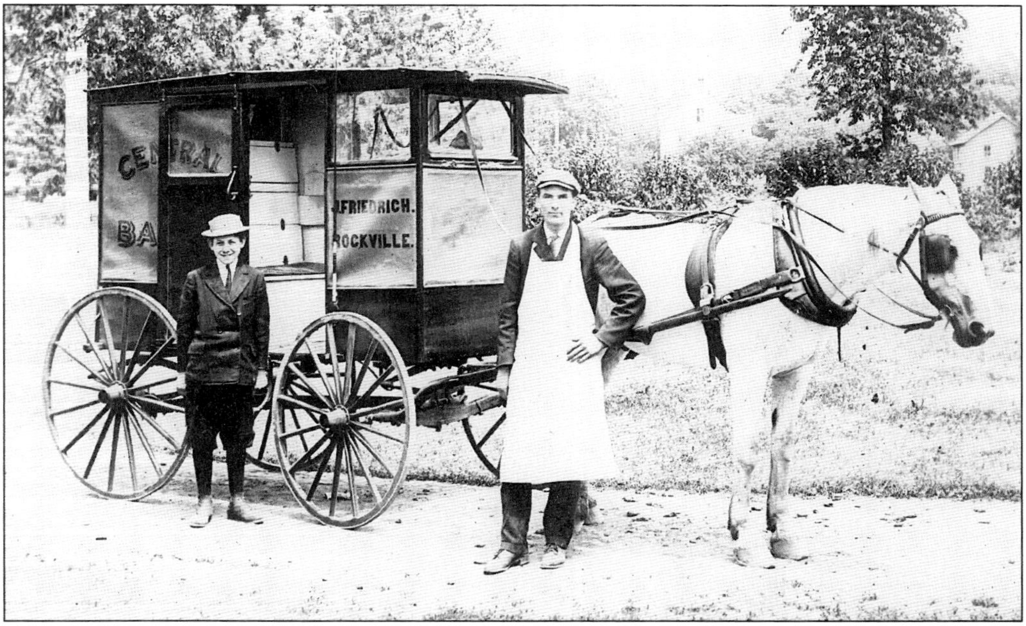

Fresh bread and other baked goods were delivered daily from door to door, as shown in this 1912 photograph. Customers could place a card in the window if they wished the bakery wagon to stop.

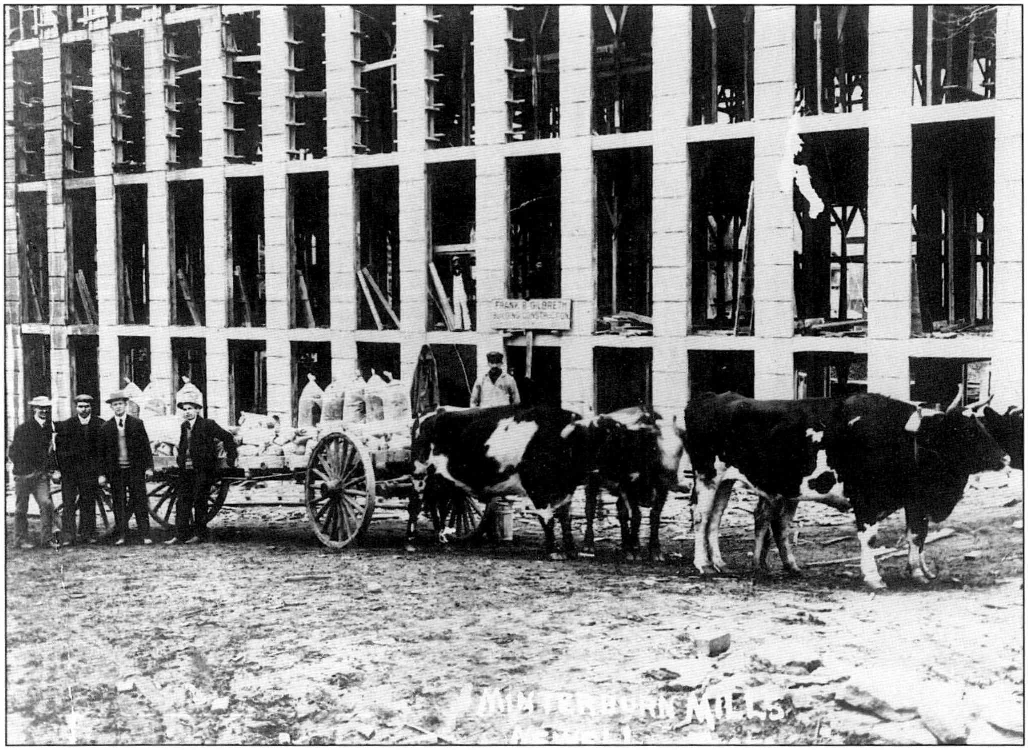

The Minterburn mill was one of the earliest factory buildings in the country to be constructed of reinforced concrete. This photograph, taken when the mill was under construction in 1906, shows that two teams of oxen were required to haul the heavy bags of cement.

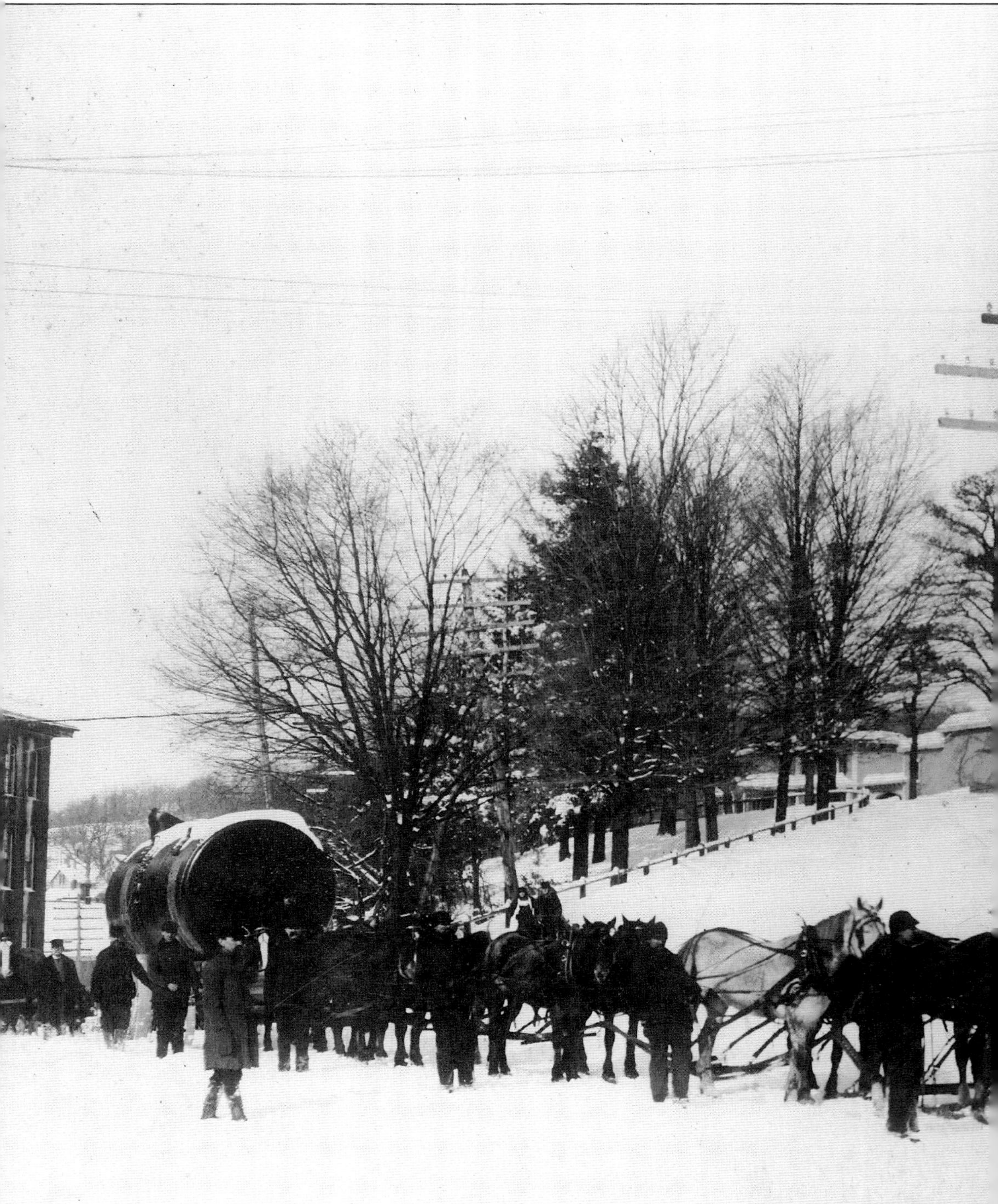

The route from the railroad station to the site of the Minterburn mill included the very steep East Main Street hill. Multiple teams of horses were needed to haul the huge boiler up the hill to the mill site. Here the horses have just reached the top of the hill and are standing in front

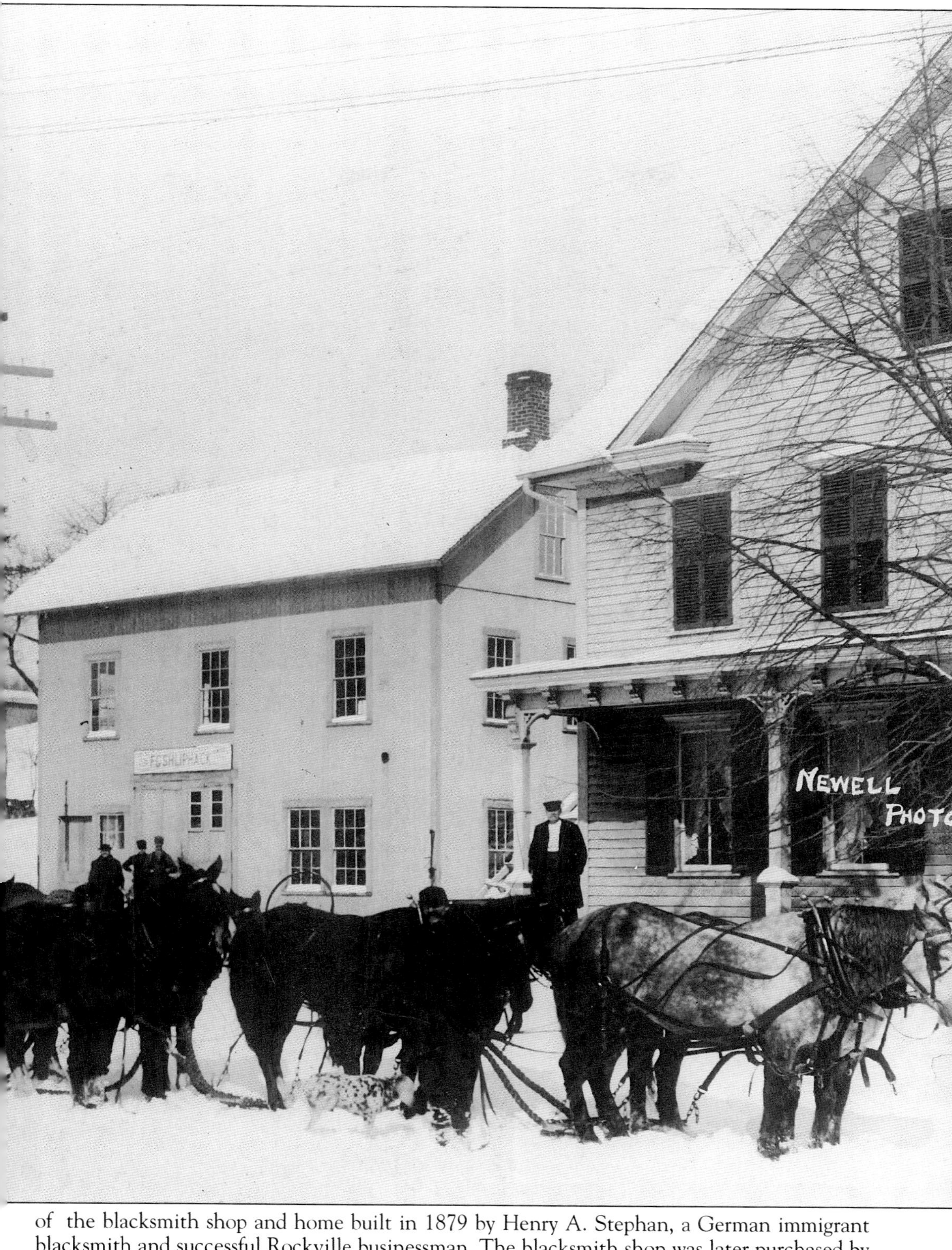

of the blacksmith shop and home built in 1879 by Henry A. Stephan, a German immigrant blacksmith and successful Rockville businessman. The blacksmith shop was later purchased by F.G. Schlipphach, whose name is visible in the sign over the shop door.

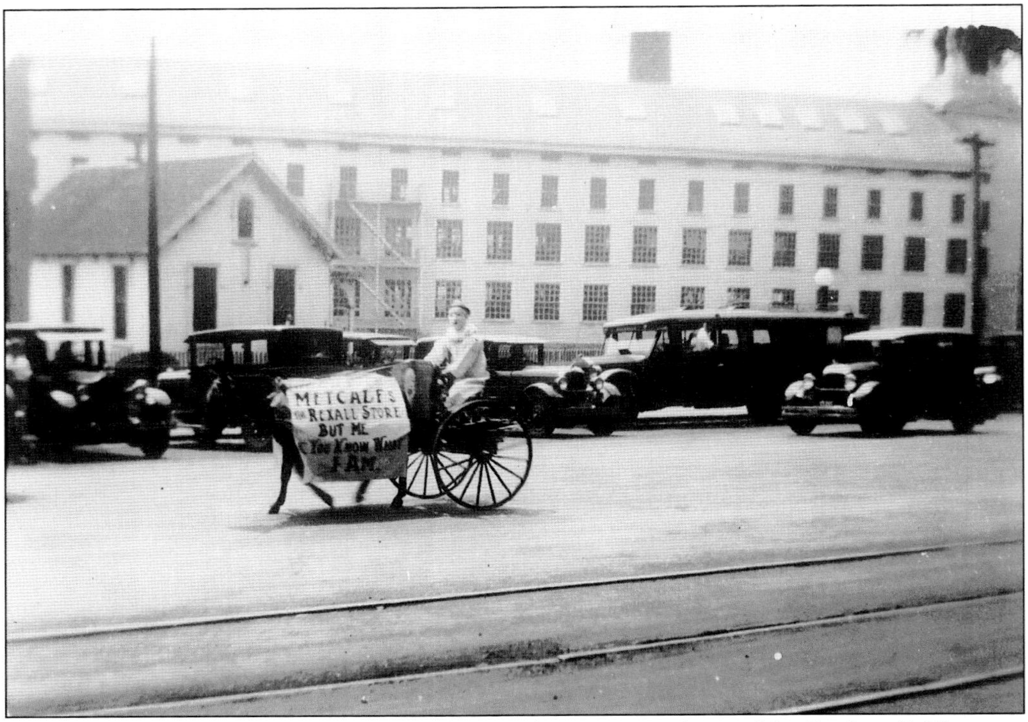

The delivery wagon from Metcalf's Rexall Store shop passes in front of the Rock mill. The time of the horse would soon be gone, as indicated by the trolley tracks in the center of the street and the parked cars in the background.

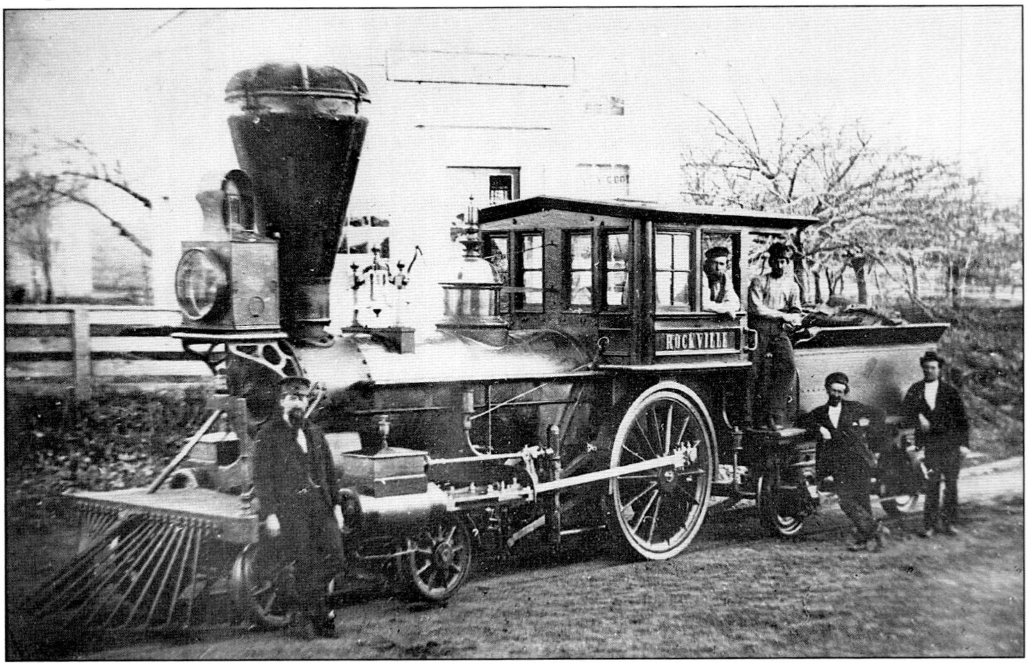

In August 1863, a spur track brought the railroad from Vernon Depot to Rockville. One of the early engines used on the line was the "Rockville," nicknamed "Old Betsey." It was long remembered for its large and noisy bell.

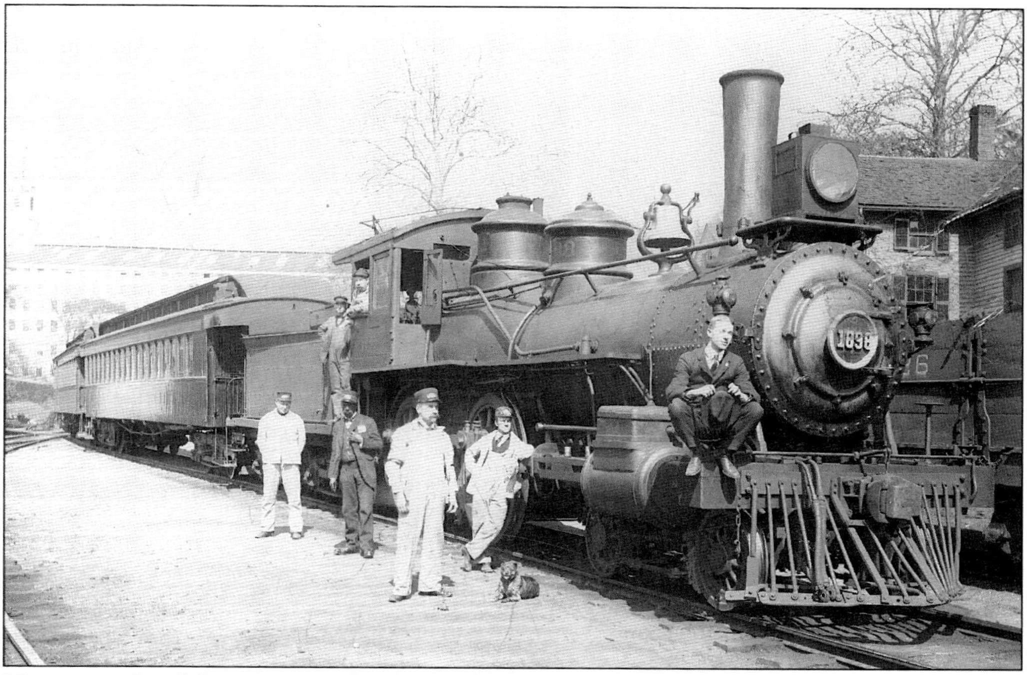

The original rail line into Rockville was built by a group of local investors, the Rockville Company, which operated it for five years. Later the line was operated by the New York, New Haven and Hartford Railroad Company. The steam engine and its crew shown here are in the rail yard which was located off Brooklyn Street. Henry VanNess, the conductor for many years, is second from the left.

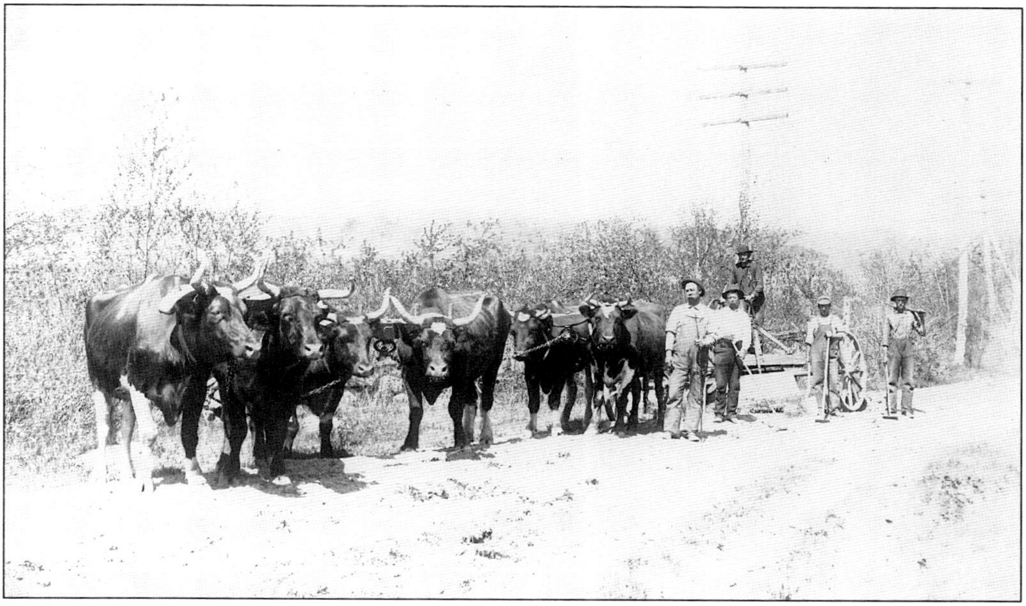

In the 1890s interurban trolley service reached Rockville. To prepare the bed for the trolley tracks near Snipsic Lake, Mr. West's oxen were used. A number of workmen were Italian immigrants who set up camp on the shores of Snipsic Lake.

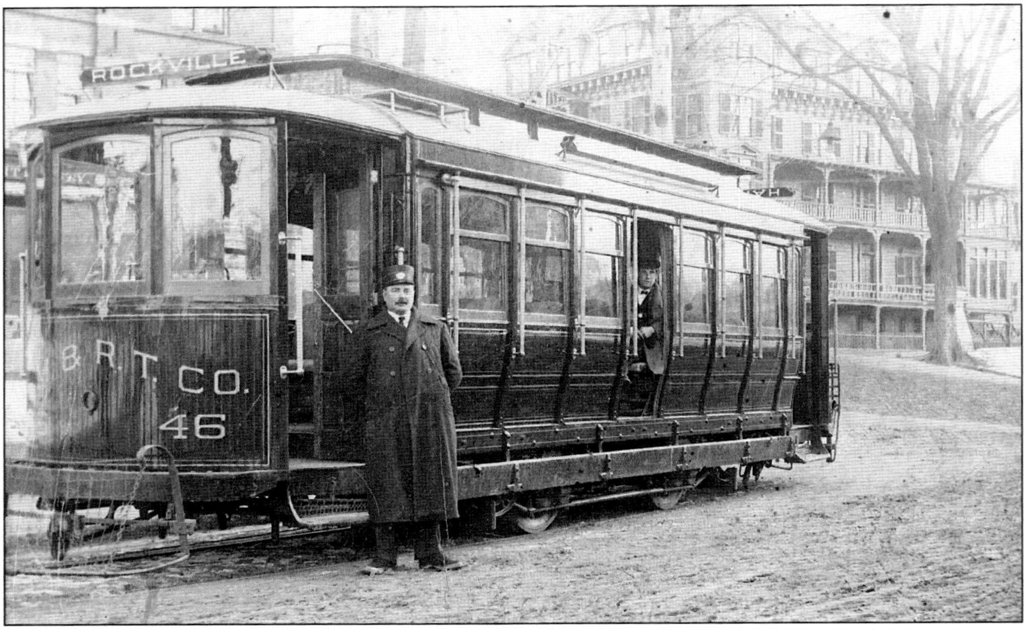

Posing proudly in front of his trolley is motorman Edward M. Thrall of the Hartford, Manchester, Rockville Tramway Company. The trolley made several stops in Rockville. In this view, the trolley waits for passengers in front of Central Park near the Henry Building and the Rockville Hotel.

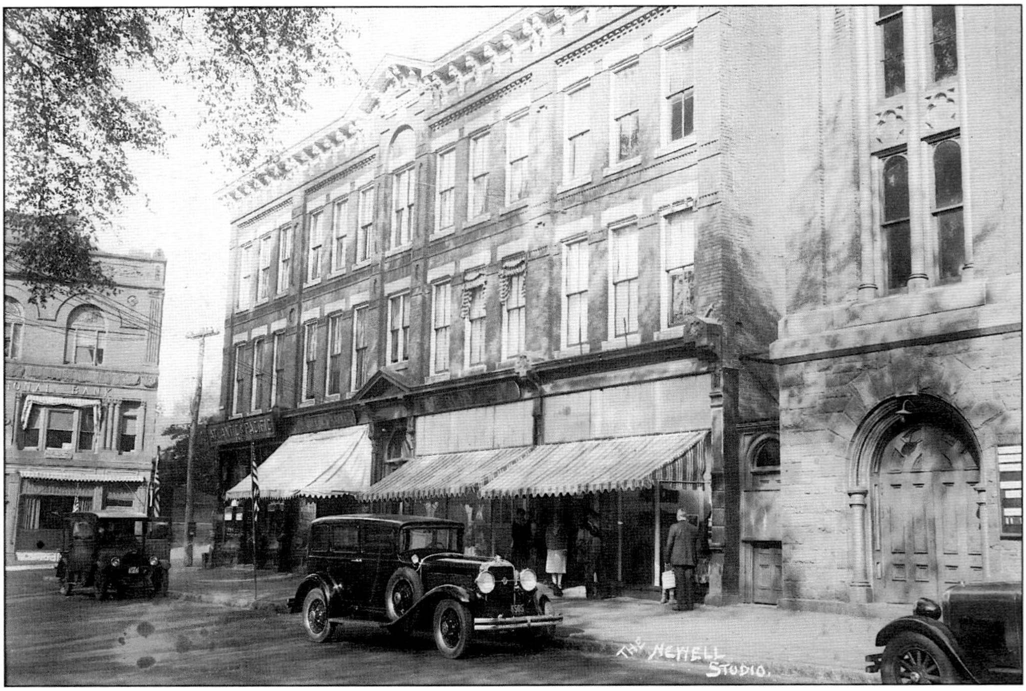

By the 1920s automobiles ruled the city streets. To accommodate them, more streets were paved in Rockville. In this picture, cars are parked in front of the Citizen's Block on Park Place. The ever-increasing demand for parking space changed the way people shopped and contributed to the rise of malls, forever changing downtown Rockville.

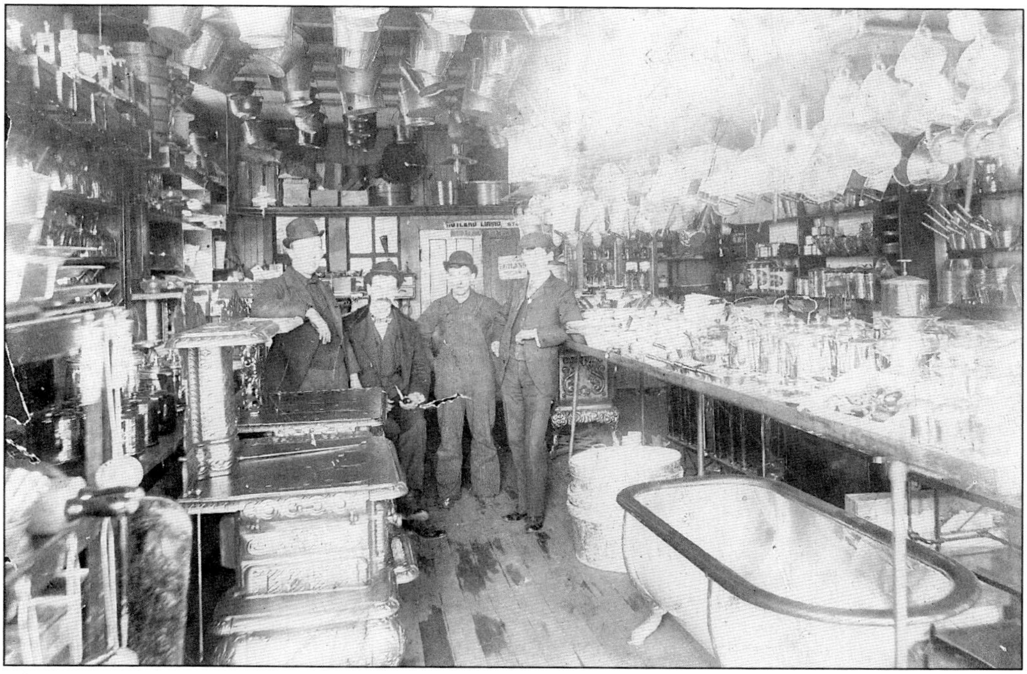

This fascinating interior view suggests the merchandise available in a turn-of-the-century hardware store. From stoves on the left to a bathtub on the right, shoppers could find many supplies in this store, where no space was wasted.

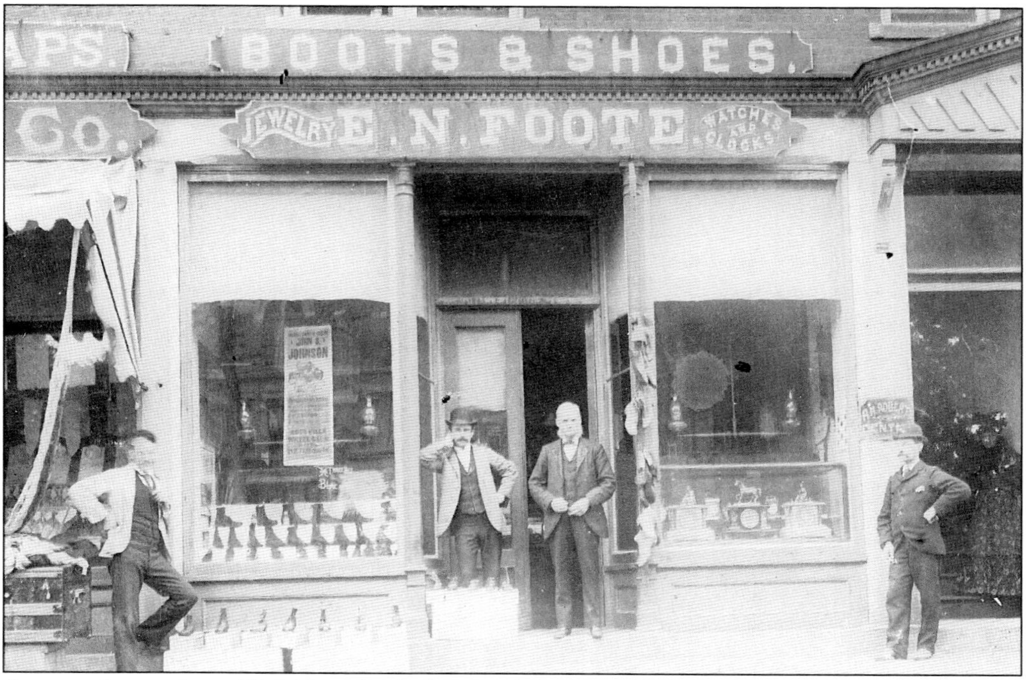

A versatile merchant, E.N. Foote had a boot and shoe store in the Fitch Block on Union Street. In the 1890s he also sold jewelry, watches, and clocks, and at one time he had a lending library in his store. Mr. Foote is shown third from the left. The men on the left in the light jackets were probably his clerks.

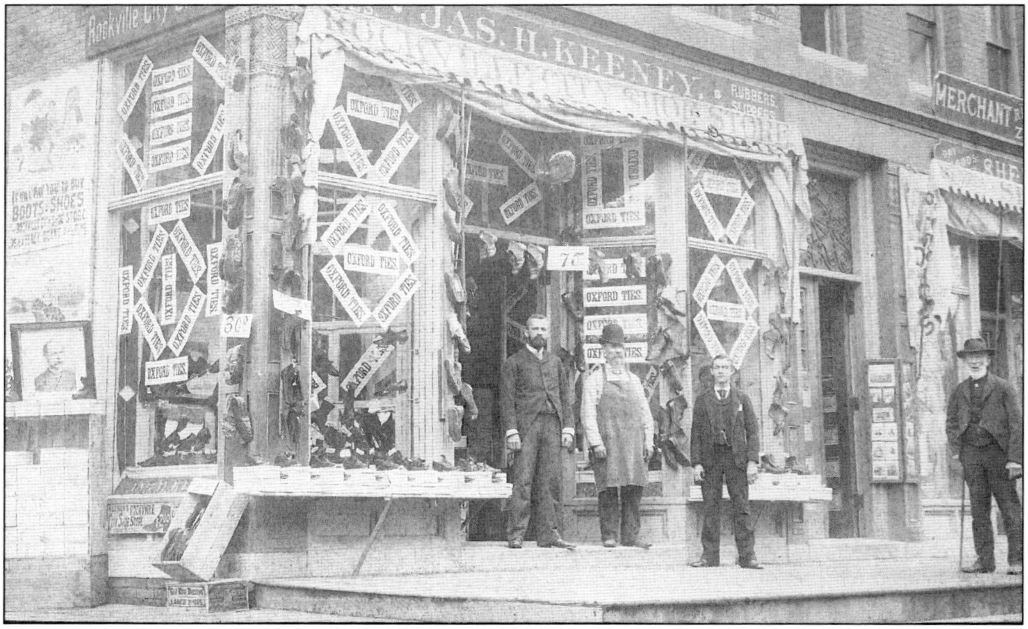

Rockville merchant James H. Keeney demonstrates his awareness of the importance of advertising in the exterior displays of his Rockville City Shoe Store. Not only are the windows covered with signs, but shoes are displayed outside in bins, around the doorway, and along the corner columns. Prices ranged from 30¢ to 85¢ a pair for the shoes displayed.

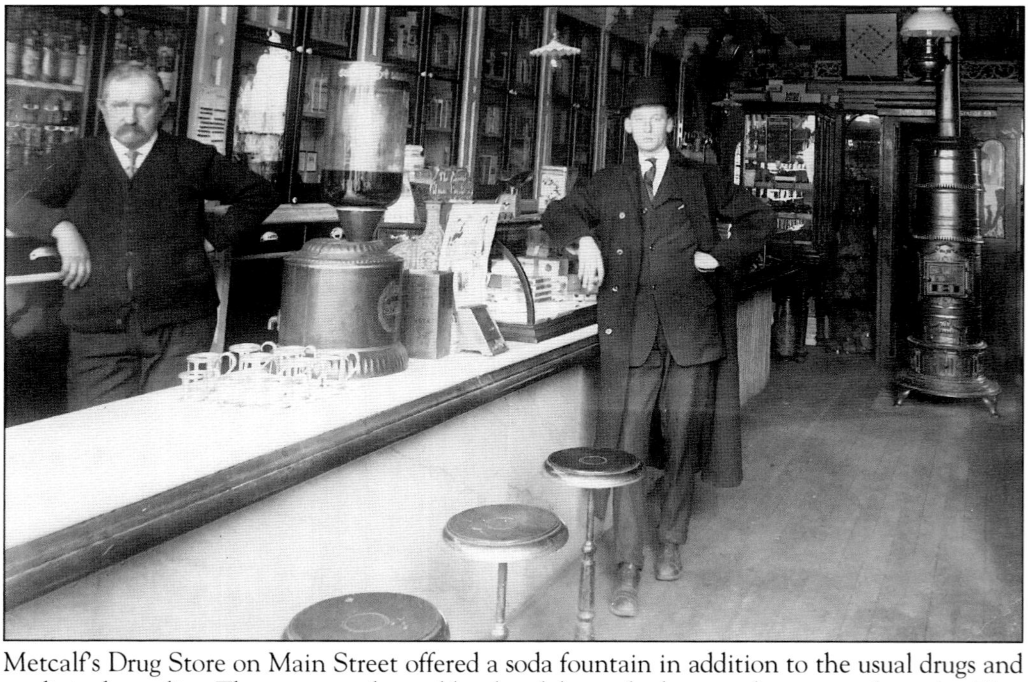

Metcalf's Drug Store on Main Street offered a soda fountain in addition to the usual drugs and medicinal supplies. The store was heated by the elaborately decorated stove on the right. This 1908 postcard view shows owner and pharmacist F. Elliot Metcalf (behind the counter) with a customer, Carl Conrady.

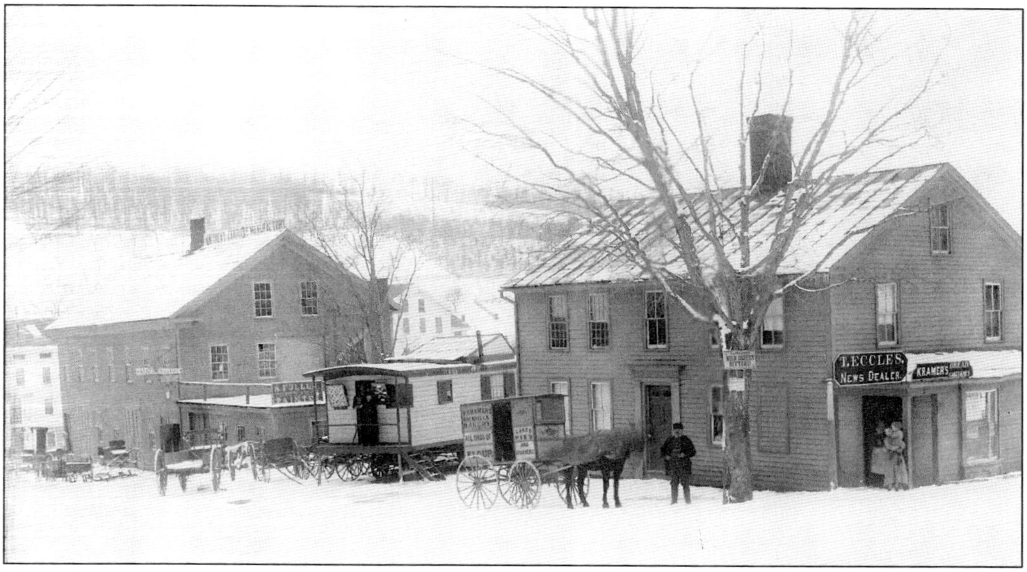

Main Street wasn't the only mercantile area. Small corner stores and tradesmen's shops were located throughout the city. The businesses shown in this photograph were located on the corner of West Main Street and Vernon Avenue. In many instances, shops and residences were combined, with the owner living "over the shop."

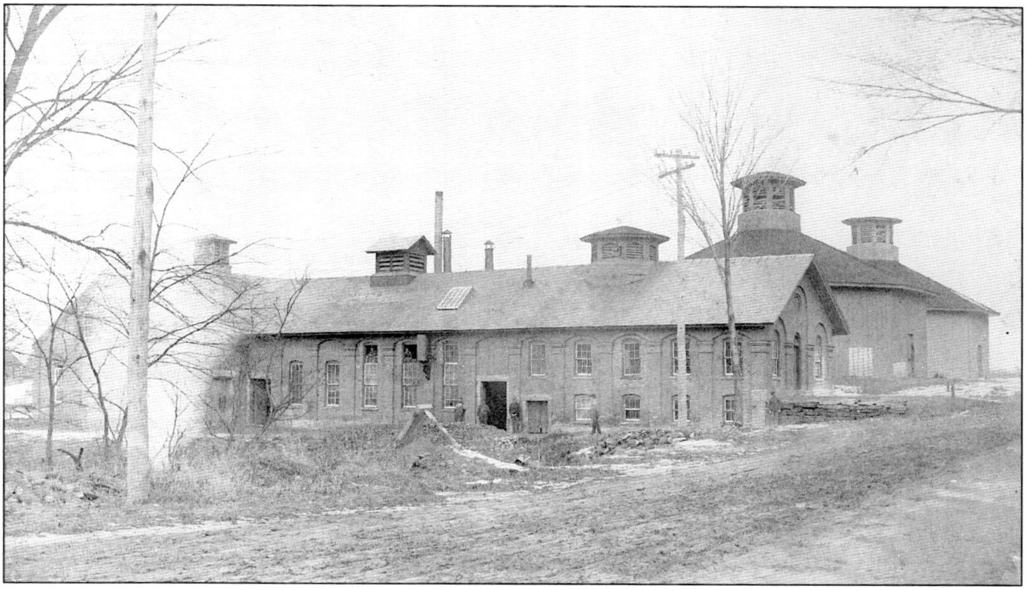

Keeping the expanding city supplied with energy was the job of the Rockville Gas and Electric Company. First established in 1862, the company built the Gas Works along Maple Street in the late nineteenth century. In 1890 it supplied the electricity for Rockville's first street lights. In 1935 the company was merged with Connecticut Light and Power.

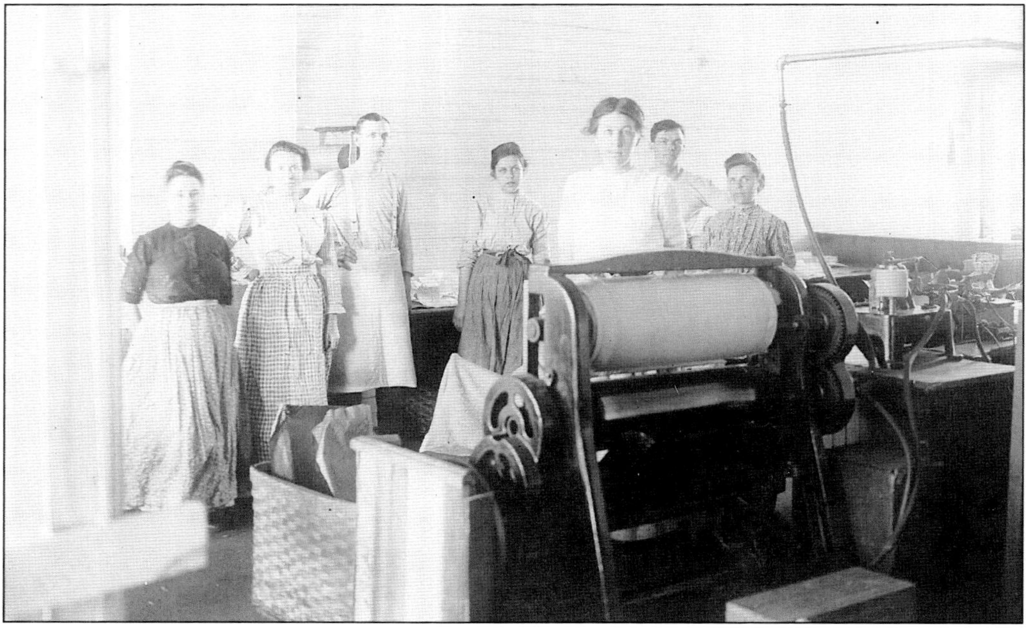

Wash day presented a tedious chore for housewives before electric washers and dryers. Some fortunate women sent their laundry to places like the Barnard Laundry on Market Street where employees, like those shown here in a 1913 photograph, washed, starched, and pressed various items to their customers' satisfaction.

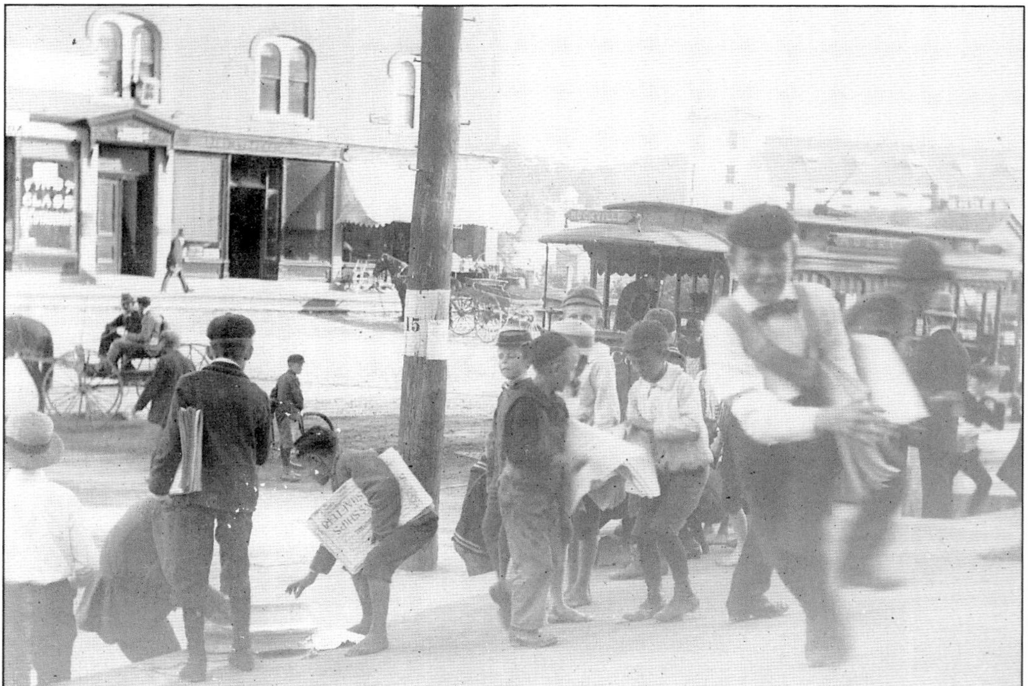

Newsboys pick up their papers at the corner of Central Park opposite the Exchange Block. Working as a newsboy, a child could supplement the family income and maybe have a little money left over for himself.

Nine

Clubs to Suit Every Taste

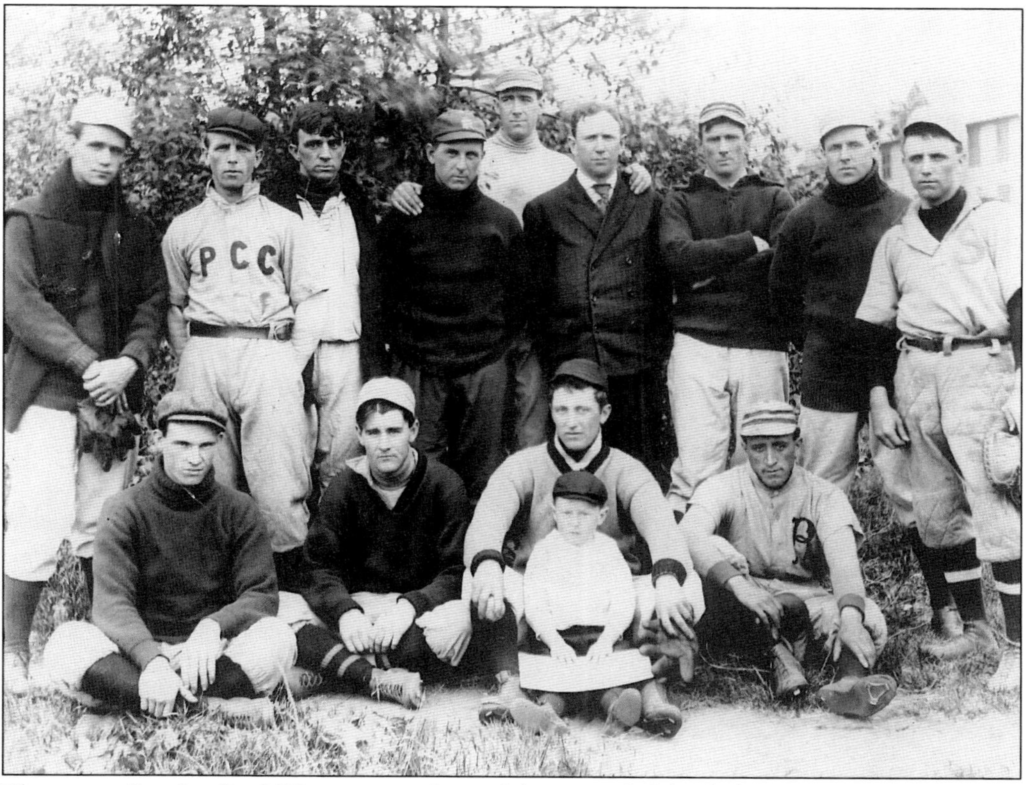

The years after the Civil War witnessed a proliferation of clubs, lodges, and societies of every description in Rockville. By 1890 citizens could choose to join any one of 55 organizations according to their particular interest. By far the most popular were the baseball clubs. Several existed in Rockville, one of which was the team "Easy Money," shown here in a 1905 photograph.

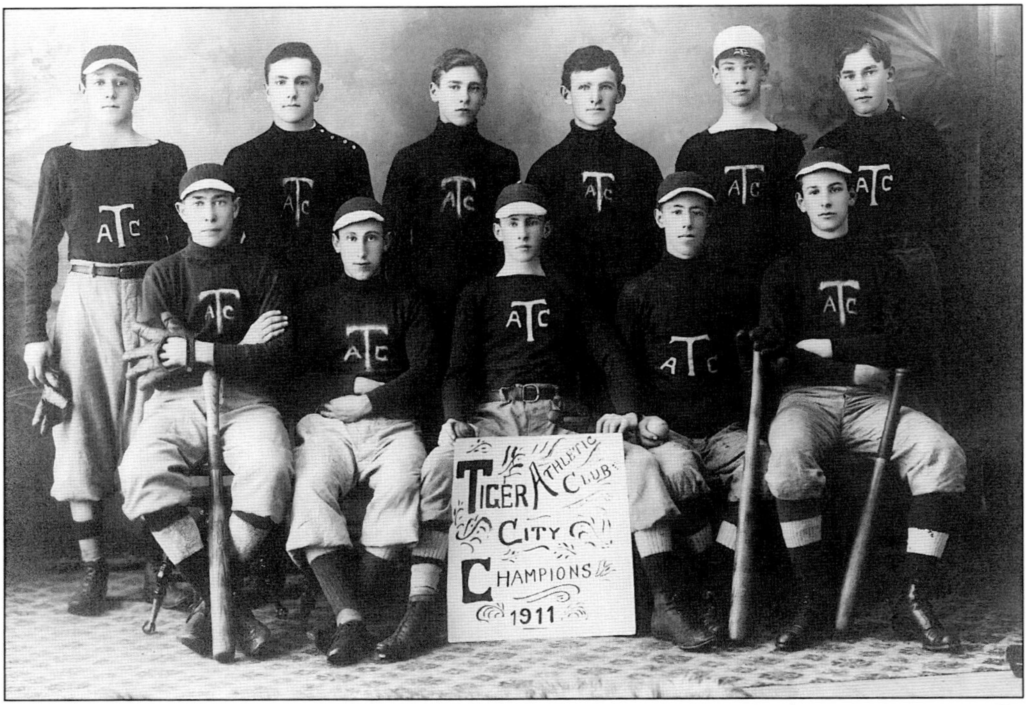

The Tigers baseball team had an outstanding record from 1911 to 1915. The team poses proudly in uniform with bats, ball, and gloves for a studio portrait.

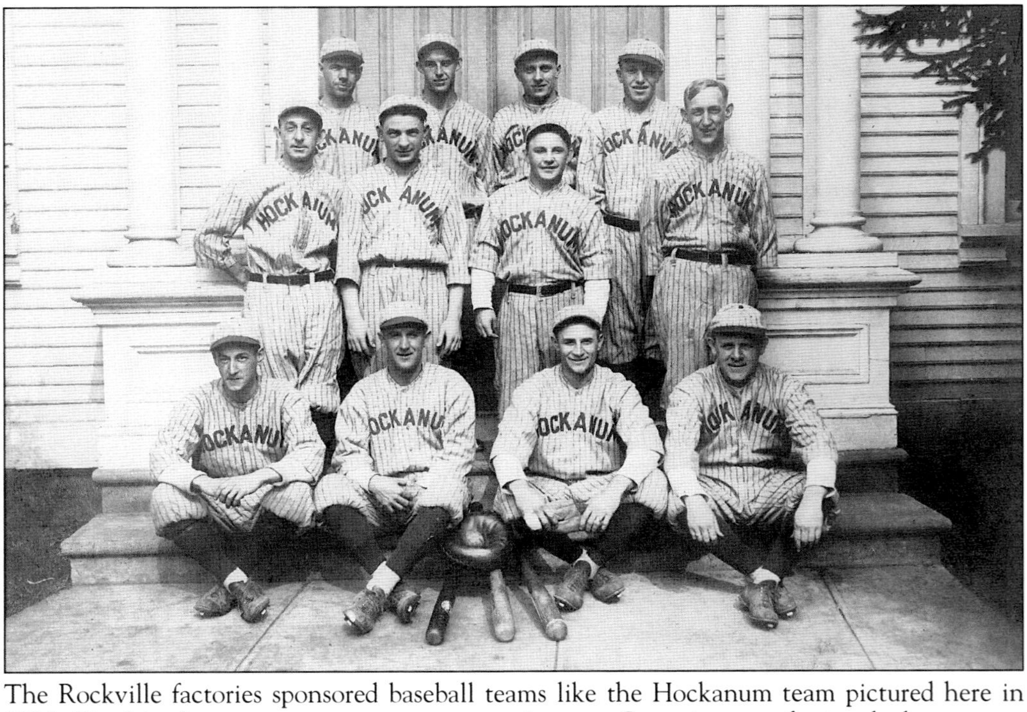

The Rockville factories sponsored baseball teams like the Hockanum team pictured here in 1930. Rivalries between company teams were intense. Sometimes professional players were brought to town for an important game. In 1904 New York Giants pitcher and future Hall of Famer Christy Mathewson came to play in Rockville for a mill team.

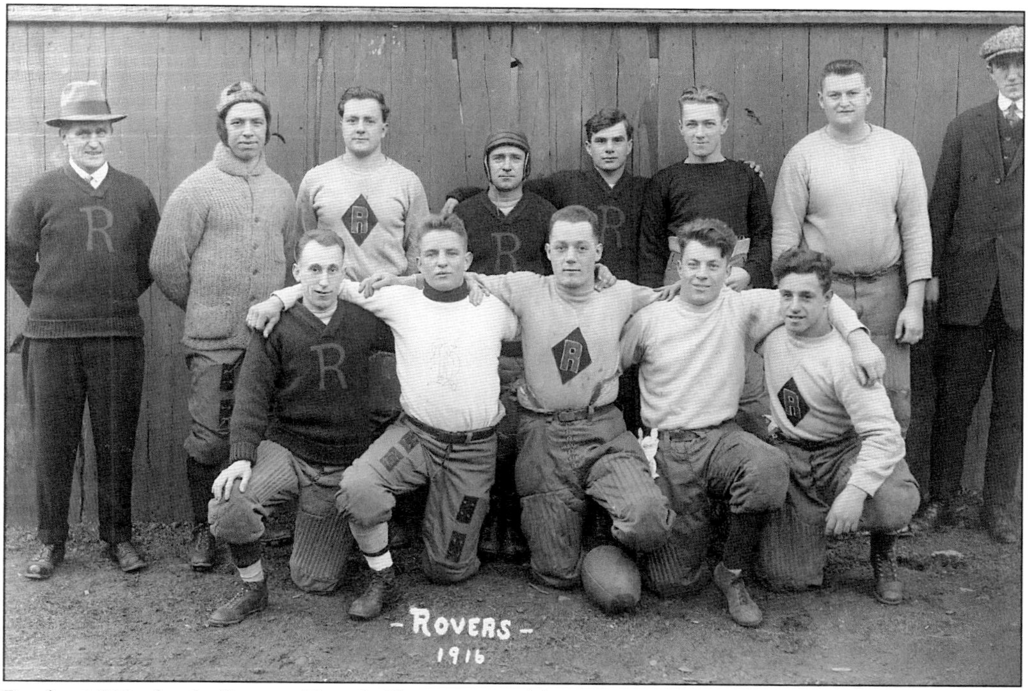

By the 1890s football joined baseball as a enjoyable spectator sport. A Rockville football team was first organized in 1896. The Rockville Rovers, a recreation league football team, had an excellent record in 1916 when this photograph was taken.

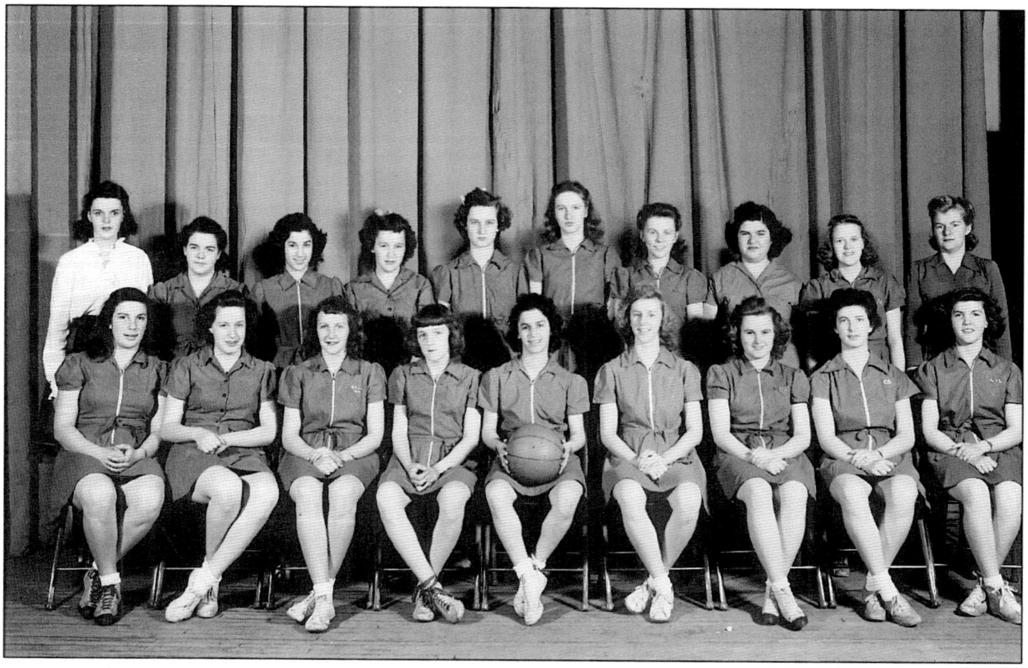

Organized sports for girls have only very recently attracted a wide-spread audience, but women have participated in high school programs for many years. This view, published in the Rockville High School yearbook for 1945 indicates that baggy shorts had not yet become the uniform for the girls' basketball team.

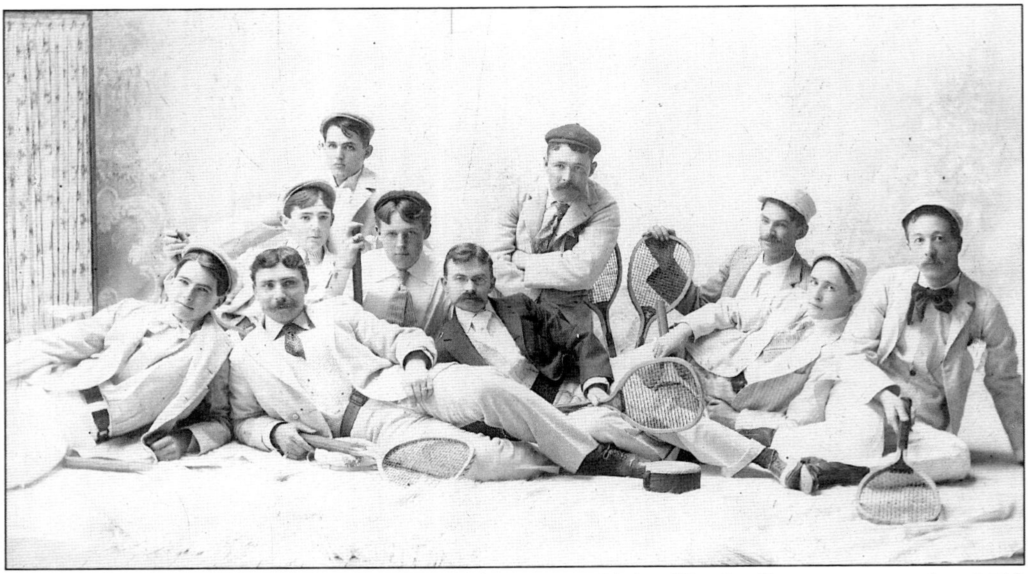

Lawn tennis became popular in the 1880s. The Tennis Club of Rockville was organized in 1912 and used a court on the grounds of mill owner Henry Adams's home on Davis Avenue. Tennis players prided themselves on looking dapper in their crisp white tennis outfits.

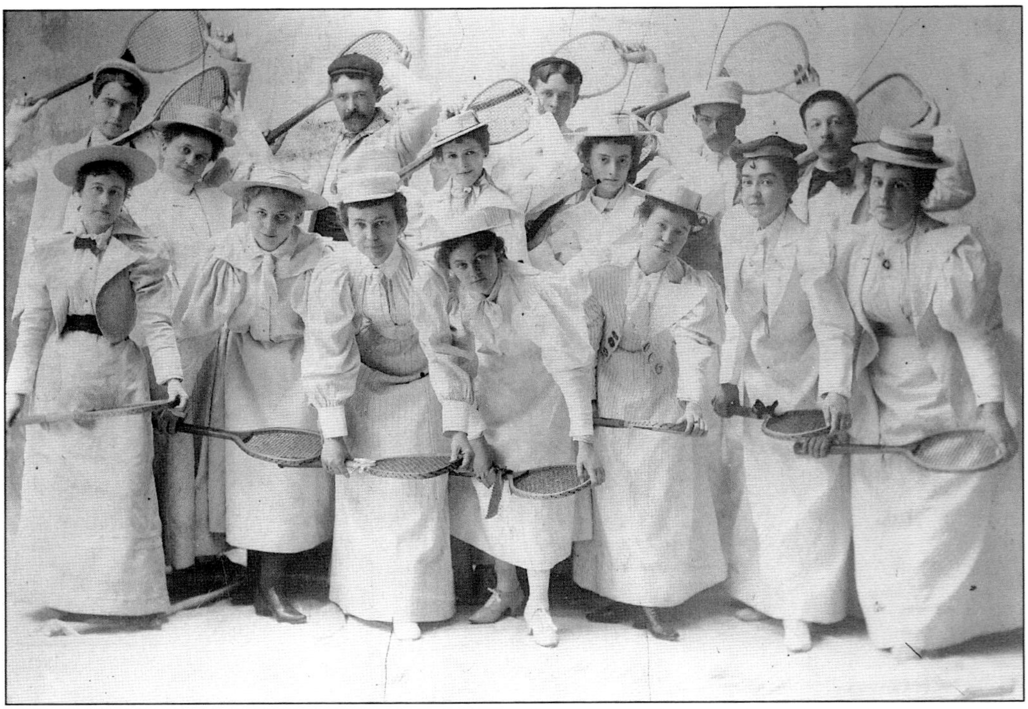

Lawn tennis was not a sport restricted to men. Women in the 1890s took up the sport when changes in fashion led to less restrictive clothing. Daring for the time, these sporty women's tennis outfits with slightly shorter skirts equaled the men's clothing in style and flair.

Musical groups, particularly silver bands and marching bands, provided much enjoyment in the late nineteenth century. In 1873 a fife and drummers convention was held in Rockville. In this view, the conventioneers parade along Main Street past the Rockville Hotel.

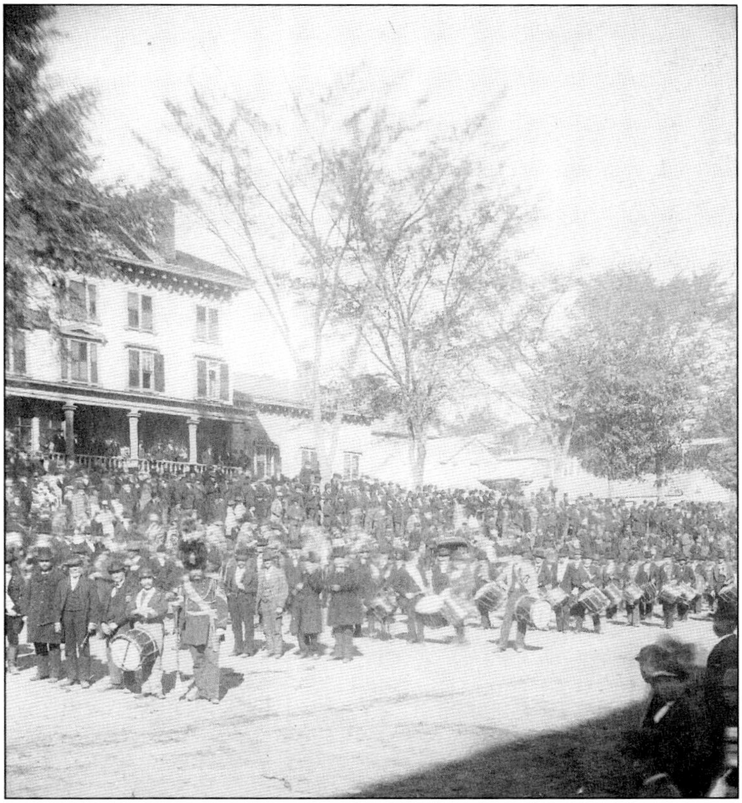

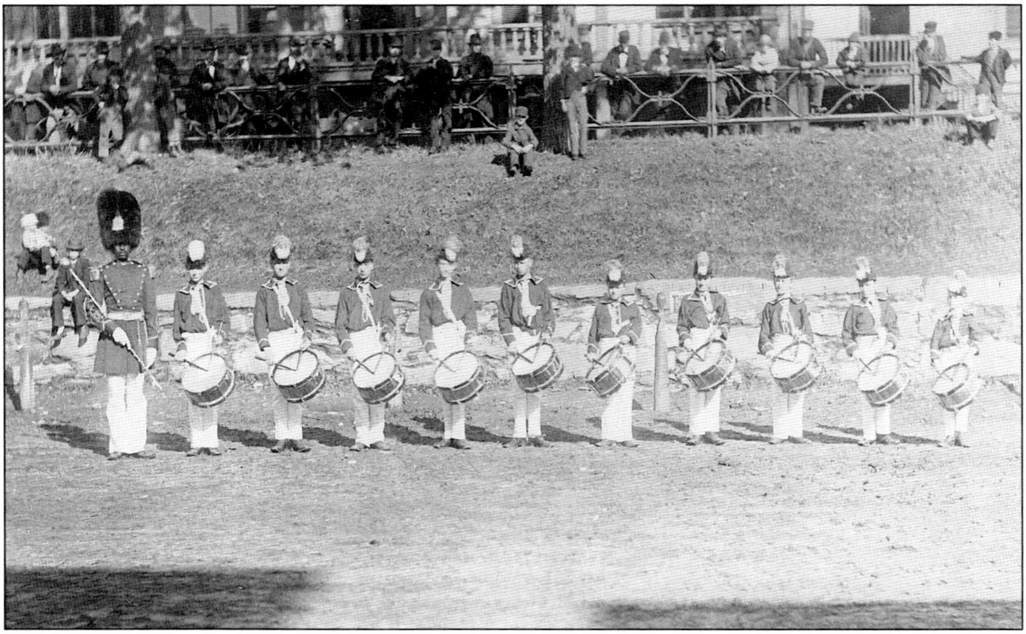

In October 1877, the newly formed Hammond Silver Drum Corps was photographed on Main Street in front of the Rockville Hotel. The band was composed of boys from 10 to 16 years of age and became famous throughout New England. One of the members, William Churchill Hammond (second from the left), went on to a career as a prominent organist.

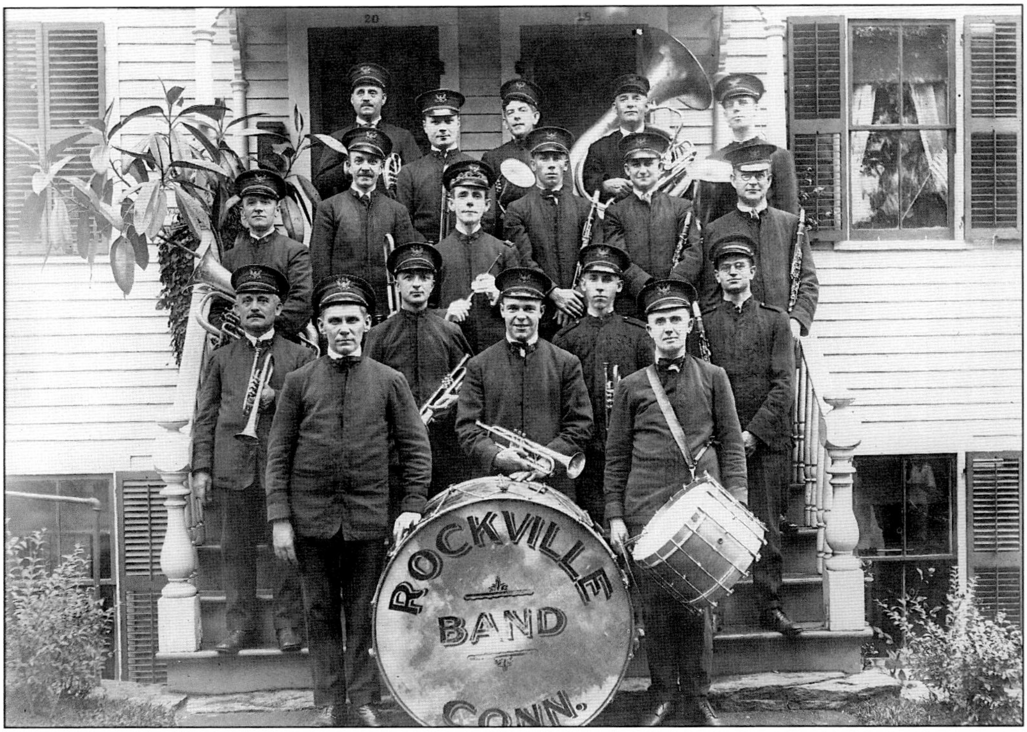

The Rockville Band, shown here in a 1910 photograph, was well known and marched in many parades and competitions.

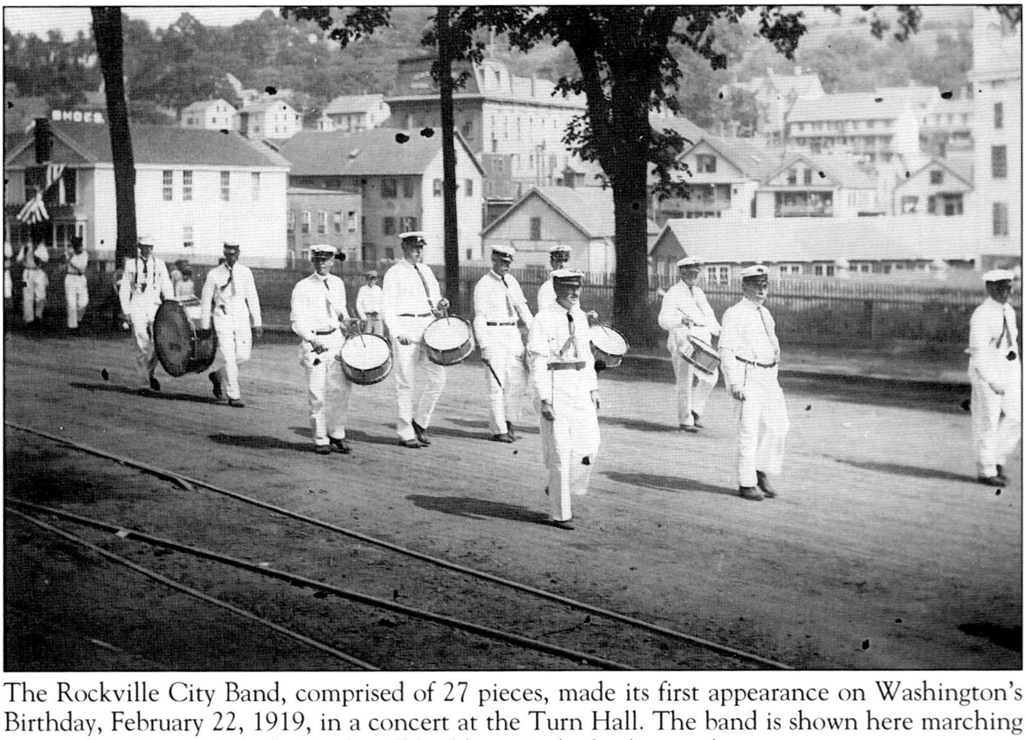

The Rockville City Band, comprised of 27 pieces, made its first appearance on Washington's Birthday, February 22, 1919, in a concert at the Turn Hall. The band is shown here marching down Main Street with the Rock mill buildings in the background.

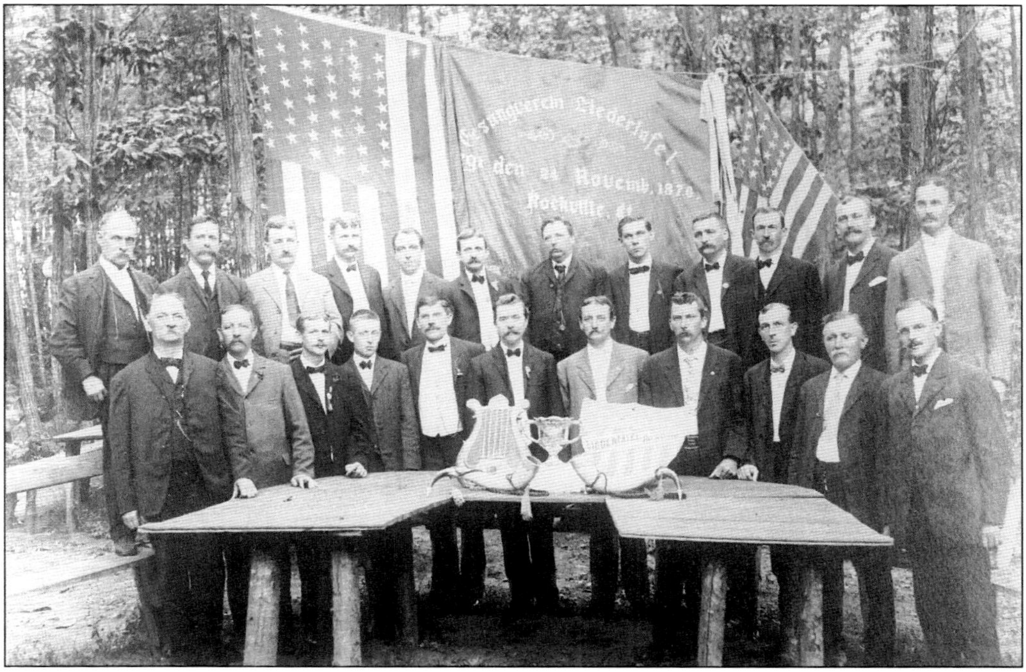

The mills attracted many immigrant workers, with a large number coming to Rockville from Germany. German-Americans formed a variety of community organizations for cultural, social, and religious purposes. Pictured here is the Liedertafel Singing Society, which won many prizes in state contests.

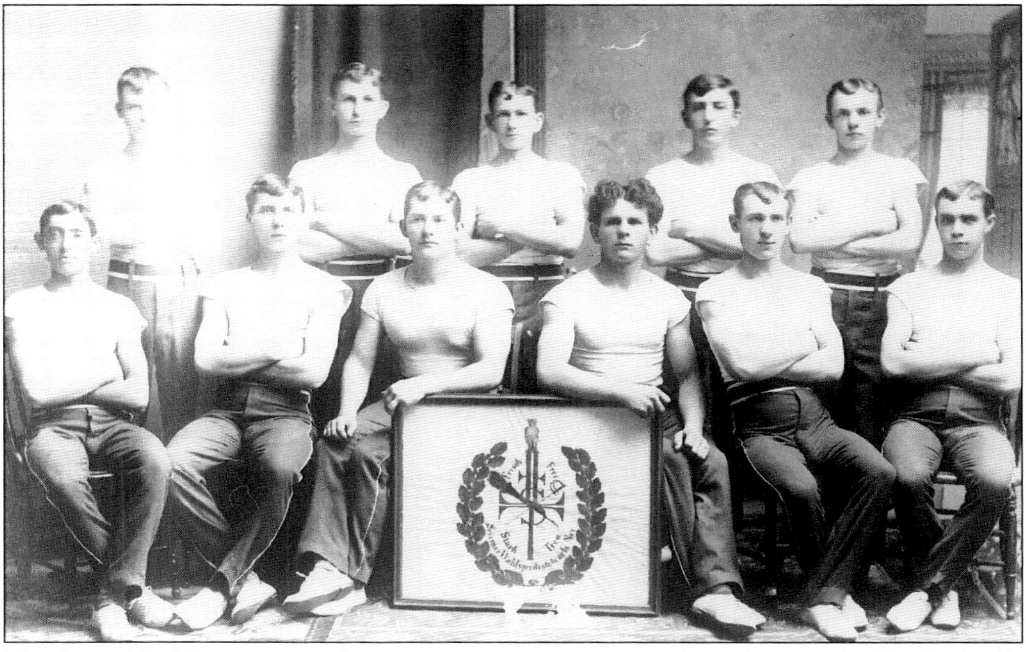

Members of the Turnverein, a German gymnastic society, pose for a photograph. The Rockville society was organized in 1857 by German immigrants. The stated purpose of the group was to promote a healthy mind in a healthy body, as exemplified by their motto stitched into their banner: *Frisch* (vigorous), *Stark* (strong), *Treu* (loyal), and *Frei* (free).

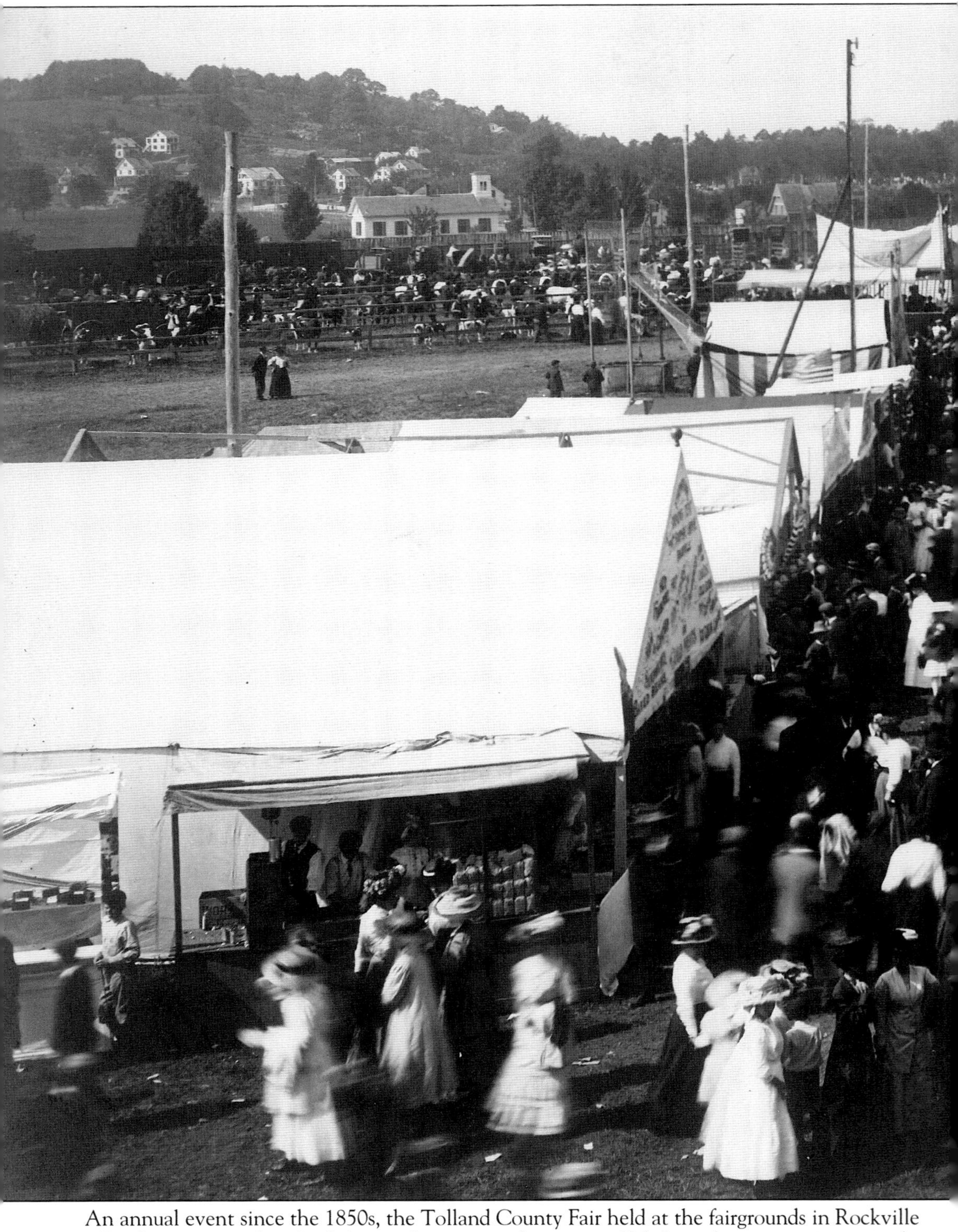

An annual event since the 1850s, the Tolland County Fair held at the fairgrounds in Rockville offered many agricultural exhibits and recreational activities. Exhibits of prize-winning animals, produce, and baked goods were on display in the tents. Local merchants like "Kibbe the Candy

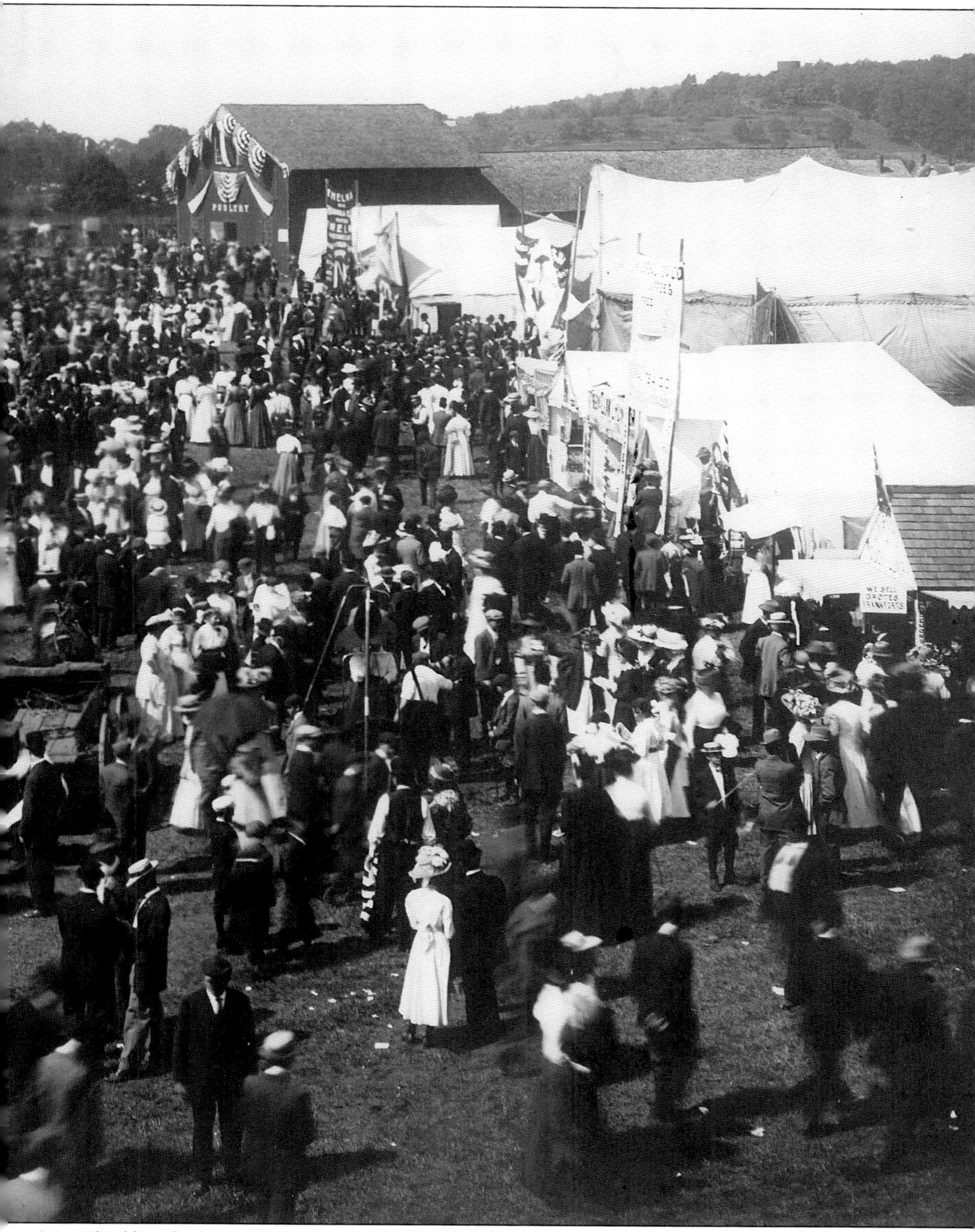

Man" had booths. A senior class of Rockville High School sponsored a food booth to raise money for class activities. Rides and games were another attraction along with horse racing on the track (at the upper left). Fairgoers in this 1910 photograph had an eventful day before them.

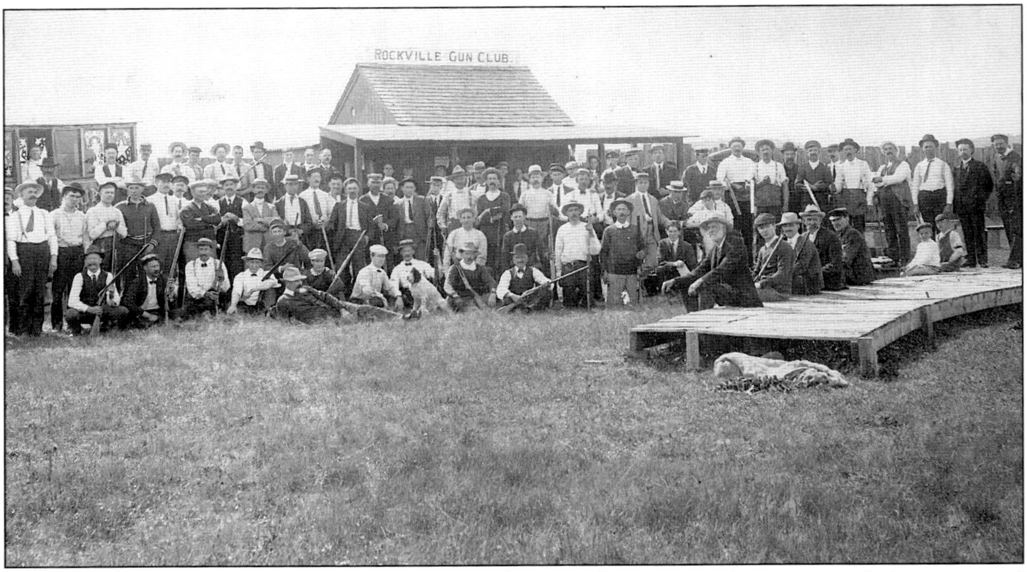

The Rockville Gun Club, shown in a 1904 photograph, sponsored recreational shooting and proved to be very popular with the gentlemen.

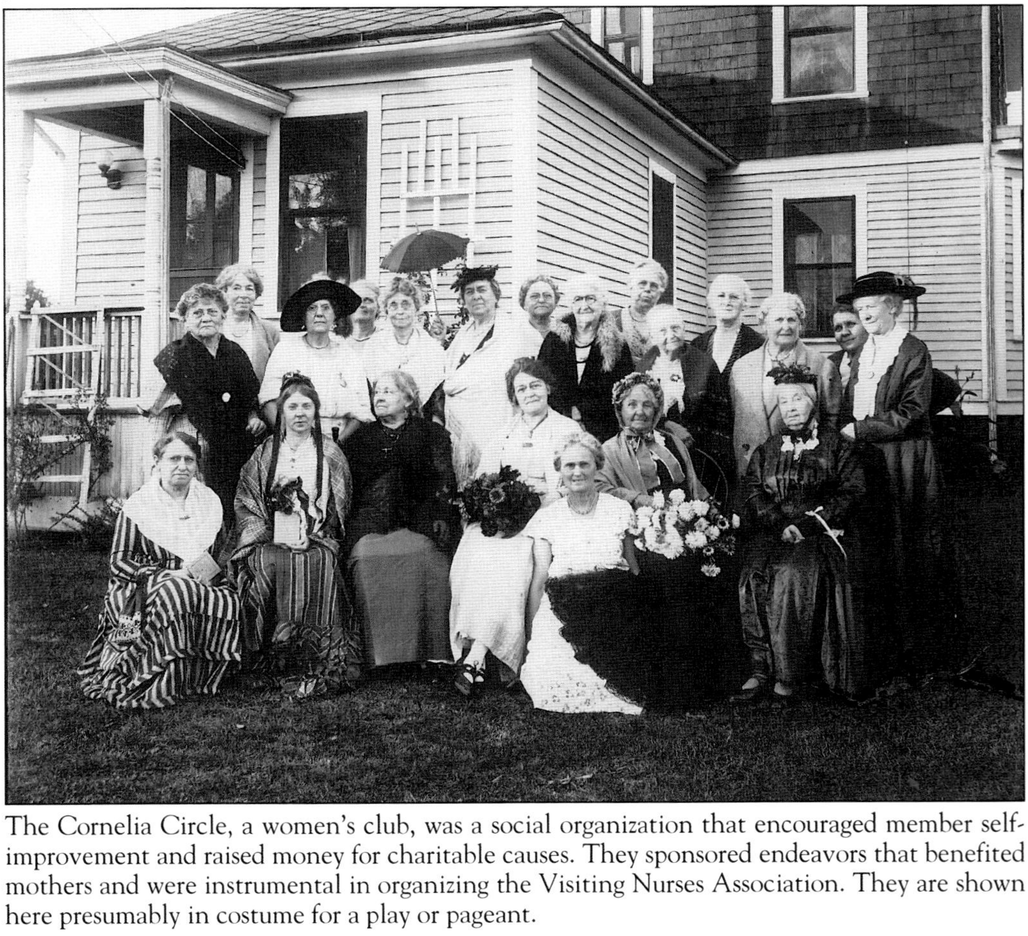

The Cornelia Circle, a women's club, was a social organization that encouraged member self-improvement and raised money for charitable causes. They sponsored endeavors that benefited mothers and were instrumental in organizing the Visiting Nurses Association. They are shown here presumably in costume for a play or pageant.

Ten

Life's Pleasures

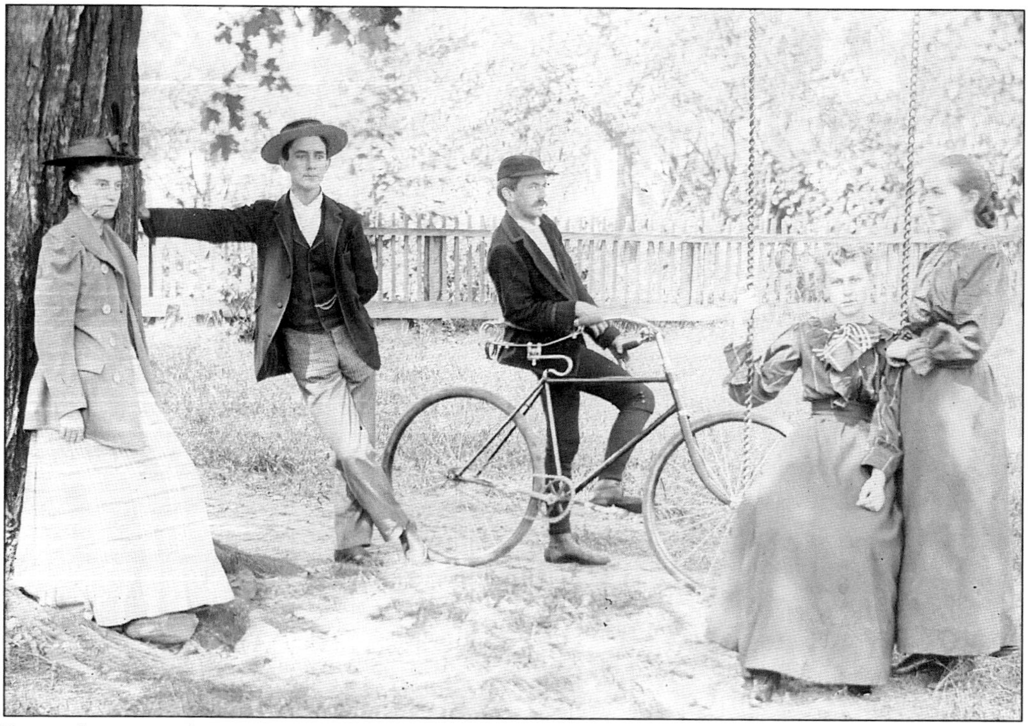

Beyond organized activities, many opportunities existed for recreation and socializing by the late nineteenth century. Bicycling became popular in the 1870s and 1880s, and was even considered healthful exercise for women. Here a sporty wheelman and his friends enjoy a sociable summer afternoon.

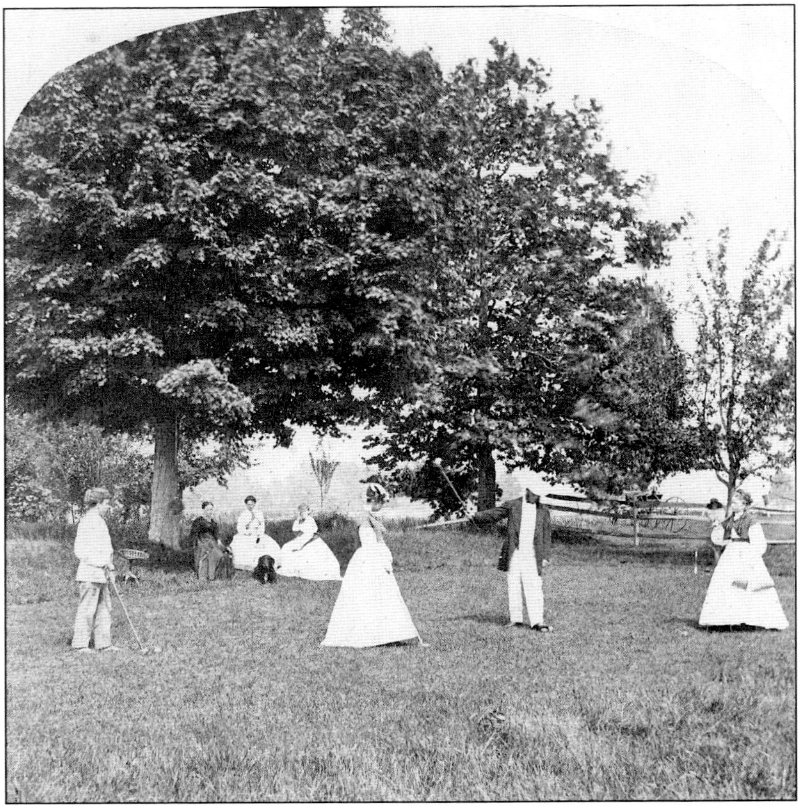

Croquet, as can be seen in this 1868 stereograph, was a leisurely game ladies could engage in despite the restrictive clothing decreed by fashion in the post–Civil War period.

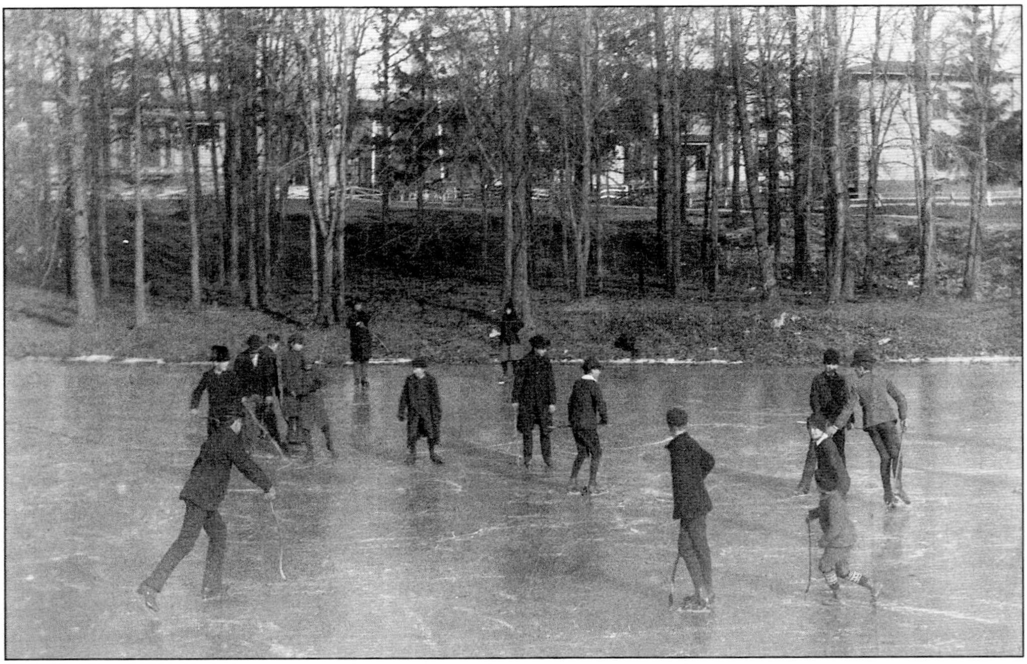

Skaters take a turn on the ice in the early twentieth century. The photograph appears to have been taken on the mill pond between Main and River Streets, near where the water flowed into the Hockanum mill headrace.

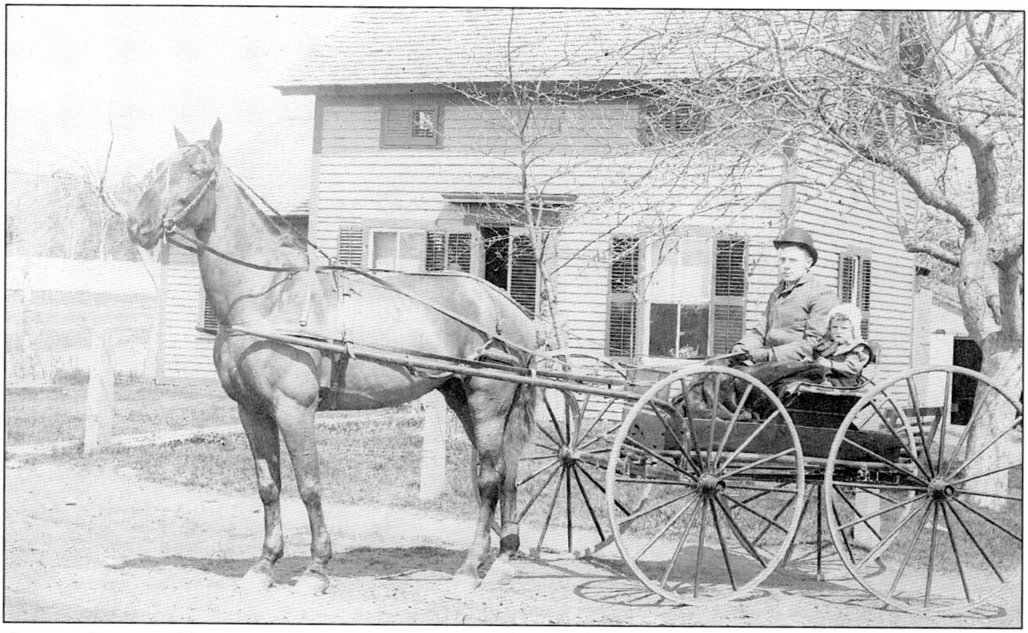

George Lutz and his sister Lena prepare to go for a ride in his horse-drawn carriage from their home on Hale Street. Many families used horse-drawn carriages for transportation. Stables were usually located near the rear of the property.

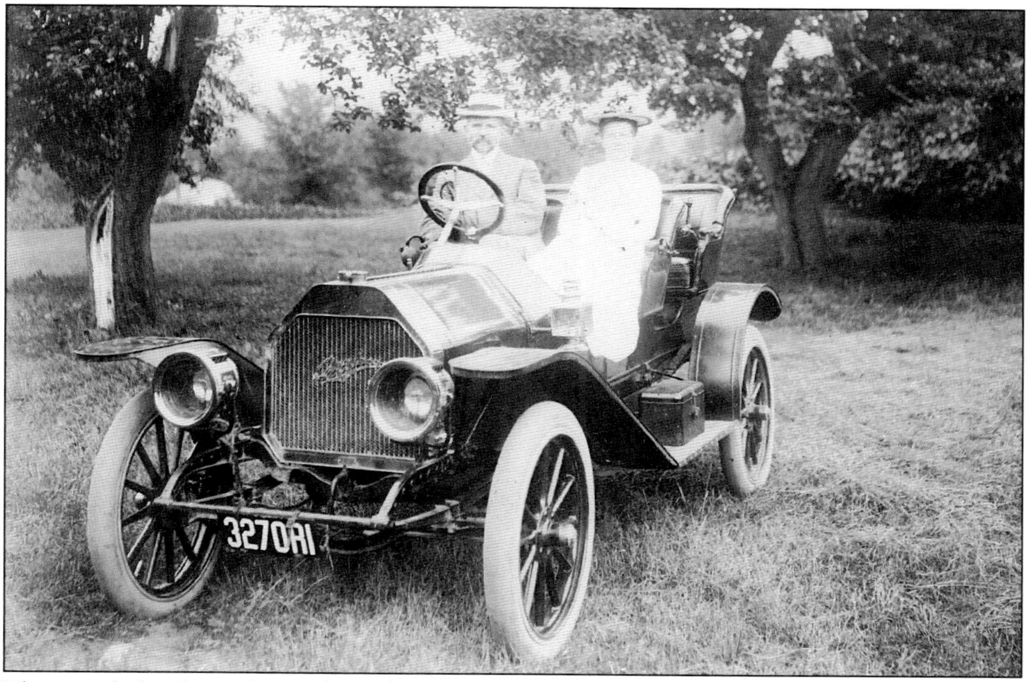

This couple has been for a ride in the country in their automobile, frequently referred to as a "horseless carriage." The weather must not have been wet nor the roads dusty since neither the driver nor his passenger are wearing the characteristic dust coats required in this period of open cars.

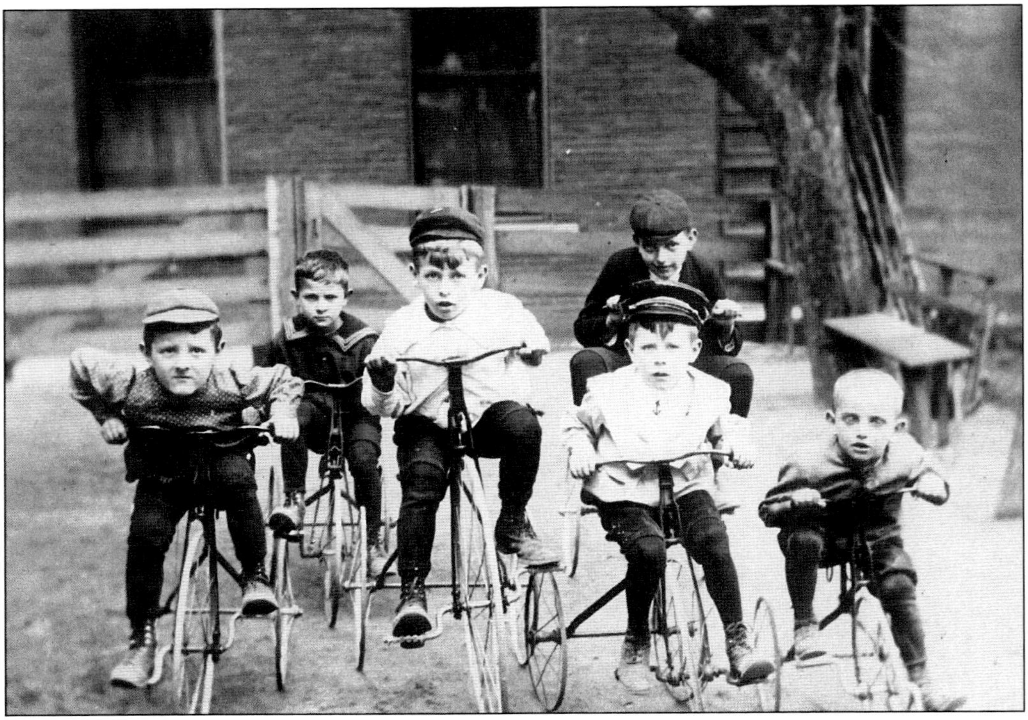

In this late-nineteenth-century photograph, boys from the Village Street neighborhood sit on their bicycles ready to ride. The wheels appear to be made of metal, which must have given the riders a bumpy trip. The boys are dressed in typical play clothes of the era—shirts, knickers with long black stockings, high-button shoes, and caps.

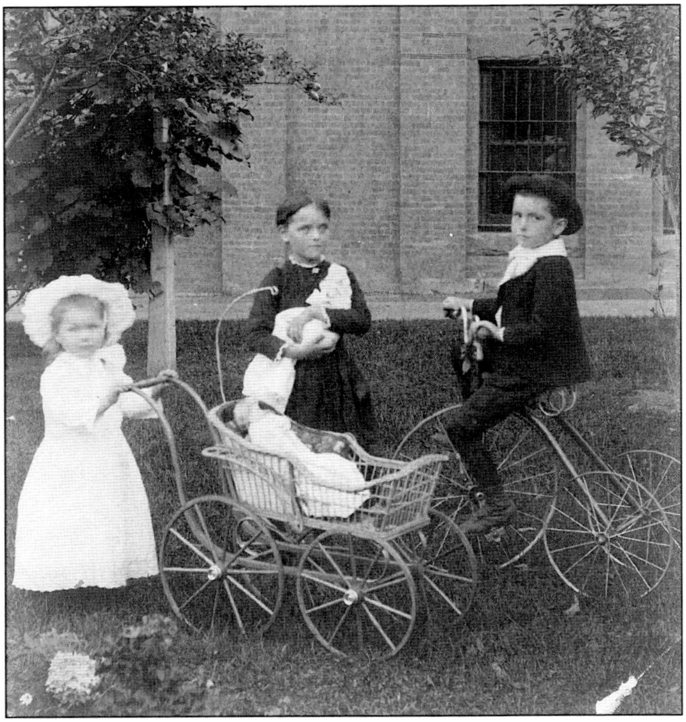

In a more formal photograph, children from the Gilnack family pose in their front yard on Elm Street with their favorite toys. One girl pushes a doll carriage while the other holds a doll. The boy sits on what appears to be a gleaming new bicycle.

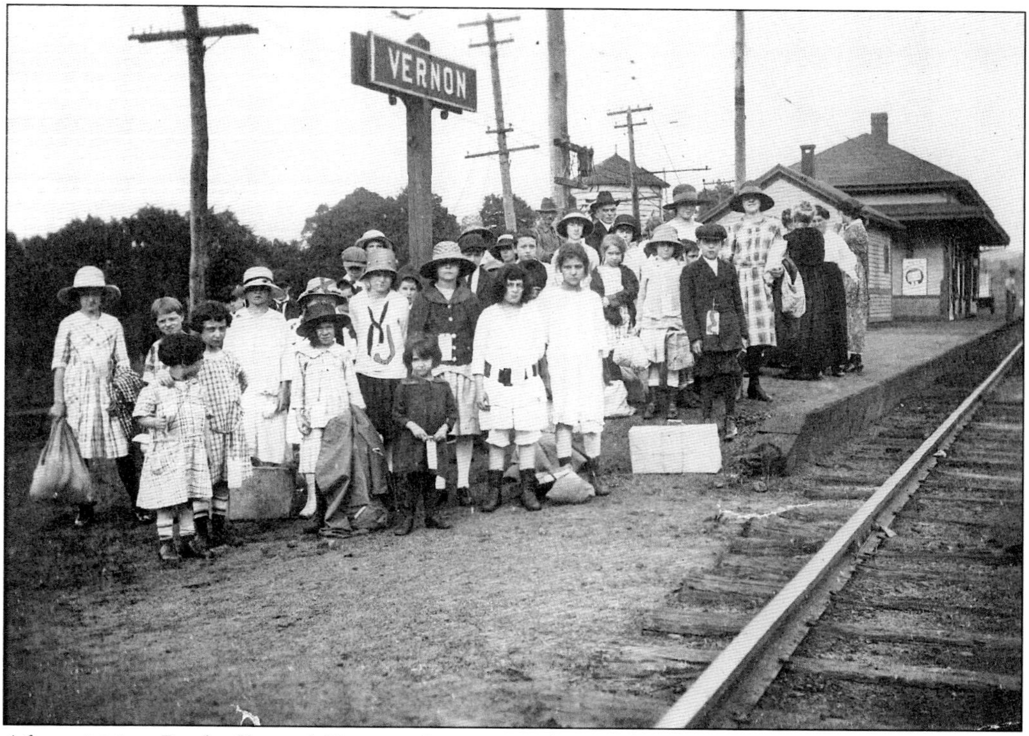

After visiting Rockville and Vernon for two weeks, Fresh Air children wait at the Vernon Depot on July 23, 1919, for the 4:15 train to take them home. Sponsored by various charities, a two-week respite in small towns and rural areas was considered a healthy change for these young urban residents.

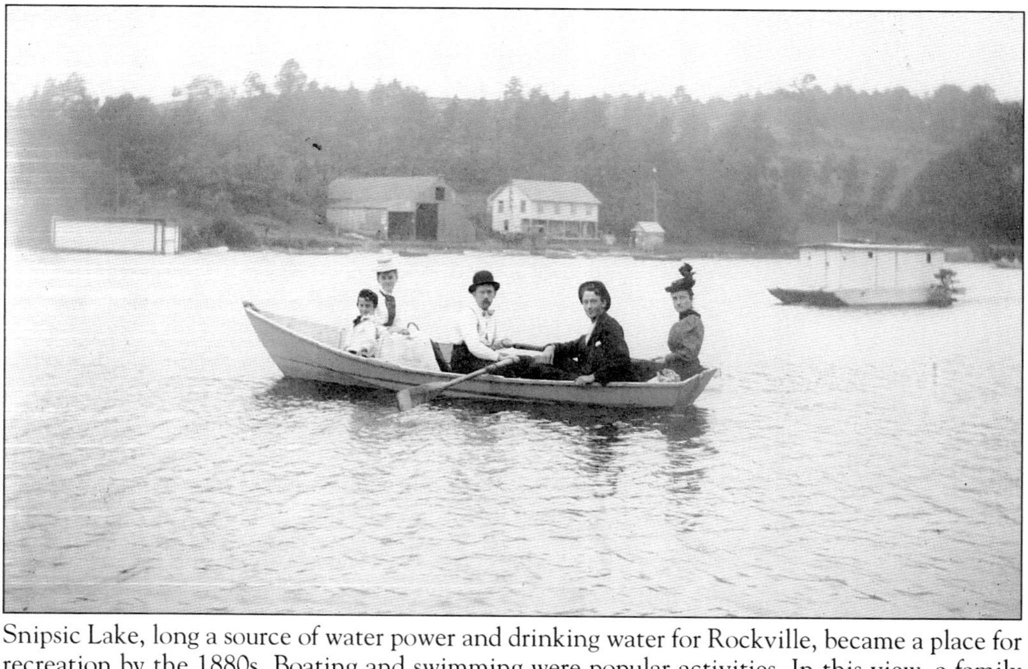

Snipsic Lake, long a source of water power and drinking water for Rockville, became a place for recreation by the 1880s. Boating and swimming were popular activities. In this view, a family enjoys a few hours on the water. Rowboats could be rented at Snipsic Landing.

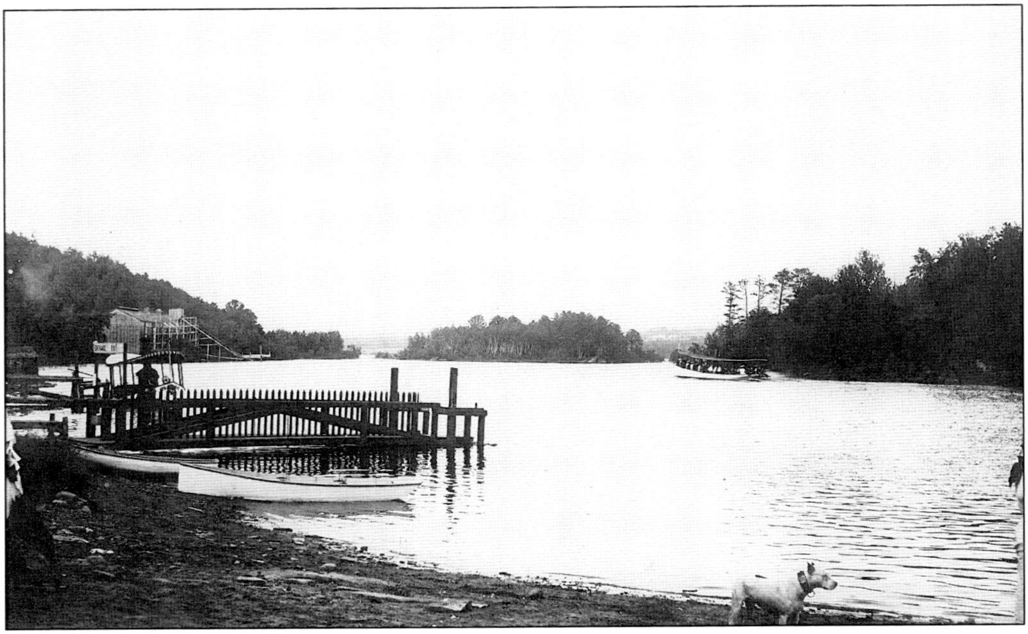

Snipsic Lake, shown around 1900, attracted summer visitors for its natural beauty as well as for Snipsic Grove, an amusement park with a dance pavilion, refreshment room, steamer excursions, and other amenities.

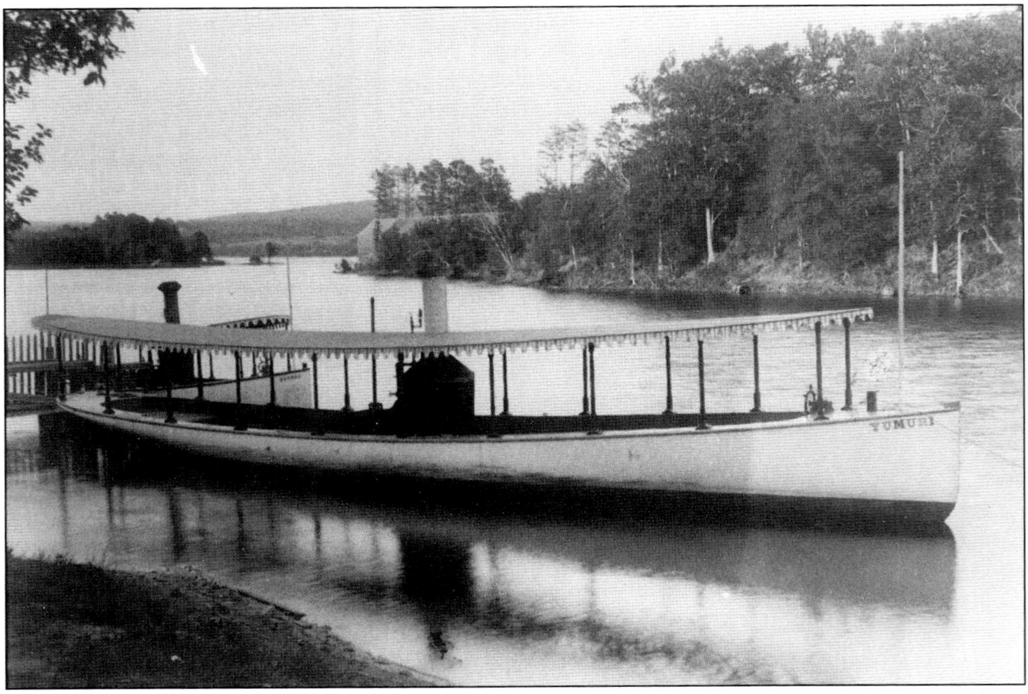

The proprietors, L.E. Thompson and his son, A.T. Thompson, operated Snipsic Grove for a number of years and added many improvements, including excursions on steamboats such as the Yumuri shown here. In 1913 the Rockville Water and Aqueduct Company that managed the lake, concerned that the large number of visitors would cause pollution, bought the Grove and closed it down.

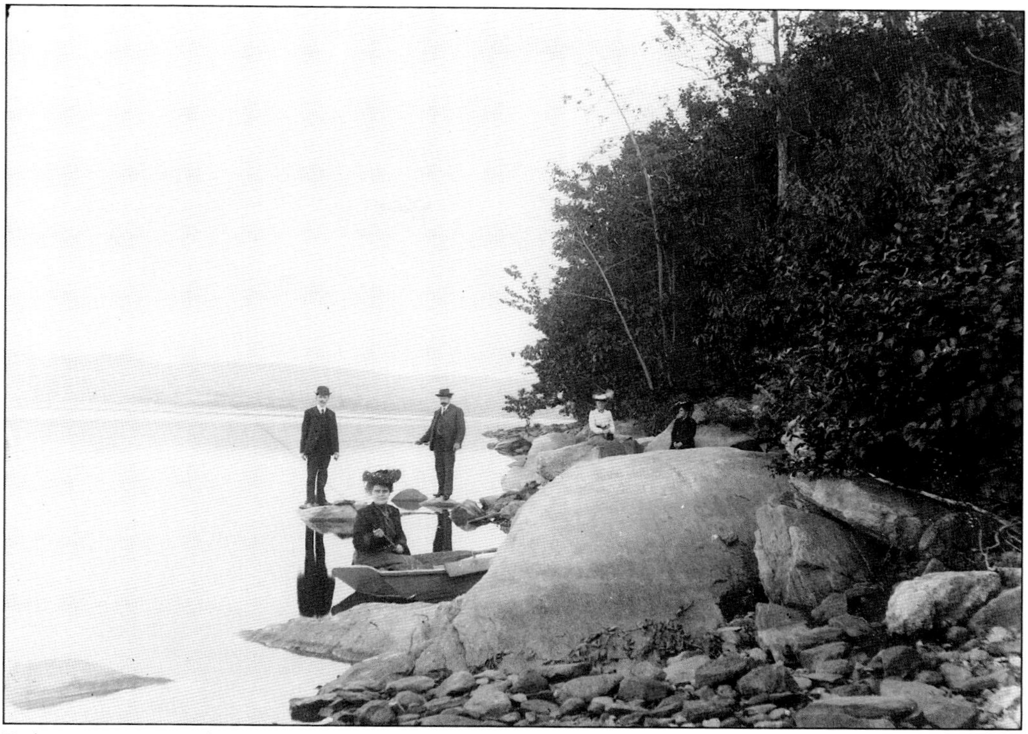

Fishing was a popular activity on Snipsic Lake and still is. This rather formally dressed group of anglers, captured on a glass-plate negative, try their luck one calm summer day.

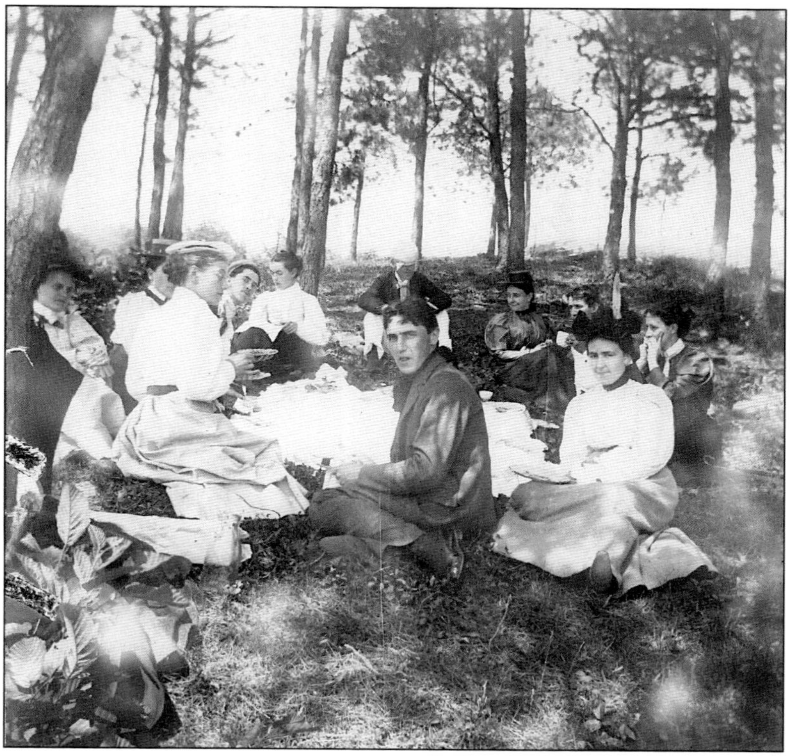

An informal group of friends enjoy a picnic at Pine Point on Snipsic Lake in July 1897.

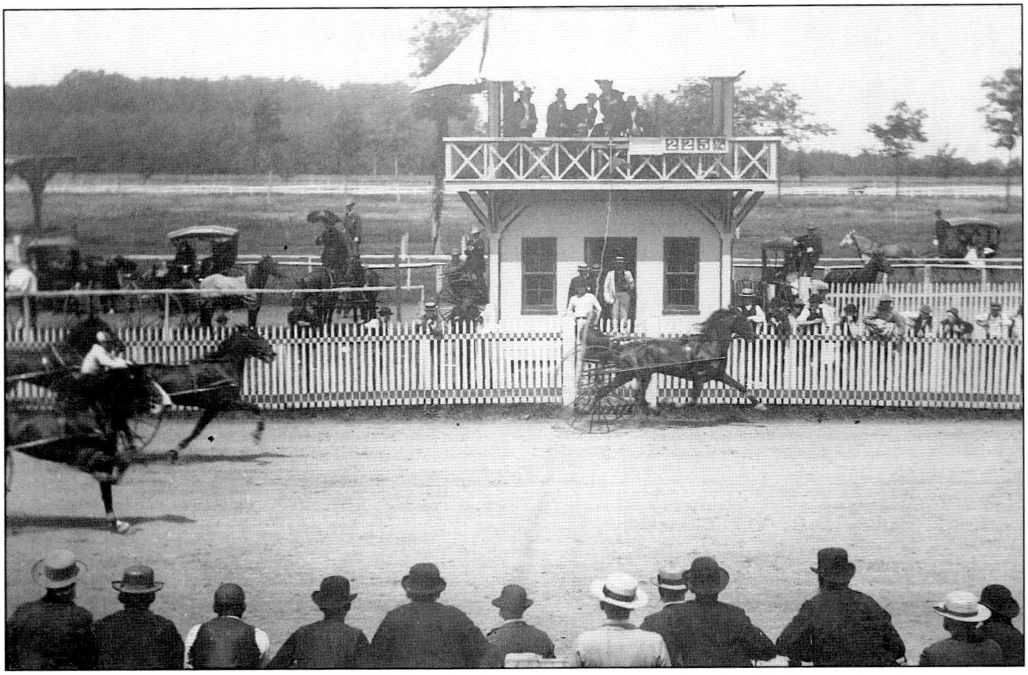

Interested spectators watch as horses and their drivers cross the finish line of a harness race during the Rockville Fair. The race track was located in Hyde Park near the Tolland town line. Young people visiting the fair admitted to wagering as much as 25¢ on a race.

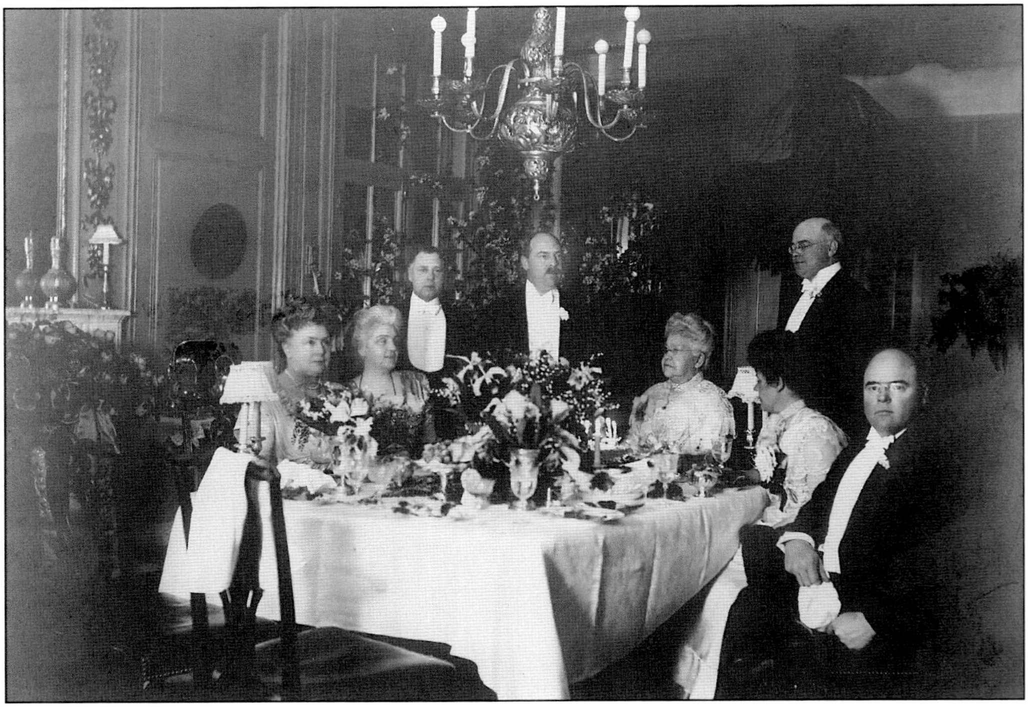

Family dinners at the Maxwell Mansion were often formal affairs featuring women in evening gowns and men in formal attire. This family party may have marked some very special occasion. Harriet Kellogg Maxwell, the widow of George Maxwell is seated at the head of the table.

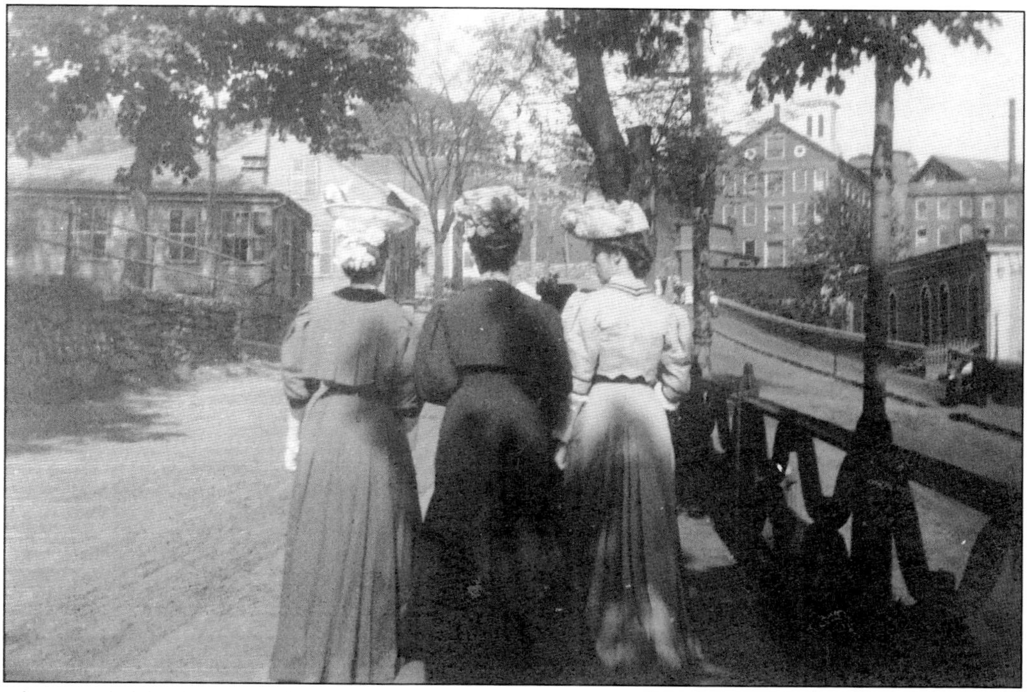

Three stylishly dressed ladies stroll self-consciously up St. Bernard's Terrace in this postcard view. Their opinion of themselves is reinforced by the comment written at the bottom of the post card: "Aren't they swell."

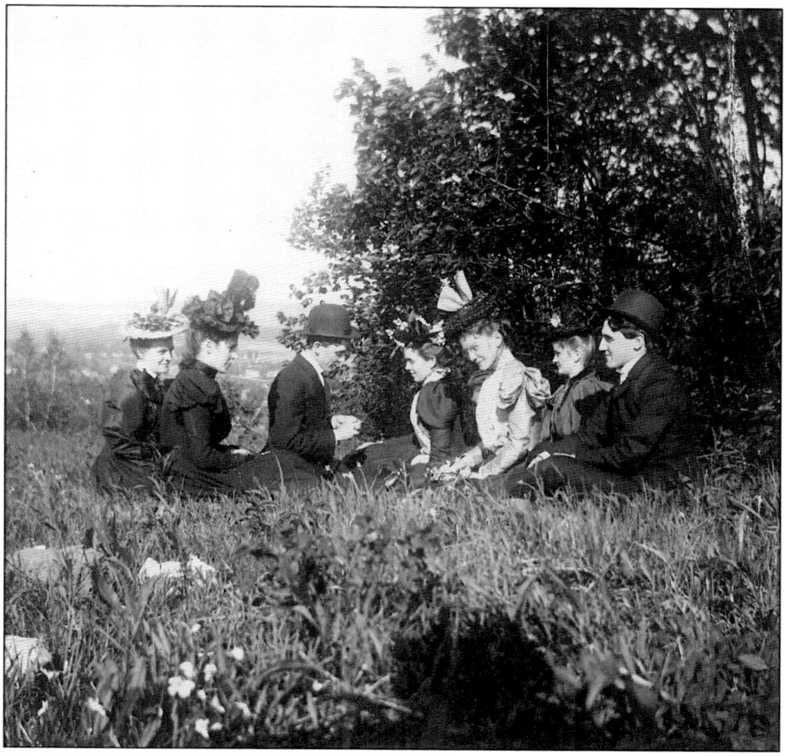

A relaxed moment during a summer picnic on Fox Hill is captured in this photograph of ladies wearing elegant hats and dapper gentlemen in derbies.

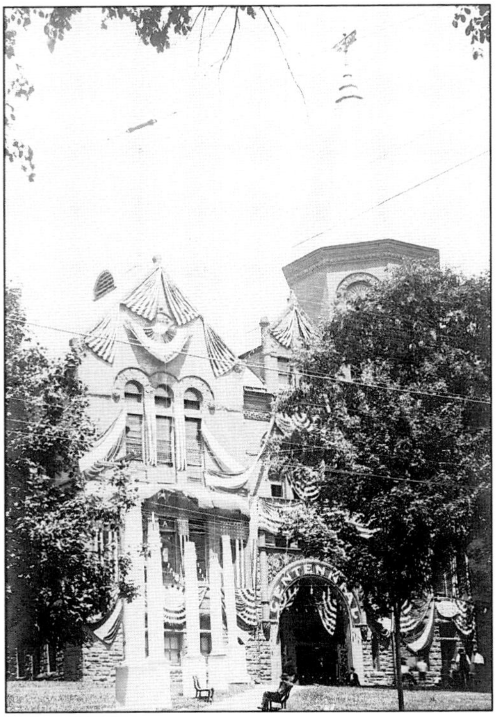

In 1908 Vernon celebrated its centennial. Plans were made for a gala Old Home Week to be held in Rockville from June 28 to July 4. The city was decorated with flags and bunting, and streets and parks were festooned with electric lights. The Memorial Building announced the "Centennial 1808–1908" in a sign over the door outlined in colored lights.

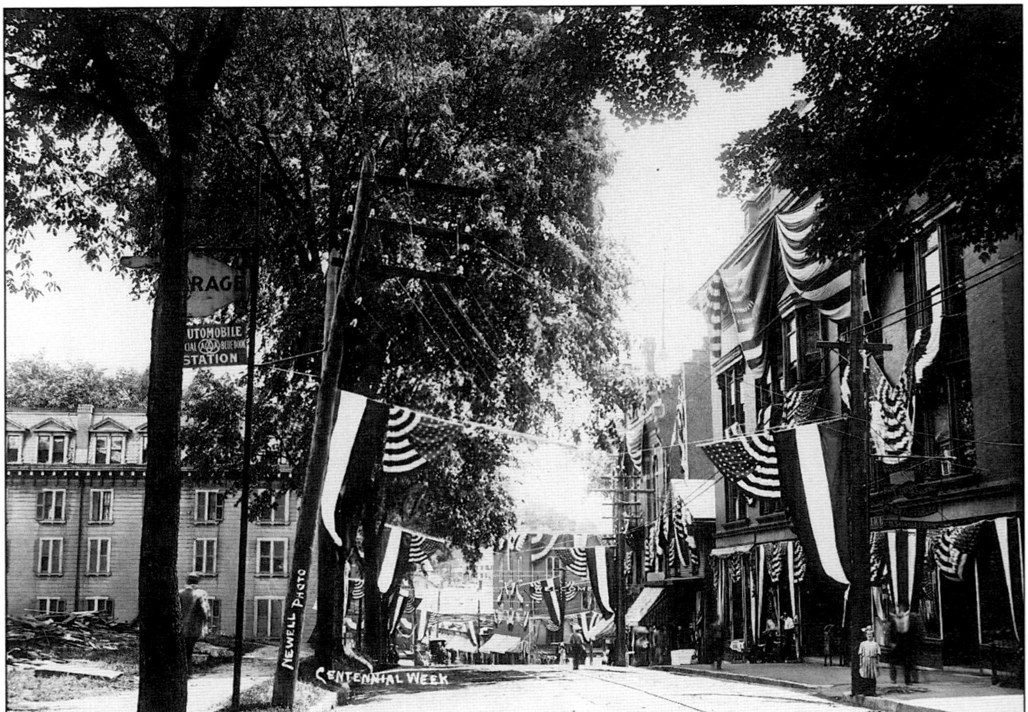

Park Street buildings covered with patriotic decorations show civic pride. The mills displayed examples of their products at a special exhibit at the Rockville Library. Balls and parades were sponsored by civic and social organizations.

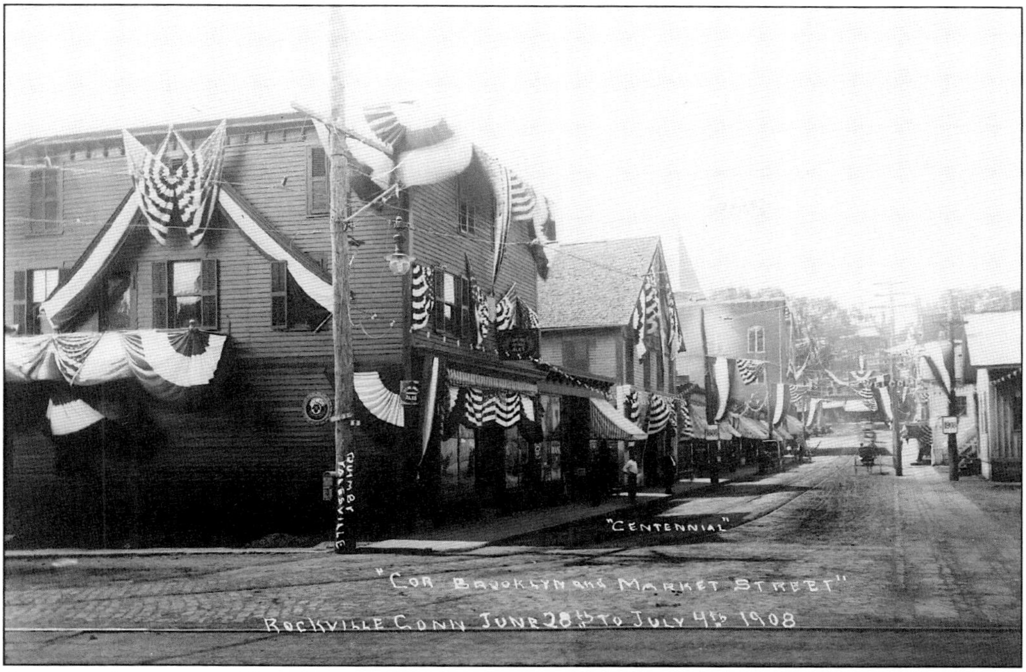

Stores at the corner of Brooklyn and Market Streets are shown here decorated in honor of Old Home Week. "Welcome" was the theme of the celebration.

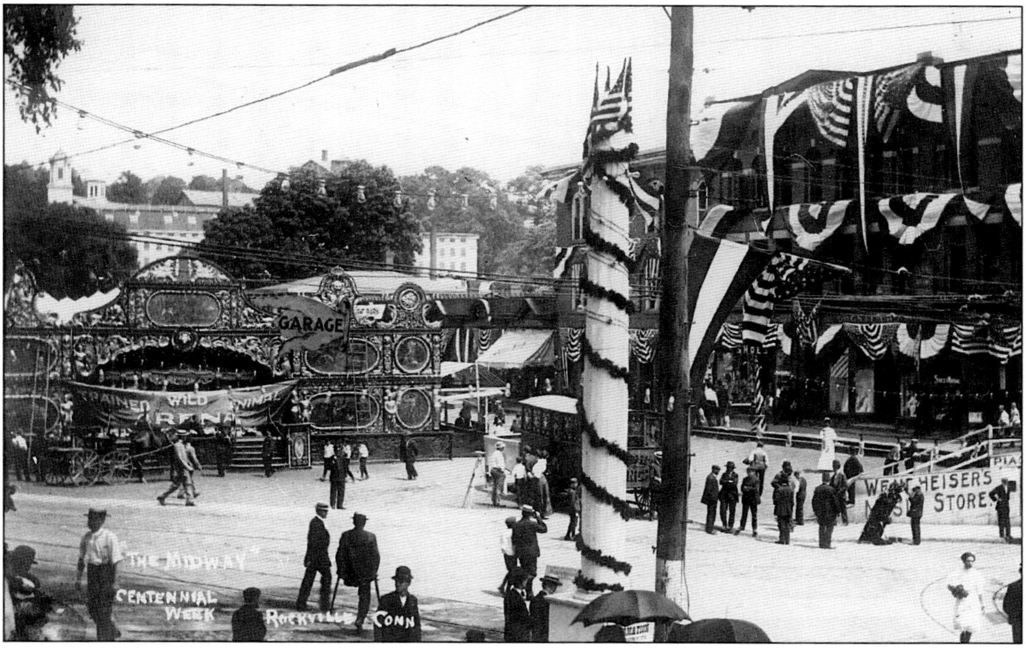

Across from Central Park a midway was erected that featured wild animal shows and other amusements. In the foreground, a white column topped by American flags stands in Central Park. Long remembered by all who attended, the celebration brought together former and current residents of Vernon and Rockville, who marveled at how far their town had come in its first one hundred years.

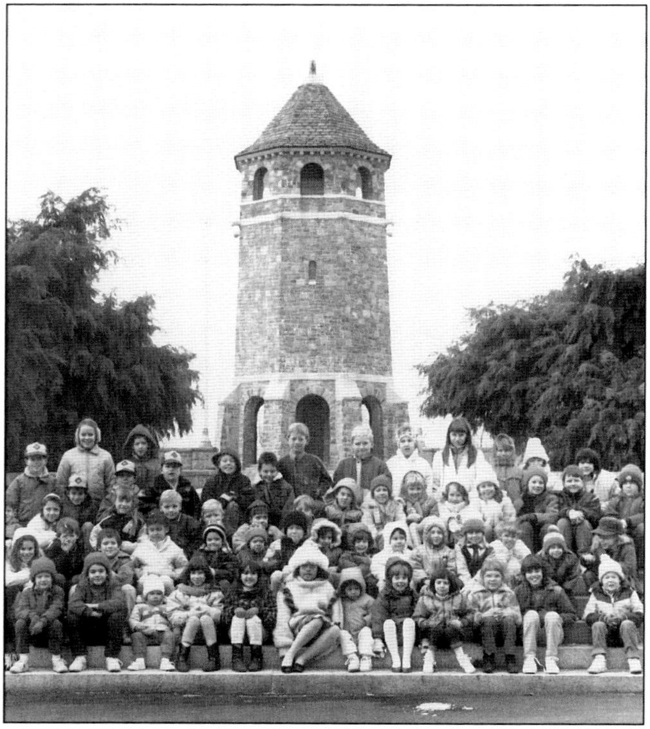

While Vernon and Rockville have much to celebrate about their past, the future is in the hands of these young citizens, who will make the history of our town in the twenty-first century.

Acknowledgments

The authors are indebted to a number of persons who have assisted us in writing and assembling the photographs for this book. We would like to especially thank Richard Steele, who allowed us to use several postcards from his collection, and Ross Dent, who provided us with a photograph of Col. Thomas Burpee and information about his military service. We are indebted to Sherwood Merk for the copy negatives and prints required in preparing some of our photographs for scanning. We are grateful to the American Textile History Museum for allowing us to reproduce the photograph of the Springville mill weave room. Finally, we want to express our gratitude to all those who have donated photographs to the Vernon Historical Society over the years, allowing us to have such a rich archive to share in this book.